To dear Victor
and Judy,
Sine quem non.

with love!
from an
Jan J

The Widening World of Children's Literature

The Widening World of Children's Literature

Susan Ang
Lecturer
Department of English Language and Literature
National University of Singapore

First published in Great Britain 2000 by
MACMILLAN PRESS LTD
Houndmills, Basingstoke, Hampshire RG21 6XS and London
Companies and representatives throughout the world

A catalogue record for this book is available from the British Library.

ISBN 0–333–68784–1

First published in the United States of America 2000 by
ST. MARTIN'S PRESS, INC.,
Scholarly and Reference Division,
175 Fifth Avenue, New York, N.Y. 10010

ISBN 0–312–22668–3

Library of Congress Cataloging-in-Publication Data
Ang, Susan, 1965–
The widening world of children's literature / Susan Ang.
  p. cm.
Includes bibliographical references (p.   ) and index.
ISBN 0–312–22668–3
1. Children's literature, English—History and criticism.
2. Children—Books and reading.   I. Title.
PR990.A84   1999
820.9'9282—dc21   99–16692
                                                            CIP

This book is printed on paper suitable for recycling and made from fully managed and sustained forest sources.

10   9   8   7   6   5   4   3   2   1
09   08   07   06   05   04   03   02   01   00

Printed and bound in Great Britain by
Antony Rowe Ltd, Chippenham, Wiltshire

To
Professor and Mrs Ang How Ghee

Contents

Acknowledgements

I am mindful of the fact that an acknowledgements page should beware of falling into hyperbole. There are, however, debts which must be acknowledged, people and institutions without whom this book could neither have been written nor revised who deserve more than a perfunctory thanks.

Among these are my supervisor, Professor John Beer, whose kindness, patience and helpfulness have been unfailing, and Mr Victor Watson, who has, over many years, unstintingly put his great wealth of knowledge of the field of children's literature at my disposal, and for whose encouragement I shall always be grateful. Both are remembered here with immense gratitude and affection. I also owe a great deal to, and wish to thank very warmly, my editor, Charmian Hearne, for her phenomenal patience and understanding over the time it took to get the script in, and helpfulness in all matters pertaining to the work. I am grateful to Associate Professor Ban Kah Choon, Head of the Department of English Language and Literature at the National University of Singapore, whose general support and generosity over matters of leave allowed me to work on the revisions; Dr Terence Dawson for his advice and help over matters of publishing procedure; Downing College, Cambridge (and especially Mr John Hopkins, Dr Martin Mays and Dr Catherine Phillips) for the Visiting Scholarship which allowed me to put the finishing touches to this work; St John's College, Cambridge, which also kindly provided me with accommodation during the period of revision, and Mr Richard Nolan, who made this possible, and who has, over the years, encouraged and nagged, according to need.

I also wish to express heartfelt thanks to Ms Kate Agnew, Mr Gwee Li Sui, Ms Venessa Lee, Mr Warren Liew, Mr Gilbert Ng and Mr Augustine Wong, who proofread, commented, and did so much else, and whose friendship has had its own importance to this work. To my parents, Professor and Mrs Ang How Ghee, however, there is a less specific but more all-encompassing debt of gratitude owed, and it is to them that this work is dedicated.

Introduction

Over the last 200 years or so of its history, children's literature has altered considerably in terms of its governing ethos, and this alteration may be understood in terms of shifts between principles of constraint and emancipation, repression and expression. This study is an attempt to trace the removal of constraints surrounding the child and his book from the eighteenth century to the present, to map the movement from the state of 'enclosure', where external shaping, defining, and constraint are active forces, to one of 'openness', where these forces have ceased to be dominant. It is also an enquiry into how these factors affect 'being' and the formation of self, how the concept of being has changed in its formulation and how these changes might best be comprehended.

In our century – and especially in the context of western culture – the notion of 'enclosure' tends, by and large, to be viewed suspiciously, being freighted with ideas of repression, constraint and imprisonment. 'Freedom', on the other hand, carries with it an almost unqualified approval. Each of the two terms, however, runs through a spectrum of meanings and intentions, and it is necessary not only to trace the history of the negotiation between the two, but also of the fluctuations along each spectrum of meanings. As Gaston Bachelard, in *The Poetics of Space* (1958), writes:

> Outside and inside form a dialectic of division, the obvious geometry of which blinds us as soon as we bring it into play in metaphorical domains. It has the sharpness of the dialectics of *yes* and *no*, which decides everything. Unless one is careful, it is made into a basis of images that govern all thoughts of positive and negative.... Formal opposition is incapable of remaining calm.[1]

1

The investigation into children's literature outlined above, therefore, is not intended to take place within a binaric framework where 'enclosure' is the negative term and 'openness' its positive opposite – nor even vice versa. Neither extreme is desirable. As Martha, the maid in Frances Hodgson Burnett's *The Secret Garden* (1911), remarks, 'Mother says as th' two worst things as can happen to a child is never to have his own way – or always to have it. She doesn't know which is th' worst.'[2] This work will examine what may ensue when those 'formal oppositions' are in place, and what happens when they are dismantled to create paradoxical territories that are both shut off *and* open, these territories being plentifully found in the literature of the period 1870–1940. After all, as testified to by the mere existence of Carroll's Wonderland and Burnett's Secret Garden, *entente* between the two is not an impossibility.

If we consider the idea of a wall, which may be understood either as an actual physical structure or a metaphor for rules and regulations, it is possible to see the above-mentioned duality in action. An illustration of the paradox may be found in the Book of Job, where the image of the hedge is used to designate protection and confinement simultaneously. Satan complains at the outset of the book that God has 'hedged' Job in, not allowing him (Satan) a free hand with Job;[3] Job too complains that God has 'hedged' him in,[4] allowing him no escape from the prison of his miserable circumstances. The circumscribing hedge is at once perceived as at once imprisoning and protecting. An example of the opposite case might be found in Phillipa Pearce's *Tom's Midnight Garden* (1958) where gaps in hedges allow Tom to get in to play with Hatty while allowing the geese to get out, which gets Hatty into trouble.

The same principle holds true in children's literature: the child enclosed within walls may find its liberty restricted and its development limited. Yet, while walls or restrictions may appear to inhibit, they may also be helpful in directing the child's growth. Certain aspects of enclosure exist for the purpose of giving necessary definition to the child: discipline and guidance are such aspects, for without them, the child's being and identity are in danger of remaining unshaped. The child may chafe against rules and regulations but, as Miss Cromwell in Antonia Forest's *The Cricket Term* (1974) points out, regulations exist and are necessary, if only to 'protect the weak from the bullies and the foolish from their folly.'[5]

The principle of enclosure may be more easily detected in literature for children written before this century, and one may find there equal evidence of both aspects of the idea: in the emphasis on control and also in the protectiveness that sought to keep the child from premature knowledge of sombre realities. Edward Salmon, a nineteenth-century critic of children's literature, described this process as 'filter[ing] the waters' of the 'great river of human thought' into which 'sewers of Zolaism and mental refuse [were] from time to time emptied'.[6] According to another (anonymous) critic, '[t]he knowledge of life's realities and the prosaic conditions of human existence w[ould] come soon enough'[7] and 'the first needs of a little child's life are light and heat and love and joyousness'. The critic continues by suggesting that happiness in childhood is a source of strength 'for the future contest',[8] this serving as a rationale for protectiveness and contraint. From Maria Edgeworth and William Wordsworth in the late eighteenth century to Hodgson Burnett almost a century later, poverty, illness and death – when these are depicted at all – are viewed through the lens of sentiment, romanticised, and so softened and robbed of their sting. Towards the end of the century, however, it is possible to see innocence/ignorance giving way to awareness: Wilde's story 'The Happy Prince' (1888) might perhaps be read as an allegorical enactment of this change. While not without its own brand of romanticism and sentimentality, the story is about the awakening of the figure of the Happy Prince to the misery and poverty surrounding him in the city. The statue of the prince recounts that while he was alive, he 'lived in the Palace of Sans-Souci, where sorrow is not allowed to enter. In the daytime I played with my companions in the garden.... Round the garden ran a very lofty wall, but I never cared to ask what lay beyond it, everything about me was so beautiful.'[9] The prince, in this reading, represents the enclosed and protected child, and the stripping of the statue's gold leaf and gems to feed the poor is reminiscent of Lear's vision of the 'bare forked animal', carrying with it the loss of innocence, as well, perhaps, as a greater-hearted awareness of the exposed world.

The instinct to define and protect, the impulse to enclose, may, however, be motivated as much by anxiety as by the more positive desire to protect. D. H. Lawrence, in his essay 'Chaos in Poetry' (1928), suggests that it is indeed this that lies at the heart of the desire to order and control:

> Man must wrap himself in a vision, make a house of apparent form and stability, fixity. In his terror of chaos, he begins by putting up an umbrella between himself and the everlasting whirl ...[10]

'Chaos', which Lawrence uses to denote the absence of order or system, is here resonant with threat, and acts as a reminder of the tenuousness and fragility of being subjected to that disorder; boundaries both serve to shut away the sight of chaos into a temporary forgetfulness, as well as to define the self more strongly by separating chaos from the self. In this connection, it might be interesting to note Nietzsche's question in *The Birth of Tragedy* (revised edition, 1886): 'what does all of science mean as a symptom of life? Might the scientific approach be nothing but fear, flight from pessimism?'[11] One might indeed posit that in periods which are marked by anxiety, method, order and control take on a commensurately greater importance. As an example of this, we might consider the 'myth' of the nineteenth century, discussed by George Steiner in *In Bluebeard's Castle* (1971) as a time of greatness and stability, reflected in the multiplicity of images of domestic bliss to be found in the literature of the period. It might be asked if these images *represent* reality or whether, in fact, they strive to *create* it, producing it according to given specifications. Often, these idyllic images ring suspiciously hollow to the reader: Dora, in *David Copperfield* (1850), playing at being David's child wife, is one example. Heathcliff and Cathy, peering into Thrushcross Grange and expecting to see the Linton children enjoying the comforts of their home, find instead 'Isabella ... screaming at the farther end of the room, shrieking as if witches were running red hot needles into her'[12] and Edgar weeping silently; in this case, the text itself ironically exposes the image as an empty one. My point here is that the myth as referred to by Steiner may represent an attempt to overwrite chaos with a vision of order.

Liberty may be seen to operate in an equally double-edged way. While mental, intellectual and imaginative freedoms and the space to develop without the constant watching and nagging of the adult are some of the more positive aspects of the idea, liberty may also signify a decline of authority and responsibility for the way in which the child will develop. Freedom can be a danger. This is reflected in a good deal of twentieth-century literature for children, especially that written since the 1960s, in which the child protagonists have found themselves increasingly free of adult control but have, perhaps, also found themselves being increasingly neglected and left bewildered in an increasingly complex world. And while some children survive – as, for example, Cynthia Voigt's Tillermans in *Homecoming* (1981), who, when abandoned by their mother in a car park, walk across America to find their grandmother – others do not. Alan Garner's *Red Shift* (1973), to be discussed in a later chapter, testifies to this bleak truth.

'Identity?' said Jack, comfortably pouring out more coffee. 'Is not identity something you are born with?'
'The identity I am thinking of is something that hovers between a man and the rest of the world: a mid-point between his view of himself and theirs of him – for each, of course, affects the other continually. A reciprocal fluxion, sir. There is nothing absolute about this identity of mine.'

Patrick O'Brian: *Master and Commander* (1971)

Children's books are written for a category of persons who are in the process of attaining awareness of themselves and the world they inhabit, and who are in the process of finding out what they are and want to be. They are thus often about being or becoming, about the quest for self-hood and identity, the attempt to discover what it is that makes an individual person or thing indubitably him or herself. The question that punctuates Kipling's *Kim* (1901) is 'What is Kim?' and this question, made general, might almost be said to articulate the quest for definition which structures many books for and about children.

However, this is not to say that all children's books are reducible to the same thing. 'Being' itself may be defined variously in, for example, social or moral terms; and in examining the body of children's literature written over the last 200 years, one may discern a pattern in the way thinking about being and self has changed over this period. This pattern follows closely that given by Terence Dawson's essay 'Jung, Literature and Literary Criticism'[13] in which he maps the evolution of a larger literary and cultural consciousness through history according to Jung's theory of the withdrawal of projections, a process which traces the development of self-awareness in the individual. His model describes, *inter alia*, a movement from collective concerns to individual ones, from assent and subscription to collective values to the working out of an individual code, from identification with one's society to alienation, and finally (ideally) reintegration into it, albeit on different terms, and also a movement from unconsciousness to awareness.[14] The larger shape of these dynamics would appear to indicate that the term(s) of reference by which being takes definition shift from their location outside the self to within it. I should, however, preface this discussion by saying that, in speaking about these various definitions of being, I do not mean to imply that there were clearly demarcated periods during which a particular formulation held despotic sway, each period sharply giving way to the next. Clearly, more than one way of thinking may hold currency at any given time and what I am attempting to sketch is a pattern of gradual and general change.

A good deal of the children's literature of the eighteenth century may be understood as expressing 'self' in predominantly social terms, that is, in terms of its contributions to society and its adherence to its collective values, how it stands in relation to the central term 'society'. 'Being', for example in Maria Edgeworth's stories for children, has little to do with individual awareness; on the contrary, it is implied that the individual only exists validly when functioning as part of society and acquiescing to its assumptions. Self is valued in terms of its usefulness and what it contributes to society, evaluated in accordance with its conformity to social dictates. Here, the power to define and shape the individual belongs to the group rather than with the individual, who has (implicitly) surrendered to it the power to pronounce on his being or non-being, existence or non-existence. Being, under this dispensation, is then externally rather than internally constructed, produced by the enclosing social system rather than arising from within. The powerful influence that society or community is capable of exerting over the moulding of one's sense of self is especially visible in literature which is predicated on the idea of the group – as, for example, the school story. The desire or the need to be accepted creates the pressure to conform to the behavioural patterns and values of the group. As Laura Rambotham in Henry Handel Richardson's *The Getting of Wisdom* (1910) discovers while at school, 'the unpardonable sin is to vary from the common mould'.[15] Divergence from the norms of the group, or transgression against them, may result in social negation or non-acknowledgement of one's being. Maria Bertram, in *Mansfield Park* (1814), after running away with Henry Crawford, is no longer spoken of by her family and ceases socially to exist.

The early English Romantic poets were responsible for formulating yet another way of looking at being, seeing it as a substance generated through a relationship with nature, and this framework was one which managed to bring enclosure and what might be called 'openness' into a creative rather than antagonistic tension. In place of the rules governing social etiquette, religious and ethical behaviour and so on, the earlier English Romantics substituted the notion of natural morality, in which Nature itself was both the living embodiment and the enforcer of moral law. The concept of 'natural being', or being that is formed by nature, was developed by Wordsworth, who, in *The Excursion*, describes this process:

For the Man, –
Who, in this spirit, communes with the Forms
Of Nature, who with understanding heart
Both knows and loves such objects as excite
No morbid passions ... needs must feel
So deeply, that, unsatisfied with aught
Less pure and exquisite, he cannot choose
But seek for objects of a kindred love
In fellow-natures and a kindred joy.
Accordingly he by degrees perceives
His feelings of aversion softened down;
A holy tenderness pervades his frame ...
So build we up the Being that we are;
Thus deeply drinking-in the soul of things,
We shall be wise perforce.[16]

The Romantic philosophy of nature as propounded by Wordsworth was thus also a philosophy of self, in which being was built up and strengthened in communion with Nature. The individual, however, was required to be open and committed to nature in order for this to happen; one had to *deeply* drink in the soul of things: this is no shallow appraisal of nature, but instead, a giving and a taking of self in communion with nature.

The difference between social and natural morality is that one is a human construction, the other an inherent order. Another – perhaps more significant – difference is that a system based on social ordering (especially if we rely on examples before the twentieth century) is relatively inflexible and is rarely tolerant of deviation from it, while the world of natural order not only accommodates asymmetry but is in fact a system whose order is one premised on the principle of change and the plurality of forms. This becomes important if we consider that this system thus manages effectually to blend principles of enclosure and openness. The Romantic natural world is one commodious enough to accommodate both liberty and law. As illustrative of this, Wordsworth's natural 'guides' in the first book of the *Prelude* are themselves imaged as fluid and dynamic: a 'wandering cloud', or 'some floating thing /Upon the river [that] point[s him] out [his] course'.[17] Being is no longer necessarily thought of as static and fixed, but as capable of change; rather than the product of outer circumstances, it is now the result of an ongoing transaction between context and self.

The philosophy of natural being may be seen to be at work in many of the better-known works of nineteenth-century children's fiction such as Charles Kingsley's *The Water Babies* (1863). Tom, a chimney-sweep's boy, escapes from a life lived in cramped chimneys into the fluid element itself (quite literally drinking in the soul of things), thereby becoming a water baby. The water world gives Tom a physical freedom, but it also creates in him an awareness of moral constraints. He is given an understanding of the natural world not purely in factual terms, but in moral terms as well – for example, in his encounter with the chrysalis whose house he breaks open. The breakage results, as the other chrysalides tell him, in the death of its occupant. The need for responsible action is enjoined on Tom even as he receives an education in natural history.

The idea of natural being continued to find expression in children's literature even up to the beginning of this century, a good example being F. H. Burnett's *The Secret Garden*, where a sort of pantheistic magic is shown to be at work in the lives of two cousins, Mary and Colin. When the novel begins, they are seen to be shut up in rooms, houses and railway carriages, and are represented – not surprisingly – as sickly, peevish children, both physically and spiritually. By virtue of their contact with the garden of which they are both nurturers and the nurtured, they grow in health and alertness. Here, the garden acts as a living, organic metaphor of space both liberated and enclosed, of growth that is both natural and cultivated.

Perhaps the most significant shifts that may be traced during the nineteenth century are those towards the establishment of the individual as the central point of reference from which meaning is made, moving from the exterior to the interior management of self and an increasing emphasis on individual consciousness and moral being. Evidence of this interiorisation may be seen in the growing nineteenth-century interest taken in the workings of the mind and psyche, in the development of psychology and psychoanalysis as disciplines, and also in the increasing value accorded to the imagination. Interestingly, an examination of the etymological history of the word 'individual' suggests that a quite radical shift in meaning has occurred. From signifying that which was *non*-dividual, or non-dividable, indivisible, from society, the word has come to mean that which is distinguishable as separate, that which stands *apart* from society instead of being *a part* of it. The date of the earliest usage of the word as signifying 'distinguished from others by attributes of its own' is given as 1646 by *The Oxford English Dictionary*, which quotes

Sir Thomas Browne: 'A man should be something that men are not, and individuall in somewhat beside his proper nature.' However, though the meaning of individualism in its modern sense began its emergence in the seventeenth century, its manifestation in literature – as seen in the conflict between characters and society – only really becomes obvious during the nineteenth century, where the Christian 'frame of things' became even more disjointed, ceasing to act as a unifying social force.

The approval of difference – of individualism in its modern sense or incarnation – may again be linked to the rise of Romanticism in England and Europe, a movement celebrating, *inter alia*, both feeling and the endeavouring self. Matthew Arnold, speaking of Goethe, calls attention to Goethe's Romantic philosophy as not only one that is emancipatory, but one in which meaning is a thing internally, not externally, determined, where the world is tested against the values of the self, rather than the self's values taken from the world:

> And how did Goethe, that grand dissolvent in an age when there were fewer of them than at present, proceed in his task of dissolution, of liberation of the modern European from the old routine? He shall tell us himself. 'Through me the German poets have become aware that, as man must live from within outwards, so the artist must work from within outwards, seeing that, make what contortions he will, he can only bring to light his own individuality....' Goethe's profound, imperturbable naturalism is absolutely fatal to all routine thinking; he puts the standard once for all, inside every man instead of outside him; when he is told, such a thing must be so, there is immense authority and custom for its being so, it has been held to be so for a thousand years, he answers, with Olympian politeness, 'But *is* it so? is it so to *me*?[18]

With the desire to 'put the standard inside' the individual, formulations such as 'social being' and 'natural being', while not disappearing altogether, began to give way to others involving the inner life, as for example the idea of 'imaginative being'. Northrop Frye, in *The Secular Scripture* (1976), has noted the importance of the imaginary or the 'not-real' in soul-making:

> the journey towards one's own identity, which literature does so much to help with, has a great deal to do with escaping from the alleged 'reality' of what one is reading or looking at ... The child

should ... send out imaginative roots into that mysterious world between the 'is' and the 'is not' where his own ultimate freedom lies.[19]

This view of the imagination – and by extension imaginative literature – as a maker and shaper of being is, though common in our century, relatively speaking, a recent one. The status and worth of the imagination was the subject of one of the greater debates during the nineteenth century concerning children's reading. Not only were fairy tales and other tales of the imagination (as opposed to didactic and moralistic stories) viewed with suspicion and initially fiercely opposed on the grounds that they were neither useful nor educational, it was also feared that they would prove morally deleterious to the developing child in exposing him to lying; for the Puritans, fiction and untruth were close cousins. To the proponents of this argument, literature was indeed a maker of being, and imaginative – 'untrue' – literature formed being that was morally warped. The Romantics (notably Coleridge) were, on the other hand, the godparents or sponsors of the idea of imaginative being – that is, both imaginative existence and being gathered through the workings of the imagination and the inner life. Through the imagination, the individual was enabled to inhabit and experience what might be called 'otherness', alternate lives, and to be fed by these. This may be seen in F. H. Burnett's *A Little Princess* (1905), where Sara Crewe, physically and emotionally starved, is sustained by her fantasies and imaginings.

While the deepening of the inner life of mind and soul may bring to the individual a sense of its own specificity and uniqueness, it is also possible for this sense of discrete personality to result in alienation and conflict if the emerging values and ideas of the individual run contrary to those held by society at large. Where it may be said that in the literature of our own century the balance has largely gone in favour of personal truths, much nineteenth-century literature, both for children and for adults, displays the often painful attempt to find an honest accommodation between the two sets of values: to be simultaneously true to oneself and one's community. Occasionally we see the attempt to abandon society altogether, as in the adventures of Huck Finn, who maintains till the end a steady defiance of the pressure to conform. His spelling remains idiosyncratically his own, symbolising his resistance to the discourse and language of his culture. But this defiance, it would appear, can only be maintained at a distance:

But I reckon I got to light out for the Territory ahead of the rest, because Aunt Sally she's going to adopt me and sivilize me and I can't stand it. I been there before.[20]

Huck's flight suggests a fear that the forces of 'sivilization' or external ordering may finally win out; it also suggests, by implication, a fear that his sense of self will be unequal to the pressure to conform: hence his flight. What this in turn suggests is that in order to continue to retain a viable existence within society and still remain one's own person, there must be a sense of self at least as strong as the social pressures being brought to bear upon it, a sense of moral being, conviction and integrity sufficient to balance the claims of social definition. One has to be, in Antonia Forest's term, 'enough'.

In this matter of moral being, it is possible to trace the concept of morality becoming ever less generalised, ceasing to refer to a collectively held set of values, and coming to mean a personally worked-out and constructed ethical code. The question of how moral being is generated and what circumstances best produce it is, however, a difficult one. In any environment purportedly structured by moral precept, morality is enjoined on the individual; however, by virtue of its being thus enjoined, there is a danger of its becoming a species of social behaviour, rather than an inner dynamic. Yet, in an environment which leaves the business of deciding what is right to the individual, the individual may often be plagued by doubt, lacking the comfort of law that has been agreed on and which is subscribed to by the community, this doubt paralysing choice and action.

Kipling's *Kim* discovers that the domain of self is one that lies outside the defining boundaries of race, religion or nationality. The answer to the question of who and what Kim is, Kipling never explicitly states; it may be that this refusal to define suggests the view that the use of categories may be precisely what obstructs the attainment of the self's wholeness. Alison, Roger and Gwyn in Garner's *The Owl Service* (1967) learn that though history shapes one's paths, it is not the sole defining force, while Taran, of Lloyd Alexander's 'Prydain Chonicles', understands that identity is not merely a matter of knowing one's parentage or station in life. While it is difficult to generalise about the development of children's literature this century, due mainly to the sheer amount which has been and is being written, one may sense a new kind of thinking coming to the forefront which involves a desire to move beyond simple formula to a more holistic idea of being.

Coveney's seminal study of childhood in literature, in *The Image of Childhood* (1967), has traced the emergence of the child in literature, and it is not my intention to reinvent the wheel here. Although my first chapter, 'The Imprisoning Image', does in fact look at the increasing emphasis on the child in adult literature, it attempts further to ascertain the impact of this on children's literature. It also deviates from Coveney's work in its rather different evaluation of certain texts, most notably *Jane Eyre*. In this chapter I discuss the 'enclosure' of the child within two-dimensional images (for example, the representations of the child as little limb of Satan or child saint), and the subsequent exposure of these myths of childhood as impediments to a real understanding of childhood. The images of saint and sinner are limited and limiting identities to the child, acting to simplify the definition of its being: here the child is defined in merely moral terms and especially according to moral polarities of good or bad; nothing can be inscribed in the space between. Neither image is an adequate or true representation of childhood, neither sufficient as a guide or prop in the quest for self definition, being partial and incomplete as ideas. The chapter will consider the history and significance of these images from Wordsworth through the nineteenth century and also their gradual attrition. The 'image of childhood', to use Coveney's phrase, was to grow increasingly 'natural'.

Wordsworth, in penning those memorable lines designating the child as father to the man, was pointing a developing and not a static entity: 'I could wish my days to be/ Bound each to each by natural piety'. The metaphor is a rich one, suggesting a book of days whose pages are bound to each other in a continuous narrative of the individual's life from childhood to adulthood. Yet, till *Jane Eyre* (1847), writers in both the adult's and children's fields persisted in treating the child as a static creature with fixed properties and needs. *Jane Eyre* presented childhood not as a separate state or condition, but as that which informed, and was continuous with, adulthood, and her child heroine was one who fought to establish her existence outside the parameters of the popular image.

Though Huck Finn, Tom Sawyer and Maisie Farange in America were significant late nineteenth-century additions to the body of literature dealing with childhood, the question of the child's needs and development ceased for the most part to preoccupy English novelists after the mid-1860s. Children's literature, however, was to benefit from all the attention which had been paid to childhood in the preceding two decades. By the 1860s, thanks to the heroic narratives of Jane Eyre, David Copperfield, Maggie Tulliver *et al.*, it was generally beginning to be recognised, as the anonymous author of the article, 'Children's Literature'(1860) said, that 'there [were] duties of *being* as well as doing ... truths of imagination, as well as truths of fact; and it [was] the inner and deeper part of man, which call[ed] for a supply of these.'[21] Works that stimulated the child's mind and imagination, leading it towards an intuitive understanding of the being of 'otherness' and away from brooding 'painfully and unhealthily upon itself', as this critic suggests, should be encouraged – and they were.

The second chapter examines 'enclosure' in children's literature from a socio-historical perspective. In the excerpt from Lawrence's essay cited earlier there is the implication that at the root of man's impulse to enclose and build, the need to construct images, lies a fear of disorder and disorientation in a basically unknowable world, and the chapter investigates 'enclosure' from this point of view. As noted by J. S. Bratton, the growth of children's literature was partly stimulated by the increasing whirl of chaos (social, religious and so forth), in that it developed in reaction to it. For example, the Religious Tract Society, which was later to be responsible for the printing of many works for children, was originally established with the aim of countering the influence of tracts calling for revolution, by printing works intended to educate the poor.[22] These appeared to be be aimed at redressing the social imbalance by helping the poor to better themselves, but the program of educating the poor was in fact a limited one and rather served to reinforce the social hierarchies already in place, thus maintaining the social status quo.

Furthermore, the tone of authority discernable in certain children's books in the late eighteenth century up to the First World War may have been intended to act as reassurance, and have been inspired by the need to combat doubt and anxiety caused by ideological and industrial upheavals. The function of children's literature was a socializing one, in that it attempted to implant a system of socially approved values in the young. Among other things, it set out to delineate social roles for the individual: male and female, master and worker and so on; these roles were perhaps as limiting as the images of saint and sinner, but may have helped to establish a socially stable framework. This kind of literature preached conformity, fearing the disruptive effects of non-conformism. Being and identity were shaped by an ethic of self-sacrifice, a paradox of acquiring (social) being through a sacrifice of private life and private aspirations.

Girls were encouraged to think of 'being' in terms of wifehood and motherhood; their identity was to be made and formed within the environs of home; they in turn were expected to make and keep each home a small nucleus of stability. What they were asked to sacrifice of themselves was the freedom to be other than wife and mother, or at least sister and aunt; they were to be guardians of future generations, responsible for passing on the doctrines that would enable the continuance of the society that protected them. Boys were taught to view identity as a corporate affair, something that could only take on form in service to a greater ideal, and/or in conjunction with other selves. 'Team', 'Country', 'Empire' – these were the terms in which male identity was conceptualised; and the boy was encouraged to see himself as part of these groupings and give himself over to them. Boys had the vision of potential heroism set before them. Self could be realised, being could be crystallised through service, or through contribution to community or country. While the duty of the girl was to strengthen society in the microcosmic bastion of home, that of the boy was to do so by helping to establish firmly the macrocosmic country and empire.

Not only were the duties of gender outlined, but a broader scheme of an ideal and stable society itself was depicted in fiction for the young, pointing out the duties of rich and poor alike, a clear-cut blueprint of desired reality. The work ethic, which is also discussed here, encouraging industriousness and condemning idleness, was no mere Puritan philosophy but one configured around the need for stability and order. Work was given the status of an epistemology, a way of organizing experience and self, a way of imparting meaning to life, and hence a means of combating the fear of chaos.

The onslaught of the First World War, however, revealed the sacrifices made to the god of Order, the veneration of tradition and community, as empty and worthless. Basil Willey has commented that, 'after the First World War, we were all debunking the nineteenth century'.[23] The pact between society and the individual, of contribution and protection, had been voided; glory was insufficient compensation for loss. As Wilfred Owen bitterly points out, there was scant glory in modern warfare, nothing heroic about death by chlorine gas. Slogans such as 'I Gave My Sons And Kept The Home Fires Burning', speaking of sacrifice and the fight to keep home and society going, were rejected and abandoned, along with whatever was felt to be a part of the teachings and traditional trappings of the society that had, after all, broken down. The disillusionment suffered as the myth of a stable society crumbled led to the further erosion of society itself, leaving the individual isolated and without support, vulnerable again to disintegration. C. E. Montague, in *Disenchantment*, wrote:

the generous youth of the war, when England could carry, with no air of burlesque, the flag of St. George, was pretty well gone. The authentic flame might still flicker on in the minds of a few tired soldiers and disregarded civilians. Otherwise, it was dead as the half million of good fellows whom it had fired four years ago, whose credulous hearts the maggots were now eating.[24]

The terrific wind referred to by Lawrence had come, and had blown the umbrella to pieces. All this would give impetus to the relocation of value from society to the individual.

Chapter 3 looks at the history of imaginative literature for children, and the opening up of a new 'emancipated' phase of children's literature signalled by the publication of Lewis Carroll's *Alice's Adventures in Wonderland* in 1865. *Alice's Adventures in Wonderland* sparked off a new flexibility and freedom in writing for children, not only structurally and stylistically, but in the choice of subject matter as well. More importantly, as so fascinatingly discussed in Juliet Dusinberre's book, *Alice To The Lighthouse* (1987), Carroll's work became a model for a new relationship between child reader and adult author in which the text was a shared space, and any number of possible meanings might be spawned in the collaboration between author and reader, with the adult present as a guide in the process of the child's *becoming*, rather than as the monopolistic shaper of the child's being.

Chapter 4 looks at the balance between enclosure and exposure in the period spanning the 1860s to about the 1950s, a period which is generally considered the Golden Age of children's literature. Books written in this period would appear to be configured around this new balance of power between adult and child. Early children's books are affirmations of adult power, and children, both fictional and real, are dominated by the structure of the text. Children's books in the later half of the present century have done much to affirm the child or adolescent, but unfortunately, the redressing of the balance of power may go too far, and the adult is made a figure of impotence, a symbol of authority to be rejected along with other elements of enclosure. During this Golden Age, however, both child and adult are seen to coexist happily, in balance with each other. The power of the adult is only exerted for the purpose of necessary discipline and protection, not the inhibition, of the child. The child is left free to develop and to find himself or herself, to enjoy the partly exposed but protected spaces as long as he, in turn, acknowledges the rightful authority of the adult. Under this happy balance of enclosure and exposure, being and self in children's literature of this period not only crystallise without unnecessary *angst*, but the resultant individual is healthy and unwarped, unlike many of the youthful protagonists inhabiting children's literature of the present time.

In children's literature of this century and especially in that written since the 1950s, which is the subject of Chapter 5, enclosure in many of its manifestations has been abandoned, not only in its ideological and sociological forms, but on occasion, in terms of narrative principles as well. Traditional patterns of narrative closure have at times been eschewed; this is especially evident in the recent genre of game books for children whose organizing aesthetic is 'make your own story', in which the participation of the child reader, his individual perceptions, knowledge and moral choices, combine to create flexible texts and story lines.

In modern children's literature, parental authority has been represented as strangely weakened or rejected; we may perhaps see in this rebellion against authority a resentment against the establishment and its values which has its origins in the disillusionment engendered by the two world wars, the sense of the social contract having been broken. Thus have the protective walls separating the child from the bleak 'real' world come down. The child within, and the child reader of, modern fiction, encounter drug addiction, abortion, rape, alcoholism, divorce and the whole gamut of societal evil, not at a decent distance, but in the full immediacy of personal experience, and under the implied defence that this *is* real life, after all. Realism has apparently become sufficient justification for representation.

But we may also identify an ideological factor at work in this aesthetic revolution, this new, defiant, valorisation of the 'real', and this has to do with the notion that 'enclosure' may in some sort be commensurate with 'privilege': that it is the privileged children who have the unpleasantness of the real world screened off from them. In the 1950s and 60s, it was felt by writers and publishers that there were significant lacunae within the body of children's literature, one of which was the absence of works 'relevant' to the child of the 'working class', no literature in which his own experience was charted and validated, no novelistic context he could 'relate to' and 'identify with'. Children's literature of the so-called 'Golden Age' had been written largely around and for middle- and upper-class children, who had maids running around after them, came into diamond mines and earldoms, had holidays in the Lake District, owned their own boats, and had 'cars 'n hosses 'n butlers 'n a rafty great house 'n loot stacked in the vaults'.[25] Even the less well-off children in E. Nesbit's novels come from homes which would by today's standards be considered comfortable, and Dickie Harding (*Harding's Luck*, and *The House of Arden*), the Nesbit character who most closely experiences poverty and privation, is in the end discovered to be the rightful Lord of Arden, and finally goes back to the time of James I, where he enjoys all that privilege can offer. 'I'm not sayin' 's I want butlers 'n that, but there's plenty other things to want for me 'n I'm startin' from scratch,'[26] says Jukie, a Teddy boy in Antonia Forest's *The Thuggery Affair* (1965), expressing a sentiment that might well stand for the views of those children's authors like John Rowe Townsend (*Gumble's Yard*, 1961[27]) who felt it incumbent on them to provide the many other things which the child who was not of the *bourgeoisie* might need and want, in a fiction constructed around and for them.

The walls around privilege had to come down, and the reader of children's or teenage fiction was to encounter no more Hundred Acre Woods, but was instead admitted into acquaintance with the real world. In this new environment, however, the child or teenager has to struggle as never before to *be* enough, to maintain self and identity in a world where authority and justice have broken down, while society is no longer able to support the individual fully in his quest for definition. The sense of threat to the self is much more strongly felt in modern children's literature, not only because of hostility in the environment, but also because the decline of authority – both moral and traditional – has removed standards by which the child can define himself. The insidiousness of moral relativism cultivated in place of objective morality[28] is a threat to selfhood difficult to ward off; and moral relativism, once a philosophy held by a minority, is becoming almost the predominant ethos of the present time. The child in the twentieth century, in its search for integrity, often flounders not through simple weakness of character, (though of course this may be a contributing factor), but because he or she is unable to distinguish clearly between right and wrong in an environment grown morally flabby.

The tone and atmosphere in many books for children written since the 1960s has thus become defeatist and hopeless. Robert Cormier's novels, *The Chocolate War* (1975), *Beyond the Chocolate War* (1985) and *I am the Cheese* (1977), convey the sense that the corruption that permeates modern society is tragically irreversible, unconquerable; the child can either succumb, give in and become one of the corrupted or be broken: there appears to be no possibility of triumph.

In Cormier's view of the world, the child can never be sufficient; his identity will either be twisted violently and warped, or wiped out. Alan Garner's *Red Shift*, though disliked, (as noted by Humphrey Carpenter in his *Oxford Companion to Children's Literature*), by the critics for its 'general atmosphere of hopelessness and degeneration', while not defeatist in the same way, is, however, equally melancholic in its portrayal of the quest for being. The quest is not doomed, but as with Browning's Childe Roland, the landscape is found daunting, and the world perceived as unhealthy; triumph and failure lie precariously balanced – infinitely so.

This work was given initial form as a Ph.D. thesis in 1992. Since then, the body of scholarship on children's literature has been considerably enlarged, and this is perhaps the proper place to take cognizance of work in the general area of children's literature, even though this study may not have had cause to use, to any significant degree, the insights provided by recent critical work, because of its non-applicability to this study's particular scope and approach. This might be described as historical rather than theoretical, and also non-ideological – at least in so far as it is possible for any work to be so. Developments should be noted, for example, in areas such as children's book illustration, which has, excitingly, been the subject of much recent thought in the field: Jane Doonan's *Looking at Pictures in Picture Books* (1993) and *Talking Pictures: Pictorial Texts and Younger Readers* (1996) (edited by Victor Watson and Morag Styles) deserve especial mention; *After Alice, The Prose and the Passion, Voices Off*, the three collections of essays edited by Morag Styles, Eve Bearne and Victor Watson, also contain a good deal of new material on this aspect of the subject. Scholarship has also moved in the direction of applying critical theory to the analysis of children's books – of particular note in this part of the field is Peter Hunt's *Criticism, Theory and Children's Literature* (1991). His more recently edited work, the *International Companion Encyclopaedia of Children's Literature* (1997), a collection of essays addressing contemporary and critical issues in children's books, such as intertextuality, reader-response theory and so on, is another important contribution to the field. Peter Hollindale's *Signs of Childness in Children's Books* (1997), which engages with the question of the perceived child to whom the text is purportedly addressed, is another significant work on reader-response theory in relation to children's literature. Interesting new readings of individual children's classics, such as those in Shirley Foster and Judy Simmons's *What Katy Read* (1995), invoking a feminist perspective, have also emerged.

In this introduction, there remains one matter to be clarified: context is of some importance to this work, and the context I have been working with is a British one. I have, however, used American children's literature in my discussion where these works have been influential and important in relation to the British scene.

1
The Imprisoning Image

We must not let loose our own subjectivity upon the pictures and make them its vehicles. We must begin by laying aside as completely as we can all our own preconceptions, interests and associations ... We sit down before the picture in order to have something done to us, not that we may do things with it.

C. S. Lewis, *An Experiment in Criticism*

All reality is iconoclastic.

N.W. Clerk, *A Grief Observed*

Children's literature has for a long time been considered a body of work separate from that intended for adult readers. However, the fortunes of children's literature were, from an early stage, intimately linked with the forces that were at work in shaping the novel. This chapter is interested in the interactions between the bodies of work, the history of mutual shaping and influence. As noted by Felicity Hughes in 'Children's Literature: Theory and Practice':

the history of children's literature coincides, more or less, with the history of the novel. What historians of children's literature often call the first real children's book, Newberry's *A Little Pretty Pocket Book*, was published within a decade of Richardson's *Pamela*. It is probable that more than coincidence is involved, since similar social conditions are conducive to both. In fact, the development of a separate body of literature addressed to children has been crucially associated with that of the novel, and the critical fortunes of the one have been strongly affected by those of the other.[1]

20

This observation is accompanied by the argument that the evolution of a separate body of children's literature was aided by the growing desire of novelists to establish the novel as a serious art form. This, however, was felt to be impossible while children continued to form a consistent part of the novel's readership: taboos and constraints existed as to what might or might not be mentioned and treated of in front of children. Family readings in the evening are a well-known fact of Victorian social history[2] and, earlier in the eighteenth century, novels and romances are known to have been easily accessible to the young. In 1802, the children's author, Mrs Trimmer, in an article entitled, 'Observations On The Changes Which Have Taken Place In Books For Children And Young Persons' in *The Guardian of Education* had complained that novels 'were at this time [the middle of the last century] frequently put into the hands of young people, and the establishment of *Circulating Libraries* a few years afterwards [gave] free access to books of all descriptions'.[3]

In these circumstances, novelists were restricted in their choice and treatment of subjects[4] for novels; this led to the growing sense that the constantly enforced awareness of child readership hindered the development of the novel as an art form, which, under the rising star of the realist aesthetic during the nineteenth century, was largely committed to the representation or depiction of real life. The problem which arose out of this concerned the possibility of creating a faithful representation of life even though there were sections of reality of which the young had to be kept in ignorance. It was felt that the art of the novel was thereby being severely limited in scope and potential and robbed of its full vitality, just as the practice of Bowdlerism and euphemistic utterance, in its refusal to confront and name, was in danger of depriving phenomena of their rightful definitions and identities.

Thus, as Dickens wrote humorously in *Our Mutual Friend*, the child, or the 'certain institution' which Mr Podsnap in his mind called the 'young person', was felt to be an inconvenient and exacting institution, requiring everything in the universe to be filed down and fitted to it. The question about everything was, would it bring a blush to the cheek of the young person?[5] Eventually, the constraints would prove too onerous, and the novelist would make a bid for freedom of expression which, paradoxically enough, also encouraged the growth of the children's novel. For it was gradually recognized that if adult literature was to be kept apart from the child, then not only was there a need for a separate literature for children, but that this separate body of work had to be capable of providing children with a degree of mental and spiritual sustenance at least equal in quality and substance to that which was being withdrawn.

If the development of children's literature was to some extent owing to a desire for literary secession on the part of writers for adults, it was also indebted to the interest taken in the child by late eighteenth-century writers and educational theorists. Without it, children's literature would probably have been slower to develop. In England, the birth of that interest owed something to Rousseau's *Émile*, which not only influenced the educational writings of the Edgeworths and Thomas Day – the author of *Sandford and Merton* – but, more significantly, inspired the work of the Romantic poets: Wordsworth, Coleridge and Blake. Wordsworth's famous 'Immortality Ode', was itself to help shape a potent image of the child and influence a whole new mode of thought regarding childhood, which attitude was to persist throughout the century and beyond.[6] The portrayal of, and scrutiny given to, children in the English novel from 1837 to the 1860s were, however, to have the greatest impact on children's literature. It can hardly be a coincidence that brought the liberated and outspoken child of *Alice's Adventures in Wonderland* (1865) into being so soon after *Great Expectations* and *The Mill on the Floss*, both published in 1860, had marked the end of a phase in the history of the English novel,[7] to which the fictional child's position had been central.

Amongst the earliest representations of childhood to be found in writing for children was that which had been given form by the Puritans, who held that children had to be completely subordinated[8] and controlled for their own good. Fictional children fashioned after the Puritan image existed only as *exemplar*: they were there either to demonstrate the effects of non-repentance, or the escape from evil through salvation, and, therefore, had no existence independent of their didactic function. The Puritan child was conceived of having a propensity for evil which had to be checked by conversion, repentance and obedience to God and parents. Books written with this image of childhood sternly exhorted the child, as James Janeway[9] did, for example, to 'get by [it]self into the chamber or garret and fall upon [its] knees and weep and mourn'.[10] In all this may be detected the desire for control of the child's inner life: of the state of his soul, what he should feel and how he should manifest those feelings.

Interestingly, the images that the reader of this type of literature – and Janeway's writing in particular – carries away with him are of children in garrets or rooms, praying and crying, Sarah Howley calling her siblings 'into a chamber with her' to perform these activities, people watching at doors to ascertain the conversion of the child. Truly, this is the theatre of claustrophobia. In any case, the child soon left the enclosure of the Puritan home for that of the grave: the unregenerate child was punished with a horrific death; the saintly child was rewarded by dying while in a state of grace. As Gillian Avery remarks in 'The Puritans and their Heirs', 'the greatest desideratum was that all children should be prepared for death, and if they died during a religious phase then they were felt to be safe'.[11] These early writings for children fail to accommodate any idea of growth or development; constrained, closely observed and monitored by its parents and the all-seeing eye of God, the Puritan child was encouraged only to define itself in religious terms while alive, and was marked for a woefully early death.

The high rates of infant mortality then current might explain to some degree the high proportion of stories in which the representation of the death experience occurs. Yet one suspects that the death of their fictional counterparts was, more importantly, a literary device intended to frighten child readers into rapid conformity with the principles that ruled the lives of Janeway characters such as Sarah Howley. This young lady spends her brief existence in tears and prayer, is submissive to her parents and dedicated to converting her siblings, until her lungs give way (doubtless as a result of all her shrieking and breast-beating antics), whereupon she dies, safe in her assurance of heaven.

Another example of writing in this tradition is Martha Butt Sherwood's *The History of the Fairchild Family* (published in two parts, the first in 1818, the second in 1847), which again presents the child as a naturally depraved being whose soul is in constant danger of perishing. The Fairchild children appear to spend their time sinning, being punished and then repenting; yet, their attempts to improve never seem to succeed, and their state of moral/religious being remains completely and negatively frozen. As with Janeway's work, there is an almost complete lack of privacy given to the children: Lucy, the eldest, is given a diary in which she is told to record her sins and which guilty narrative she is then required to show to her mother. The Fairchild parents stand on the stairs to listen in on the children; Mrs Fairchild enters Lucy and Emily's bedroom to overhear their conversations.

Children's books of this sort operate on a principle of restriction, miming the supervisory function of the adult, and seeking to convince the child that he is being continually observed, reminding him that God knows his heart as well as his actions. Even in the physical absence of the parents, the psychology of being watched continues. Emily dreams, for instance, that God's Eye keeps watch on her wherever she goes – this is depicted as a frightening experience rather than as an exercise of a benevolent concern on God's part. The dream sends her into a fever which nearly proves fatal, and Sherwood intends that this should signify to the reader both punishment and threat. To the modern reader, however, the fever may be construed as a sign of a minor psychological breakdown inflicted by the oppressiveness of her environment. After all, if Emily does suffer from paranoia, the constant sensation of being watched, of feeling that Someone is after her, she is hardly to blame: Someone is.

Changes in aesthetics are often the product of alterations in perspective, and in Wordsworth's poetry, and also Brontë's *Jane Eyre* (1847) which is discussed below, there may be found important instances of such 'revisioning' which were to have far-reaching consequences for children's literature. The influence of *The Prelude* and especially the 'Ode' should be noted,[12] but even the children in his *Lyrical Ballads* – as, for example, those encountered in 'Anecdote for Fathers' and 'We are Seven' – may have had some part to play in the changing perception of the child. If the 'Ode' provides the general template for the Romantic child, then the children in 'Anecdote for Fathers' and 'We are Seven' may be thought of as particularised products of that template. Their childish vision effectively reconfigures the perception of the world as well as restructuring the power balance between child and adult.[13]

In 'We are Seven', for instance, the adult's insistence on the strict demarcation of space into physical and conceptual, where the living occupy the one and the dead the other, is countered by the more coherent understanding of the little girl to whom life and death, the living and the dead, exist in a temporal and spatial continuum. Her family members dwell in the churchyard cottage and, to her, the churchyard is 'near', their graves only 'twelve steps or more from [her] mother's door', located in what is only an extension of that familial space – again, we may note the trope of the widened childhood world. Both poems suggest that the instinctual wisdom of the child, which lies outside language, is superior to the habituated thinking of the adult who subjects the world to his quantifying mind, and they show how the adult's attempt to intellectually colonise the new world which the child's vision translates into being is frustrated. As Susan

Wolfson notes, the child's response often eludes 'the terms in which the [adult's] question has been posed'.[14] The child's answer demands understanding on its own terms, and the child thus becomes the determiner of meaning.

In the 'Ode', Wordsworth sought to give the child his manumission from the older, grimmer image espoused by the Puritans which had held the child defined within the limitations of a sinful nature; the image of childhood he substituted was ultimately, however, one equally constricted, albeit by innocence, and thus as unfit to represent the needs and the real nature of the child. While Wordsworth's child of the 'Ode' is *itself* still subject to temporality and hence to the possibilities of change, the idea of childhood that was inspired by it was unfortunately static, tending to valorise an innocence which could not be over-written and which therefore limited the potential for development. In any case, no child, as Dusinberre says, 'wants to be part of an iconography: slip of Satan or cherub, baby Jesus or changeling boy, man's only inspiration or someone who always tells lies.' To be part of an iconography is to inhabit a two-dimensional world, to be unable to step outside the limitations of the image; 'the literal world is freer'.[15]

This caveat aside, Wordsworth's 'Ode on Intimations of Immortality from Recollections of Early Childhood' (1802) none the less deserves discussion as demonstrating most clearly the new aesthetic and philosophy of childhood that replaced the Puritan view of things. One cannot afford to underestimate the effect which Wordsworth's work was to have on attitudes to childhood. Coveney comments that

> Even so early as 1899, James Fotheringham ... remarked on Wordsworth's importance to the nineteenth century's interest in the child: 'It is owing to the movement he so well interpreted, ... that we have studied the child-nature so much, and so carefully as we have been doing.[16]

Nor is it possible to wade far through nineteenth-century criticism and essays on children's literature without finding the 'Ode' often and lovingly quoted; Wordsworth's views on childhood came to be the shaping factor of many children's books. For instance, the epigraphs of each chapter of Kingsley's *The Water Babies* (1863), as Victor Watson observes, are quotations from Wordsworth, Coleridge and Longfellow, and Kingsley attempts to convey the spontaneity and liberty of the Wordsworthian spirit of childhood through the liquid medium in which the fictional child, Tom, moves.[17] Perhaps the most important (though not the most obvious) part of Wordsworth's vision of childhood was that he *did* see the child as a figure capable of growth and development, a being whose most vital growth and development was stimulated from within and not by the teachings of those around him.[18] In this, Wordsworth departed significantly from the views of his time. Despite the tone of regret that shades the inevitability of growing up in the 'Immortality Ode', the necessity of growth is acknowledged and seen as a condition of wholeness and total selfhood.

The 'Ode' contains many of the seeds from which the refurbished image of childhood was to germinate; the image which emerges is impressionistic, painted in pleasing colours, but a trifle blurred around the edges. To some degree, this slightly blurred luminosity with which the fictional child was endowed was inescapable; nostalgia dictates the tone of the poem and influences its contained images of childhood. The image of the child which the 'Ode' presents is fluid: distinct at times, indefinite at others (the word 'indefinite' is not, however, intended to carry here any strongly pejorative overtones). The child of the 'Ode' exists within a structure of memory, a mood relating to the not-present, a state inaccessible to and non-ascertainable by the empirical senses of eye, ear and touch. As such, the artistic issue is likely to be emotively coloured impressions of childhood, rather than objective and accurate delineations of it.

The language of description in the 'Ode' plays an important role in creating these impressions; much of this language is of a connotative rather than of a denotative kind. It contains many 'unparametered' words: words whose meaning cannot be exactly or precisely defined and whose resultant flexibility may be used to create a sense of enlarged space. The language also contains a preponderance of light and sense impressions. All this, taken together, works to achieve the 'soft focus' effect with which childhood is depicted in the 'Ode' which begins by establishing a state of things where 'every common sight' seems 'apparelled in celestial light'. This might be said to operate in a manner analogous to that of Moses's 'burning bush', rebuffing any attempt to approach too closely. The word 'celestial' gestures towards an area of experience which the human imagination can only brush against or aspire after; the objects which the celestial light bathes are thus distanced and to some degree hallowed. The light which the poetic vision emits is one that causes the beholder to avert his eye; thus, there is a failure of direct confrontation on the part of the observer. The opening is also intended to establish a mood of wonder, a mood perhaps not naive, but childlike, which again serves to create distance between reader and subject. Partly because of this distance, and partly because of the poet's technique in pulling the eye from object to object, the 'light' and the 'freshness' permeating the poem and surrounding the child do *not* result in clarity; the reader is allowed little time in which to pause and examine each image, his vision awash with image as he is whirled from 'meadow' to 'grove' to 'stream' and so on.

'Glory' and 'dream' are likewise words that strain after precise and clearly definable meaning.[19] The struggle to elicit exactness from a word like 'glory' (which would later in the century be glossed by Humpty Dumpty as 'a nice knock-down argument', during a debate whose linguistic issues would make the question of precision look very unimportant indeed) in order to recall the particularity of a dream, is mimetic of the attempt to recover or recreate that state of idyllic childhood which the poet claims to remember. Words such as these swathe childhood in a haze of luminosity, making it difficult to apprehend fully. Thus, right from the start, the reader is faced with terms of reference that do not contain experience, but reach outwards and upwards to the unencompassable. And thus, the child of the Ode cannot be strictly defined or fixed.[20] The figure of the child, when he first appears within the poem, does not occupy a fixed or specific temporality or spatiality. Similarly, the 'Child of Joy' who suddenly appears does so not as a concrete and tangible entity, but as a poetic and symbolic, almost archetypal, manifestation cordoned off by memory and the aesthetic doctrines at work within the poem. The qualities associated by the poet with the state of childhood are couched in terms associated with light, and hover in the realm of the indefinable and thus non-possessable:

> Whither is fled the visionary *gleam*
> Where is it now, the glory and the dream?   (lines 56–7)

Following this are the now-famous and oft-quoted lines about the child arriving from his heavenly and eternal home, trailing clouds of glory in his wake. It was in this scanty, if lovely, array that the Romantic child was sent forth into the nineteenth century, and as with so many of the abandoned waifs of fiction, his clothing at least provided a clue to his origins: heaven. Thus, the intrinsic nature of childhood, if not quite semi-divine, was at least closer to God than that of adult mankind. The 'Ode' portrays childhood as a naturally enlightened state of being and one from which enlightenment may in turn be derived. This was – unfortunately – an idea that was easy to sentimentalise. Heightening the potential for sentimentality already inherent in the mental picture of the cherub wreathed in rosy clouds and dimples is the lassitude of words like 'trailing'. Existing for the adult as inspiration and as subject for adult sentiment, the romantic image of childhood was one lacking in vitality and energy.

Though adulthood is spoken of as 'bringing the philosophic mind', it is spoken of with a regret too strongly accented to be mistaken. Maturity is almost a consolation prize rather than a state to be sought after. The child is not so much freed to grow up as reluctantly resigned into the hands of the inevitable. There is a narrowing rather than widening of horizons:

> *Shades* of the prison-house begin to *close*
> Upon the growing boy ...   (lines 67–8)

The corona of light surrounding the child that till now has shone forth is darkened and diminished, and light becomes a thing apart from him; he becomes beholder rather than source:

> He sees it in his joy ...
> The youth, who daily from the East
> Must travel ...
> And by the vision splendid
> Is on his way attended;
> At length the man perceives it die away
> And fade into the light of common day ...
>   (lines 71–7)

Not only does he travel away from the source of light in the East, but the sun's 'splendour' (a Wordsworthian synonym for 'glory') fades also into commonness, in direct contrast to the opening lines, where what was common had appeared clothed in celestial light. Although the terms of enclosure are, in Wordsworth's mind, applicable to the 'growing boy' and not the child, adulthood is represented as a time of imprisonment, and the child becomes unwilling to grow up, to leave the spaces for the prison house, and this reluctance may be seen as a limiting factor to growth.

Despite this, Wordsworth's treatment of childhood should not be thought of as totally regressive. The 'Immortality Ode' may be atypical of the general sense of concreteness – 'the rocks and stones and trees' of his other poetry – but the characteristic toughness is still present here, though in a muted way:

> We will grieve not, rather find
> Strength in what remains behind;
> In the primal sympathy
> Which having been must ever be ...
>
> (lines 180–3)

Despite the sentimental lingering over childhood, the poet in the end accepts the inevitability of growing up, and in this acceptance is the beginning of strength. The symbolic child of the 'Ode', rather than the more ordinary but less distinctive one of the *Prelude*, was to shape the popular attitude and tempt future writers into vistas of increasing saccharine sentimentality. Though Wordsworth cannot be entirely blamed for this sentimentalising trend, the child of the 'Ode' and the tone of regret for a lost innocence and sunlit happiness was to mould much of nineteenth- and early twentieth-century literature.

Nearly half a century on, traces of the Wordsworthian legacy were still discernible. In *The Nemesis of Faith*, written by Froude in 1849, sentiment is shaped by the 'Ode':

> God has given us each our own *Paradise*, our own old childhood, over which the old *glories linger*, to which our own hearts *cling,* as all we have ever known of *Heaven* upon earth. And there, as all earth's weary *wayfarers* turn back their toil-jaded eyes, so do all the poor speculators ... *turn back* in thought, at least, to that old time of peace – that village church – that child-faith, – which, once lost, is never gained again.[21] [emphases mine]

The matrix of ideas embedded in this passage, its vocabulary, the tone of desire and memory – all these recall the 'Ode'. The languor of the earlier 'trailing clouds' may be detected here in the lingering glories and clinging hearts; the 'wayfarers' echo the journey taken by the growing boy in the 'Ode'. In a strange way, too, even the parentheses and phrasing: '– the village church – that child faith' are like scrapbook images or ideas hesitantly fingered, which, however, the writer cannot link to a stream or sequence of fully remembered things.

Wordsworth's vision of childhood was also to influence George Eliot, whose *Mill on the Floss*, published in 1860, although presenting to the

Victorian reader a wider and fuller picture of childhood painted in tones that avoided the absolutism of earlier images, yet bore the imprint of Wordsworthian yearning for the imagined golden age. As the first volume closes, the reader observes Tom and Maggie going forth

> ... together into their new life of sorrow, and they would never more see the sunshine undimmed by remembered cares. They had entered the thorny wilderness, and the golden gates of their childhood had forever closed behind them.[22]

All this is laden with Biblical overtones; the thorns and thistles promised to Adam and Eve on their eviction from Eden, and the closing of Eden to them for eternity. What lies under this passage is the mythos of innocence and its loss. The end of the novel again alludes to this lost idyll of childhood, crystallised in the image of daisy fields in which the children had roamed, and 'clasped their little hands in love'. Here, too, is detected the psychological reluctance of both author and character to depart from the enclosed happy circle of Romantic childhood for an adult, and therefore lesser, state of being. Maggie's reluctance, and, perhaps, inability to grow up and out of what Coveney calls the 'structure of regret' is, ironically, the cause of the spiral into tragedy. At the century's end, this mood of reluctance was to crystallise into the figure of the boy who never did grow up: Peter Pan.

Further testifying to the triumph of Wordsworthian sentiment were the proliferating figures of child saints, child saviours and child sages that flooded the pages of children's literature, through whose death or suffering the fallen world might be redeemed. Ironically, it appeared that the child of sweetness and light had nearly as little survival instinct as its predecessor. *The Story of Little Henry and His Bearer*, written in 1809 and published in 1814 by Mrs Sherwood, serves a dual function and bestrides both traditions of children's writing. Little Henry (who was modelled on Mrs Sherwood's own son who died young in India), never grows up to become Big Henry. His mother having died young, he is brought up a veritable heathen. The first part of the story follows the guidelines set out for redemptory literature: a young lady arrives in India and teaches Little Henry about God, and how to read his Bible. This section is purely catechistic, structured as a question-and-(orthodox)-answer session between the lady and Henry. After his conversion, he learns to write Persian characters and read Hindi so as to be able to read the Bible to his Indian bearer,

Boosy: this is Henry in his new role of child saviour coming into play. Henry's death, described as the 'glorious progress of the departing saint', is the catalyst for the conversion of his bearer and also of his adoptive mother. Jessica, the heroine of *Jessica's First Prayer* (1867) by Hesba Stretton, is another child-saviour cast in the same mould, and the structure of this children's book follows the same pattern: the salvation of the child who then becomes the instrument of an adult friend's salvation. In the course of the story Jessica falls very ill, and nearly dies. In this, however, she is more fortunate than her predecessors in the tradition: her death has become unnecessary to the success of the story's intention, for her illness is sufficient to soften the heart of the man who has befriended her, and who subsequently repents of the dissipations of his life.

Little Henry (1814), Jessica (1867), Little Lord Fauntleroy (1886) and Pollyanna (1913) are fictional children of the saint/reformer category, involved in the making of the moral being of the adults with whom they come into contact. Possessing more power than the Puritan child, in that they are capable of acting on others rather than only being acted upon, they are none the less constrained by their adherence to the formulae of narrative and type. In the case of Henry and Jessica, their 'soul-making' is central to the function of the books in which they appear. But it may be observed that in both *Jessica's First Prayer* and *The Story of Little Henry and his Bearer* – and indeed in other works in their tradition – the stuff of soul is manufactured at the expense of body. In acquiring their own spiritual being and also the power to form that of the adults, Jessica has to become ill, and Little Henry to relinquish life altogether. Although these two children's stories seem to reverse the traditional roles of adult and child where the formation of character is concerned, the authorial posture of control and authority remains essentially unaltered, for the text is addressed to a child reader whose spiritual being the author hopes to develop.

Little Lord Fauntleroy and Pollyanna go to work in a different and more positive manner, (re)forming the substance of being through the power of positive thinking, and the strength and conviction of their belief in the moral excellence of adult friends and relatives. Though to some extent still prisoners of a literary tradition, they are no longer enclosed in a literature of pure didactic intent, and instead of the adult controlling the child through the projections of image, the child reshapes the adult by projecting an idealised image onto him.

Fauntleroy comes to England to be brought up as the heir of his grandfather, the Earl of Dorincourt, a crabby old aristocrat who cares nothing for the welfare of his tenants. The rehabilitation of the Earl begins with the arrival of his grandchild, who believes him to be a good and benevolent man. He plays a game with the child, which distracts him from his bad temper and his gout, and, as the author Frances Hodgson Burnett notes, from himself.

> If a week before anyone had told the Earl ... that ... he would be forgetting his gout and his bad temper in a child's game, ... he would without doubt have *made himself very unpleasant*; and yet he had certainly *forgotten himself* when the door opened ....²³ [emphases mine]

Here, the reader sees the Earl's power to 'make himself' being abrogated in favour of the child. He begins by forgetting the nature of his being and his power of forming it and the child, and in so doing, opens the way for the child to take over. On a later occasion, after the Earl has grown to be fond of Fauntleroy, and has become less egotistic and self-oriented, Fauntleroy says,

> 'I shall tell him,' ... glowing with enthusiasm, 'that you are the kindest man I ever heard of. And you are always thinking of other people and making them happy, and – and I hope when I grow up I shall be just like you.'
> 'Just like me!' repeated his lordship, looking at the little kindling face. And a dull red crept up under his withered skin, and he suddenly turned his eyes away and looked out of the carriage window ....²⁴

The Earl is not only made ashamed of what he has been; lurking at the back of his mind is the fear that the child *may* become like him – may have his nature corrupted – and this fear is part of what stimulates the change in him. His being imperceptibly alters to take on the nature and likeness of Fauntleroy's, and this is aided by the energy of the child's positive belief.

This is also the case with Pollyanna and her aunt. Pollyanna's practice of seeing something to be glad about in everything has the effect of enhancing what is good in all that is around her. The characters she interacts with are encouraged to build upon what positive moral being they possess. They are not twitted into destroying what is negative, but a central idea in the novel is that the negative qualities of a person will wither if time and energy are spent in cultivating opposite virtues.

Eleanor Porter's entire philosophy of being may be found in the magazine which the pastor of the community reads in his disappointment over the townfolks' quarrelsome behaviour:

> What men and women need is encouragement. Their natural resisting powers should be strengthened, not weakened ... Instead of harping on a man's faults, tell him of his virtues... Hold up to him his better self, his real self that can dare and do and win out![25]

Pollyanna is the mirror which reflects people's better selves back onto them, remaking them in a more positive image.

Oliver Twist (1837), as Kathleen Tillotson has noted, was the first English novel to make the child the centrepiece.[26] As such, it is important, though its incorruptibly innocent protagonist, Oliver, is none the less an obvious Romantic descendent; there is nothing either new or unique in the character and presentation of the child Oliver, a scion of the eighteenth-century novel of sensibility pressed into the service of the nineteenth-century social novel. Oliver is not endowed with either the temperament or the vitality to revolutionise attitudes concerning children, though he may indeed have served to draw attention to their sufferings in an industrial environment. Firstly, he does not really represent childhood at all, nor the point of view of the child. If he (and children in general) were intended to be the main focal point of the novel, it is strange that in Dickens's preface to the novel, Oliver only comes in for one mention:

> I have yet to learn that a lesson of the purest good may not be drawn from the vilest evil ... In this spirit, ... I wished to show in little Oliver, the principle of Good surviving through every adverse circumstance and triumphing at last.[27]

Moreover, Dickens describes him as the embodiment of a principle, metaphorising the figure of the child rather than presenting him as a psychologically realistic being. The rest of the preface, continuing over a few pages, reveals Dickens's true concerns, which may be summed up thus:

> It appeared to me that to draw a knot of associates in crime as did really exist ... to show them as they really are ... would be to attempt a something that was needed, and would be *a service to society*.[28] [emphases mine]

The question of privilege is invested in the whole novel. It is about privilege, the haves and have-nots; it suggests how the system should or might be restructured, asking for an equalisation of the two states. The posture assumed by the text is that of the unprivileged, which is embodied in its titular representative, a child whose implicit statement to the reader is: 'I am both smaller and younger than you.' This representative is also poor, nameless and an orphan: what greater proof of being unprivileged? The adoption of this unthreatening position in relation to the reader constitutes an act of flattery, and asks for his patronage, both for the text and also the causes espoused by it. The novel, however, privileges the discourse of the poor over that of the child, and thus attention is given to his state of poverty but not to his lack of expressive facilities, or to the problem of his incomplete representation.

Dickens tries to divest vice of its fancy trappings, to de-romanticise it:

> Here are no canterings on moonlit heaths, no merry-makings in the snuggest of all possible caverns, none of the attractions of dress, no embroidery, no lace, no jack-boots, no crimson coats and ruffles, none of the dash and freedom with which 'the road' has been time out of mind invested.[29]

But no attempt is made to de-romanticise the child, who remains uncomfortably decked out in his halo throughout the novel (after all, it is necessary that he do so if he is to come into his portion of his inheritance). Oliver's soulful quality makes it impossible for him to fight back, only to resist morally, and thus, he is trapped and rigidly held a prisoner by his own angelic image, which denies him the resources of the real.

Oliver Twist, on one level, is about the acquisition of a social identity rather than moral being, with which he is well supplied. The name 'Oliver Twist' is not the infant's true name, this symbolising his ignorance of his true identity, without which he is very much at the mercy of the rogues in the novel. The name is arbitrarily given, 'invented' by Mr Bumble:

> 'We name our foundlings in alphabetical order. The last was a S, Swubble, I named him. This was a T, – Twist, I named *him*.'[30]

The name 'Oliver Twist' leads neither the reader nor Monks to the person signified by the name, but ironically serves to blur his identity and hide him from those who are his friends and enemies alike. The arbitrary name misleads Agnes's friends away from Agnes's child, though his face serves as a truer guide to his parentage and his identity. The search for identity is, however, in a way restricted to the acquisition of a name, for there is in Oliver no real development of self-knowledge, no awareness of the search *qua* search even while it is ongoing. At the end of the novel, identity is given rather than won, and the giving leaves him unchanged in the same way as his earlier contact with vice has made no impression upon his virtue: he is a *tabula rasa,* a blank tablet on which nothing has been, or can be, written. This is partly due to the fact that Oliver, as I have suggested before, is not a real child, but only a literary symbol for Good and the sufficiency of moral being, a vehicle for the author's social critique. Oliver, his own feelings and responses to the picturesque horrors of Victorian London, is never the real focus of the novel.

In any case, Oliver's repertoire of responses is an extremely limited one, and almost purely emotional, though this may have an explanation. With the rise of the cult of sensibility in the late eighteenth-century, feeling had become, in a sense, an index to moral worth, and Oliver's excessive sensibility, his tears and trembling are thus, at one level, signs to the reader of his goodness. As Janet Todd writes: 'The sentimental work reveals a belief in the appealing aesthetic quality of virtue, displayed in a naughty world through a vague and potent distress.'[31] At another level, the display of emotion is aimed at evoking a response from the reader's emotive rather than rational faculties, intended to evoke pity for the child and his circumstances.

Oliver's initial appearance prepares the reader for what is to prove a frequent Twist characteristic: 'Oliver cried lustily.' The second mention of him is equally bedewed with tears and carries an unconscious irony: 'It was no difficult matter for the boy to call tears into his eyes... he burst into an agony of childish grief.' Upon being reminded of his orphaned state (and its implicit attendant social miseries), Oliver commences crying again:

> 'You know that you've got no father or mother, and that you were brought up by the parish, don't you?'
> 'Yes sir,' replied Oliver weeping bitterly.
> 'What are you crying for?' inquired the gentleman ...
> And to be sure it was very extraordinary. What *could* the boy be crying for?[32]

Just in case the reader has managed – somehow – to overlook the point, Dickens underlines it with a heavy pencil. Locked up in a dark room, Oliver (again) cries 'bitterly all day; and, when the long, dismal night came on, spread his little hands before his eyes to shut out the darkness, and crouching in his corner, tried to sleep: ever and anon waking with a start and a tremble'. Again, both syntax and visual image are artfully arranged for the reader's benefit. Four pages on, at the sight of a basin of gruel, 'Oliver began to cry very piteously'; on being told he is going to be made an apprentice, he trembles; on being reminded yet again of his orphaned state, tears roll down his face and he sobs bitterly. And so on and so forth.

Perhaps the most ironic point about the novel is that though it criticises the social ills of the day, amongst which was the exploitation of children, it utilises, albeit unconsciously, the evil it seeks to destroy. Apprenticed to Mr Sowerberry, the undertaker, Oliver is enjoined to take the part of the mute at children's funerals.

'There's an expression of melancholy in his face, my dear,' resumed Mr Sowerberry, 'which is very interesting. He would make a delightful mute.'[33]

We are told, 'many were the mournful processions which little Oliver headed, in a hat band reaching down to his knees, to the indescribable emotion of all the mothers in the town'. Here, Dickens relates the exploitation of Oliver by Mr Sowerberry: the facts of his childhood and his unhappiness as manifested in his melancholic expression are used to evoke emotion at children's funerals; he is a living advertisement for his employer. Moreover, he is a 'mute'; not only made to serve a function, but denied the opportunity to speak on his own behalf. Oliver at this point embodies the 'seen and not heard' principle that dominated the child's world in the nineteenth century. Far from being allowed to express his own feelings, his job with the undertaker consists of giving expression to, and working on, the emotions of others. However, Dickens does exactly the same thing as Mr Sowerberry, being himself the ultimate puppet master behind Oliver, though operating at one degree removed from the action. He too financially exploits the youth and sadness with which he has endowed the child for his own purposes, namely to increase the appeal of the work with his readers. The irony of this was probably lost on the majority of readers.

Oliver Twist is written around themes of enclosure, imprisonment and escape.[34] Oliver moves from places which hem him in, like the dark room where he is locked up, to Mr Sowerberry's, where he is pushed down a steep flight of steps by Mrs Sowerberry into a stone cell, and made to sleep among the coffins in a 'grave-like' recess. He escapes, only to fall into the clutches of Fagin, from whom he is rescued, and into whose hands he again falls, in a sequence of things constantly repeated, repetition itself being a form of structural imprisonment. The fictional child in this novel, apart from his constitutional inability to develop and his untarnishable image of innocence, is never able to establish himself as a free agent: his very nature acts as a form of imprisonment. Even when he finally escapes from Fagin and his gang to come under the benevolent patronage of Mr Brownlow, the terms of his new existence are still terms made by another adult, not by the child.

Oliver Twist's popularity was outstripped four years later by another Dickens creation also belonging to the tribe of Romantic innocents: Little Nell, of Dickens's *The Old Curiosity Shop*, a girl of marriageable age, who is, however, constantly referred to by the narrator as a child:

> For my part, my curiosity and interest were at least equal to the child's, for child she certainly was, although I thought it probable from what I could make out, that her very small and delicate frame imparted a particular youthfulness to her appearance.[35]

The Wordsworthian heritage is again, as with Oliver, obvious: children, the narrator writes, are 'little people ... fresh from God', and Little Nell's function is to protect and lead the adult (the Victorian seeing-eye child). This theme is sounded by the narrator in the text, who walks Nell home,

> ... the little creature accommodating her pace to mine, and seeming rather to lead and take care of me than I to be protecting her ...[36]

and corroborated by her grandfather: 'It is true that in many respects I am the child, and she the grown person ....'[37] Though Dickens compounds this image with overtones of Cordelia's care for the old, half-mad Lear, still the predominant idea is again that of the greater, innocent wisdom of youth guiding the blind. Nell, like Oliver, is constantly fleeing the forces of enclosure, but the way she finally escapes the bonds of marriage to Quilp is through dying. Though Nell's tremendous popularity with the public is legendary, her appeal was of the sentimental type, her delineation conforming to, rather than turning from, the recipe for the Romantic child. Her death marked the wearing out of the self in the service of her function, that of child-saviour, and again indicates the limitations inherent in this tradition of childhood.

It might be argued that when the Romantic movement adopted the child, writers such as Wordsworth, Coleridge and Rousseau were rendering childhood a service by helping to substitute one image of childhood – that of the child sage/visionary/ saint, representative of an era of lost innocence and beauty – for that of the young limb of Satan, hell-bound unless saved through confession and repentance. At any rate it is true that they encouraged and nurtured what was altogether a more positive view of childhood. However, the Romantic image of childhood, feeding off and fed on what is popularly termed 'the cult of sensibility', held within it the seeds of a decadent sentimentality that was ultimately to weaken the child as symbol. Moreover, the primary qualities that defined the Romantic child – innocence and goodness – were qualities which unfortunately rendered the child passive and unable to fight back effectively. Innocence may be defined in part by its lack of acquaintance with evil; the inability to recognise evil through the lack of first-hand knowledge of it renders the child more vulnerable to its onslaught. Paradoxically, the child who is unrestrained by the code of good behaviour may possess a greater power to counter evil or unpleasantness. Mary, in Frances Hodgson Burnett's *The Secret Garden* for example, has recourse to anger and negative qualities which are unavailable to the innocent child, and which allow her to combat her cousin Colin's bad temper and hysteria:

> "You stop!" she almost shouted. "You stop! I hate you! Everybody hates you! I wish everybody would run out of the house and let you scream yourself to death! You *will* scream yourself to death in a minute, and I wish you would!"
>
> A nice sympathetic child could neither have thought nor said such things but it happened that the shock of hearing them was the best possible thing for this hysterical boy whom no one had ever dared to restrain or contradict.[38]

Mary, who is *not* a 'nice sympathetic child', has power which passive innocence lacks, power which enables her to alter the image of sickly childhood set before her. The difference between Mary and Little Lord Fauntleroy is a distinct one.

Huckleberry Finn, too, derives power from outside the bounds of innocence; he is able to free Jim because his vision transcends the conventional goodness which his society has striven to imprint on him (law and social morality define and deplore his action as theft). There is a sense in which moral being can only be made through the action of moral choice, and choice does not exist until and unless the possibility of 'wrongful' action is there to act as a pull on the individual. Huck is able to make a choice because he does not belong to the tribe of Romantic children inhabiting a two-dimensional morality, and is in that sense freer than they are. Having access to moral choice, he can then develop, where Oliver Twist, with his endowment of goodness, can only remain unchanged. The innocents, sadly enough, are vulnerable to those who would control and enclose them, and those who escape are those who are able to acknowledge their own potentially negative impulses.

This, however, was to occur much later; it was with the publication of *Jane Eyre* in 1847 that the most significant breakthrough occurred. In *Jane Eyre*, Charlotte Brontë set out to break down the existing stereotype of the child, at once giving the fictional child primary status within the text, and also helping it to break down the walls of its imprisoning image. This work was to set in motion the revolution in the appraisal of childhood, drawing strength from the truth and honesty of its representation of childhood feelings and needs, stripping away the innate falseness of previous images. It was the first major work written for adults that used the persona of the child to tell the story in the first person, without the mediation of a detached authorial presence to frame and shape the tale around the child as Dickens had done with *Oliver Twist*. Without the overt authorial presence mediating between reader and fictional subject, the reader is shown the child's world, enabled to experience its terrors and joys directly, and also to inhabit fully, and complexly, the world and people of the novel. *Jane Eyre* was also the first novel to take the fictional child into the experience of adulthood, to survive physically as fictional children of both Romantic and Puritan schools rarely did. Thus, the fictional child was liberated from the tropes of childhood that would have kept him enclosed in childhood.

Jane Eyre is a complex work to discuss, containing so much that is germane to the discussion of both identity and enclosure. Before coming directly to the image of childhood sponsored by the novel, however, it would be interesting to note some of the terms in which the role of Jane has been misunderstood. Peter Coveney has commented on the novel in his book, *The Image of Childhood*, and has this to say:

> The early chapters of *Jane Eyre* establish the heroine as the victim. They insist on her victimization, her loneliness, her isolation. The autobiographical form itself serves to create this sense of an isolated, trapped psyche.... But whereas with Dickens the method evokes a feeling of reality and an attitude to Oliver Twist, say, as a child, the purpose of the emotional realism of *Jane Eyre* is used to establish certain basic attitudes towards the heroine, sympathy which is transferrable to Jane Eyre, the adult.[39]

There are many points which one might contest here. Coveney, while granting earlier in the chapter that Jane Eyre was the 'first heroine to be given a psychic whole', then goes on to imply that she belongs to a class of stereotypes, this being the class of victim whose sufferings are designed to purchase the sympathy of the reader for a cause. This is a severe misunderstanding, doubly so in my view, as the respective strengths and weaknesses of *Jane Eyre* and *Oliver Twist* are, by Coveney, imputed to each other. For as I have suggested above, Oliver is not a real child, but a symbol affirming the values associated with Romantic childhood; and to say as Coveney does, that Dickens's method of depicting Oliver's plight evokes a sense of reality, is, at the very least, arguable.

While Jane is certainly isolated and lonely at the outset of the book, she is not trapped, unless one counts the incident of the Red Room, where she is locked up by her aunt, Mrs Reed. But the point of *Jane Eyre* is that the child Jane resists imprisonment, even if she must fail because of her size. Fighting her loneliness and her isolation, she also fights against being the kind of child which her relatives would have her be. Coveney's grievance that the heroine grows up and draws the reader along with her, away from the contemplation of her childhood state, is a curious one; indeed one may conclude from this that Coveney feels that the section of the novel dealing with Jane's childhood has served merely as prelude to her adult experiences, and that insufficient weight has been given to this passage in her life. If this, indeed, is the sum of his complaint, then he has missed the point, for the adult Jane is produced by the child.

To describe Jane as a victim[40] is misleading; we are told by the first-person narrator,

I resolved in the depth of my heart that I would be *most moderate,* – most correct; and having reflected a few minutes in order to arrange *coherently* what I had to say, I told her all the story of my sad childhood. Exhausted by emotion, *my language was more subdued than it generally was* when it developed that sad theme; and *mindful of Helen's warnings against the indulgence of resentment, I infused into the narrative far less of gall and wormwood than ordinary. Thus restrained and simplified, it sounded more credible: I felt as I went on that Miss Temple fully believed me.*[41] [emphases mine]

This caution against extremism refutes in part the terms in which Mr Coveney wishes to view Jane: the text does *not* insist on her victimisation because she is constantly being cautioned against self-pity and the tendency to see herself as victim. It is difficult to view Jane Eyre as of this crushed species, if only because what the reader is constantly made aware of is the strength of character in the child, her retaliatory resistance. Neither does the 'autobiographical' form convey the sense of a trapped psyche; on the contrary, by bestowing on the individual narrator the prerogative of self-representation, it takes the fictional child one step further on the road to freedom.

The realism of *Jane Eyre* and the sincerity with which the child is depicted are largely due to the tone of moderation already referred to, which the author also uses to deflate popular images of childhood. Brontë works by parading a series of alternative images, which are *not* Jane and do not fairly represent her, but whose existence has contoured the being and existence of the image of childhood of which Jane *is* the embodiment. Indeed, the images of child saint and child sinner are demonstrated to be both flat and false. The isolation which Mr Coveney ascribes to Jane at the commencement of the novel serves notice of her severance from both the idealised and idolised household pet which the Romantic child was becoming, and also from the Puritan exemplary child. The text begins with the process of defamiliarising, by parting the reader from his previous cherished notions of childhood. The tensions in the novel, arising from the inconsistency between the sentimentalised views on childhood that Mr Brocklehurst and Mrs Reed subscribe to in public, and their attitude towards Jane and the inmates of Lowood institution in private, spiral out to touch the reader, making him aware of the duality and hypocrisy practised here. Consistency is advocated by both Brocklehurst and Mrs Reed, she piously pronouncing: 'Consistency, my dear Mr Brocklehurst – I advocate consistency in all things', he unctuously replying:

'Consistency, madam, is the first of Christian duties ...'[42] Yet, as will be shown, there is a singular lack of consistency between the reality of the child and its public image.

The novel opens with Jane kept indoors by bad weather, initially half-imprisoned by the ideas she has been brought up to accept of her own 'physical inferiority' to her cousins, superficial appearance being the foundation on which the image of childhood is shown to be based. The scene moves on to a tableau:

> The said Eliza, John, and Georgiana were now clustered round their mamma in the drawing room: she lay reclined on a sofa by the fireside, and with her darlings about her (for the time neither quarrelling nor crying) looked perfectly happy.[43]

This little scene, posed as if for the painter, is reminiscent of a similar grouping to be found in Dickens's *Master Humphrey's Clock* (1840):

> A little knot of playmates – they must have been beautiful, for I see them now – were clustered one day round my mother's knee in eager admiration of some picture representing a group of infant angels.[44]

He then goes on to relate the dawning of the realisation that his crippled state exiles him from the group. The difference between the two pictures is that Dickens intends one to take this charming miniature with its romantic terms of reference seriously, whereas Charlotte Brontë holds up a magnifying glass to the cracks in the varnish. Dickens's piece of wistful sentimentalia excludes the narrator because the narrator accepts the aesthetic terms on which his exclusion is based as being just. Jane does not.

Jane not only questions her exclusion from the group, but demonstrates the falsity and artifice of the domestic myth. The part of the sentence held in parenthesis, 'for the time neither quarrelling nor crying', is a candid shot slyly taken between official sittings, the dissonant reality behind the popular image, a syntactic bomb within the sentence that explodes the picture of the 'happy contented little children' referred to by Mrs Reed. Jane's enforced distance from the domestic tableau underlines her non-involvement with the saccharine image of childhood, a break which, after the incident of the Red Room, is accentuated:

> ... since my illness she had drawn a more marked line of separation than ever between me and her own children ...[45]

Her exclusion from the domestic myth is partly the outcome of her refusal to play at any of the roles which Mrs Reed would have found acceptable, such as child-dependent or waif, and in her refusal, she denies Mrs Reed the satisfaction of playing the part of benefactress, which that lady would have liked. Jane's difference, the stubbornness that refuses to conform to known and understood roles, disturbs the family, because it challenges and distorts the smug self-image they wish to broadcast to the world. Jane knows she is different:

> I was a discord in Gateshead Hall; I was like *nobody* there; I had *nothing* in harmony with Mrs Reed or her children, or her chosen vassalage ... They were not bound to regard with affection a *thing* that could not sympathise with one amongst them; ... I know that had I been a sanguine, brilliant, careless, exacting, handsome, romping child – though equally dependent and friendless, Mrs Reed would have endured my presence more complacently.[46] [emphases mine]

Ostracising Jane from the group is a temporary means of preserving this image; her presence in it immediately causes the 'angel' children to show their true colours in their reaction to her. The language used by Jane in the passage above describes and mimes the process by which the Reeds seek to nullify her existence. The first sentence, beginning, 'I was a discord ...' is split off by semi-colons, each successive negatory section a logical offshoot of the preceding words, and the structural equation in

> *I was* a *discord* = *I was* like *nobody* (emphases mine]

continues ruthlessly to cut off, one by one, the ties with everyone at Gateshead – 'I had *nothing* in harmony with Mrs Reed or her children, or her chosen vassalage' – with even the words 'they were *not bound*' emphasising this idea of ties being cut. This rejection of the bonds of relationship, marking her separation from the image of childhood sponsored by her aunt, however, eventually frees her to find her own destiny. The reiteration of the word 'thing' in the passage quoted above mimes the process of its being dinned into the ears and consciousness of the child, to render her into a faceless, nameless entity. Because she does not do what Oliver Twist does, that is, play on her position as child and inferior, flattering the adult, she is silenced and shut out. All this may be summed up in Mrs Reed's reply to Jane's earlier question:

Jane, I don't like cavillers or questioners ... Be seated somewhere; and until you can speak pleasantly, remain silent.[47]

The domestic myth of sweetness and light continues to shatter, and Jane continues to grow away from the limitations which images of childhood impose. Finally, the worm turns. Jane bursts out:

I am glad you are *no relation of mine*. I will *never call you aunt again* as long as I live.[48] [emphases mine]

This echoes the cutting of familial bonds spoken of earlier, but now the severance takes place on Jane's initiative, and on Jane's terms, a sign that her emotional dependence on the Reeds is ending. The threat of exposure, and the energy of its utterance, strangely terrifies Mrs Reed, as she, too, attempts to placate Jane, to re-assimilate her into the 'safe' structure of the domestic idyll. She forgets, however, in her semi-panic, that the terms of endearment and feigned concern she thinks to tame Jane with are unfamiliar to the child's ears, and as such, unlikely to hypnotise or soothe her back into dormancy:

Why do you tremble so violently? Would you like to drink some water? ... Is there anything else you wish for, Jane? I assure you, I wish to be your friend ... now *return to the nursery – there's a dear –* and *lie down a little*.[49] [emphases mine]

Of all this, the last three phrases are the most revealing of what she is up to. 'Return to the nursery' – the nursery is the place where the child can be safe and cared for, but it may also be read here as a symbolic place of psychological containment, Jane's re-entry into which would allow Mrs Reed to re-enforce the power relationship between adult and child. 'Lie down a little' is intended to work in a similar manner, re-inculcating the habit of passivity (lying down) and former subdued state of the child. But 'there's a dear' is unfortunate, for it fully awakens the child to two things: the truly artificial nature of what is going on, and the power she has gained over the older being. The 'dear' fails to lull; the attempted resurgence of the domestic myth fails. As Jane says, 'I am not your dear; I cannot lie down.' The balance of power between child and adult has shifted.

During Mr Brocklehurst's visit, which takes place just before this encounter between Jane and Mrs Reed, a deconstructing of childhood images has occurred which makes possible the final breaking-out discussed above.[50] This deconstruction happens when two, mutually exclusive, versions of childhood are juxtaposed, each undermining the other. Earlier, Brocklehurst and Mrs Reed had agreed on the value of consistency; yet what becomes evident is the absence of this quality. Mr Brocklehurst attempts to cast Jane in the role of the naughty, hell-bound, little child, presenting her with a Calvinist tract, the *Child's Guide*, which contains 'an account of the awfully sudden death of Martha G——, a naughty child addicted to falsehood and deceit'.[51]

However, Jane belongs to a completely different breed of child from the unfortunate Martha G—— and Janeway's Sarah Howley; she recognises that the literature of the hell-fire tracts is a fiction of control, one that attempts to manipulate the child through terror. When Mr Brocklehurst asks Jane how she thinks to escape falling into the fiery pit, her answer is that she 'must keep in good health and not die'. As with the children of 'Anecdote for Fathers' and 'We are Seven', the catechistic structure breaks down as the answers given depart from any expected orthodoxy, an assent to which would have meant assent to the image of childhood used to control Jane. Brocklehurst then refers to his own son who, he asserts ponderously, loves the psalms; when asked whether he would prefer a ginger-bread nut or a psalm to learn, the infant prodigy says he would like the psalm: angels sing psalms and he would like to be a little angel here below. Having made this endearing reply, his son is given two ginger nuts as a reward for his infant piety. What he fails to understand is that his little angel is a little hypocrite who has learned to manipulate the image of childhood that his parents, in blind wilfulness, subscribe to. The child, instead of retaining the true innocence of childhood that Jane still possesses and which is manifested in her frankness and lack of hypocrisy, is corrupted into playing at innocence. By juxtaposing the image of his son as angel child with the image of Jane as 'limb of Satan', Mr Brocklehurst demonstrates a failure of coherence which deconstructs both images, for this failure demonstrates that he, and by extension the images he projects of childhood, are not to be trusted: there is no health in either.

In this connection, it might be useful to examine Charlotte Brontë's use of the term 'angel'. Like the term 'darling', it is frequently used by Mrs Reed and Mr Brocklehurst to refer to their own children. Terms such as these were part of the standard Victorian vocabulary for women (for example, 'angel in the house') and children, and thus became a species of debased cliché, an over-familiar term containing little in the way of real significance. What the author tries to do in this novel is to defamiliarise these terms by showing, quite clearly, their trivialised connection with women and children, and in so doing, to release the child from the non-signifying cliché.

In chapter 12, speaking of Adèle, the author/narrator writes,

> She had no great talents, no marked traits of character, no peculiar development of feeling or taste *which raised her one inch above the ordinary level of childhood; but neither had she any deficiency or vice which sunk her below it* ...
>
> This, *par parenthèse*, will be thought cool language by persons who entertain solemn doctrines about the *angelic nature of children*, and the duty of those charged with their education to conceive for them an idolatrous devotion. But I am not writing to flatter parental egotism, to echo cant, or prop up humbug; *I am merely telling the truth* ... [52] [emphases mine]

'Moderation' is obviously a term of approbation; in speaking of the mutual regard of Mrs Fairfax and herself, she refers to Mrs Fairfax's '*moderation* of mind and character'. Again and again, the word occurs, and this is the key to the intention of the author in the depiction of the child. Though it is not used to refer to the child directly, it occurs almost immediately after the description of Adèle, which is given in a mode almost deliberately bland. The author indicates that 'angelic' here is not her own word, but that of the general parent, and shows the inappropriateness of its general and debased usage. 'I am merely telling the truth' might be the legend hung over *Jane Eyre*: it 'tells the truth' about childhood and children, which is that they are neither the darling angels spoken of by some, nor the 'infantine Guy Fawkes[es]' (as Abbott puts it), spoken of by others. *Jane Eyre* is about discovering the average, the real, but also about proving that the average can be, and is, arresting. Jane Eyre herself is not particularly distinguished, either as a child or adult; the author deliberately created her small and plain, to prove that a heroine need not be ravishingly beautiful in order to be interesting.[53] There is nothing in the text to show her greatly above the ordinary level of childhood, even if her status as 'heroine' causes us to shrink from saying of her what she says of Adèle.

The child in *Jane Eyre* differed from her predecessors not only in being the first to escape from the hands of the image makers and to attain an ordinariness, a sense of realism, but also in being the first fictional child whose growth of being and self was the author's main concern. The development of identity in the novel is linked not only to the growing independence of the child from stereotypes and from restraining and inhibitive relationships, but also to the growth of moderation and courage in the child. (The gaining of space and imaginative freedom, and the role played by books and literature in *Jane Eyre*, is part of this process of self-development, an issue to be discussed in a subsequent chapter. In the opening chapters, there are references to the as yet 'undeveloped and imperfect' feelings, the inability to analyse and put into words the sum of the thought processes as well as the timidity and lack of self-assertion of the child. Within an amazingly brief period, however, all this is changed; beginning with the hurling of the book at her head, she begins to retaliate, to dare to speak, and to analyse her reactions and the true state of her debts, if any, to the Reed family. After her attack on John Reed, she is borne off from the scene by Bessie and Abbott, but noticeably, she 'resist[s] all the way'. 'The fact,' she says, 'is that [she] was a trifle beside [her]self; or rather, *out* of [her]self as the French would say.'[54]

The words speak for themselves, but the metaphor brings with it images of an expanding being. Brought to the Red Room, she refuses to be tied to her seat, choosing instead to sit still – the first rudimentary signs of self-control, not enforced control. She looks in the mirror and the reflected image she sees there and describes does not appear to correspond to that of a child. The self as described here has an amorphous undefined quality, lacking specific features and colour, neither imp nor fairy, in fact not only refusing the traditional categories available such as that of the saintly child and taking instead its terms of reference from the world of faery, but refusing even classification within that world. In this we may not only read a resistance to the extant images of childhood but to the very notion of classification, as a representation of the enclosing impulse. Looking into the mirror, Jane appears to have difficulty in recognising herself:

> the strange little figure there gazing at me with a white face ... and glittering eyes of fear moving where all else was still, had the effect of a real spirit. I thought it like one of the tiny phantoms, half fairy, half imp ... [55]

What is interesting here is the burgeoning of power and self which, in the beginning, comes and goes in pulses:

'Unjust! – unjust!' said my reason, forced by the agonizing stimulus
into precocious though transitory power ... [56]

the word *book* acted as a transient stimulus ... [57]

Speak I must: I had been trodden on severely and *must* turn ... I
gathered my energies and launched them ... [58]

Ere I had finished this reply, my soul began to expand, to exult,
with the strangest sense of freedom, of triumph, I ever felt. It
seemed as if an invisible bond had burst, and that I had struggled
out into unhoped-for liberty ... but this fierce pleasure subsided in
me as fast as did the accelerated throb of my pulses ... [59]

The child, not as image, but as an entity capable of growth is here
pointed. Yet it is possible to see here the even more sophisticated realisation that the process of growth is not necessarily constant, nor
always sustainable. This idea, to be given fantastic and visual life in
Alice's Adventures in Wonderland, was a powerful one, and signified a
departure from the simple formulations of childhood, self and development that had preceded it.

After 1849 and the publication of *Jane Eyre*, the fictional child
tended to possess a greater degree of freedom, which was owing to
Jane's rebellious efforts. Nor was this the only benefit it enjoyed
through Jane's good offices, for the fictional child who was successor
to Jane Eyre found himself endowed with a greater measure of
naturalism instead of being made to conform to stereotypes of childhood. Though one still occasionally discovered angel children, the
species gradually became extinct, referred to only ironically, as in
E. Nesbit's *The Enchanted Castle* (1907), where 'Gerald's look assure[s]
[Mademoiselle] that he and the others w[ill] be as near angels as
children could be without ceasing to be human'.[60] *David Copperfield*,
and *Great Expectations*, arguably the best of the Dickens *corpus*, are
works that follow along the path trodden by *Jane Eyre*, borrowing its
literary structure and ethos as one appropriate for the study of being.
David Copperfield, in particular, declares itself her heir. Many are the
correspondences of incident, such as David's imprisonment by Mr
Murdstone before he is dispatched to school, where he is made an
example of through the malicious offices of his stepfather.

The Mill on the Floss (1860) and *Great Expectations* (1860–1) were the
last major English novels of the nineteenth century to employ the

structure of child-to-adult exploration of self. *Silas Marner*, written a little later, already betrays the shifting of interest away from the child that had been its focus for the past two decades or so. Though the child Eppie is one of the novel's lynchpins, Silas is at the true heart of the novel, and Eppie is merely the means by which the balance of things is restored, and Silas moved from the margins and recentred in human society. The movement from Maggie to Eppie, from real child to child-redeemer signified the ending of the period of dominance of childhood in the nineteenth-century English novel. The golden age of children's literature, however, was waiting to happen, with *The Water Babies* (1863) and *Alice's Adventures in Wonderland* (1865) to come within half a decade, and it was surely no coincidence that the children's classics emerging from the chrysalis were to continue where the novel had left off, in exploring themes of growth and development.

2
An Ordered Universe

A society is the awareness of the people who maintain its formal substance according to the image of society imprinted on them. That collective awareness is made up of many individual awarenesses which do not appear to be as functionally different as, for example, the cells of the body are. Yet in action the awarenesses differ: some hold the shape of things; some alter; some build; some destroy. All change constantly, and the formal substance of societies and civilizations changes with those changing awarenesses.

Russell Hoban, 'Thoughts on Being and Writing'

We are a garden walled around
Chosen and made peculiar ground
A little spot enclosed by grace
Out of the world's wide wilderness.

Isaac Watts

As seen in the previous chapter, image may possess the power to shape and confine. The debate between the images of child saint and child sinner had been, in a sense, a manifestation of the much older conflict between the philosophies of Original Innocence and Original Sin. But there were other kinds of images to be found in children's books of the nineteenth century which were not so much the products of a religious or philosophical system, as the intended producers of a social one. It is these 'social' images and the concept of social being that this chapter sets out to examine, and also the beginnings of the development of the inner code of self in place of the exterior definitions so far adopted. It may be argued that the impulse to order, structure and define, traceable within the domain of children's fiction in the late eighteenth and nineteenth centuries, arose in response to feelings of insecurity and anxiety which were caused by an undermining of the social, economic and religious status quo. There was an impulse to retreat behind the fastnesses of society in order not to be blasted by the winds of desolation and isolation, and for this purpose, society itself had to be made secure. It was with this end in mind that the ethics of usefulness, self-sacrifice and subservience of self to society were implanted in literature both for adults and children, forms of social and moral codification that would offer a sense of stability. In such conditions of enclosure, the concept of being and selfhood could only be partially expressed, for it stressed certain facets of being, (for example, the moral and social), at the expense of others, (for example the artistic), with the result that the individual in literature emerged, in Dr Miyoshi's phrase, as a 'divided self'.[1] Individuals constructed by these codes came to be at war with themselves, as they struggled to suppress or excise portions of their personality and being which came into conflict with the performance of their social duty.

In the categorisation of 'boys' fiction' and 'girls' fiction' during the nineteenth century, the idea of the divided self becomes additionally pertinent as the body of children's literature itself became split into sections, each catering for a separate class of persons, who were by implication barred and excluded from the other classes of fiction. One may also postulate in the pointing away of boys from girls' fiction and girls from fiction for males, a stunting of both the feminine side of the male personality and the masculine side of the female personality; this too may be held to constitute a division of self. However, with the gradual hardening of resistance against enclosure (in the form of social definitions) through the nineteenth century, being began to be seen more as a cohesive entity, less as a composite of aspects; this new view was to make possible deeper investigations of the self.

A picture of social control emerges from children's literature where social classes each have a clearly marked-out place and clearly marked-out duties, and the same is true regarding the roles of male and female, adult and child. A good deal has been written on the subject of what is commonly called 'sex-role stereotyping' in children's literature of the nineteenth century, and here the most interesting work has been done by Claudia Nelson in *Boys Will Be Girls* (1991), which argues that it is possible to trace in children's books of the period under discussion a feminisation of the male. In this reading, the 'feminine' virtues of patience, gentleness, and so forth are the ideal to be embraced, and some of the physical descriptions of boys given are notably feminised as well. This is all fascinating stuff, and in some sense may be used to argue my own case for the divided self. Though in *Tom Brown's Schooldays*, the ideal is to be equally proficient in Greek and games, the more reflective or feminine side of the personality developed in tandem with the more actively masculine side, this work does not necessarily represent the norm. More often, the gentler, 'feminine', side of the male personality is kept for situations involving the home and family, the more aggressive instincts channelled outwards – this seems to me to demonstrate a dichotomisation of self. In any case, most writers on the subject of sex-role stereotyping have been content to note the phenomenon, but have not suggested any reason *why* it should have been important that 'women should be womanly and men, manly', and why it is also that a high proportion of Victorian children's books should be so concerned with order, authority and duty, and portray societies with firmly ingrained patterns of function and place.

A possible answer to this question might be that feelings of insecurity prompted a response of authority and the setting up of patterns of living and being both calculated to keep up morale by a show of extreme order, and to maintain a sense of individual comfort. These responses strove to establish known systems of duties and shapes of being into which one could retreat; they constituted lifelines and guidelines to hold on to in the rough seas of doubt. Children's literature also had a special function in an age of anxiety, for it was a place where, owing to the desire to protect the child's peace of mind, insecurity was not openly spoken of, and the authority of the text's utterance which left scant room for questioning was a valued quality to its adult readers, of whom there were many.

In his essay 'Chaos in Poetry' already cited in the Introduction, D. H. Lawrence writes of man's need to 'wrap himself in a vision', to 'make a house of apparent form and stability [and] fixity'. It is terror of chaos, of unstructuredness, according to Lawrence, which inspires the need to define the territory and in so doing, to fix it in a form knowable to oneself. Man may sometimes deliberately cling to that which appears limited and inhibiting – that which I have called 'enclosed' – because this to him betokens the safe and the encompassable. In response to the tendency towards disintegration and confusion, he seeks to build and establish; fixity, even rigidity, is his answer to the forces that threaten to sweep away all that he has hitherto known.

It might be possible to see the trend in architectural design during the eighteenth and nineteenth centuries, the return to Classical idiom and proportions which conveyed the sense of strength and reassurance, as a response to this notion of man's desire for order in the face of a threatening chaos.[2] This idea, presumably, lay behind the motto expressed by the Victorian architect, Gilbert Scott: 'Gothic for churches. Classical for banks.' An underlying insecurity is perhaps revealed also by the increasing degree of compartmentalisation and structuralisation to be found in everyday life. Within homes, this was manifest in the way that rooms were increasingly set apart for the carrying out of separate functions: nurseries, day-rooms, school-rooms, dining-rooms, and so on. There was also compartmentalisation in the way that home life was kept discrete and at a distance from the working life of the male.[3] One finds this mirrored in fiction in Dickens's *Great Expectations*, when Mr Wemmick takes Pip home and sheds his sterner work-day persona to become the caring and dutiful son at home. Ira Bruce Nadel has also noted in '"The Mansion of Bliss"' the increasing degree of structure within the sphere of play or games:

> Play taught the Victorians, individually and collectively, the importance of rules, the basic code that defines and establishes every game. In an increasingly complex world, the Victorians felt the need to create an existence that was manageable, self-contained and regulated. The existence of rules thus gave instantaneous meaning. The irony however – an irony the Victorians soon realized – was that rules were not absolutes, as Alice learned when she stumbled down the rabbit hole.[4]

Nadel also adds in a footnote that the fact that

> ... the Victorian period was an age of rules, regulations and discipline, particularly in sport, can be seen in the establishment of the Cambridge Rules for football in 1863, the Queensbury Rules for boxing in 1867, and the English Rugby rules in 1871. The first manual for golf appeared in 1857, although the St. Andrews' rules for playing were set up in 1754.[5]

In all this, one senses the careful erection of rigid barriers around personality and daily activities, a programme of structuring designed to support the individual in the midst of a period of continuous change in which the traditional props of religion and sense of community were being knocked out from under; it was an age broadly defined by evolution and revolution. Darwin's theory demanded a reassessment of man's basic nature and origins, and *apropos* of this it may be asked if the idea of common ancestry with the apes, and by extension, the implications of a basic, bestial, nature tenuously overlaid by a veneer of civilisation, might not have somewhat undermined the notion of the child trailing clouds of glory as it came from its heavenly home. Furthermore – offering what was essentially an alternative Creationist 'myth' – *The Origin of Species* instituted uneasy questioning as to the status of the Bible as the repository of divine truth, by implication challenging the validity of the Christian faith. The Industrial Revolution not only remapped Britain demographically but also had deeper philosophical implications for man's conception of himself and his place in society. The French revolution, with its reconfiguration of the social and political structures in France, was also to affect Britain even if only indirectly, through the sense of threat of social upheaval spilling over and dissolving social codes at home.

Although society was in a state of flux during this period, children's literature reflects little sense of change, or of anxiety with regard to that same momentum of change that was rapidly sweeping away the familiar world. While literature written for adults betrayed some of the sense of upset caused by change, children's literature, however, maintained its calm façade. Partly, this was because it was felt that children should not have to be subjected to the same trauma and doubt that paralysed the adult exposed to the external realities of change and disintegration. Partly, the sheltering of the child was undertaken out of the desire that the child, symbolically and literally representing the hope of the present generation for the future, should have a period of calmness and stability in which to shore up 'strength for the future contest', instead of being made to grow up a slave to anxiety. For this reason, insecurity could not be openly discussed, fear not directly mentioned. Morale could best be kept up by keeping a cheerful face and tone of voice, and refusing to acknowledge any causes for worry or anxiety. As Claudia Nelson notes, when Buchan's *Prester John* (1910) was run serially as *The Black General* in *The Captain* magazine, the editors eliminated the narrator's occasional confessions of weakness or fright.[6] One might also wish to consider T. E. Hulme's comment, in *Speculations*, that '[t]here are certain doctrines which for a particular period seem not doctrines, but invisible categories of the human mind ... They [people] do not see them [the categories] but other things *through* them.'[7] Despite never having its name spoken aloud, insecurity was the invisible reason behind the enclosure and stress on order and structure found in works written for children. And conversely, just as one might ignore unpleasant reality in the hope that it would somehow alter its lineaments, one might also attempt to give a more concrete existence to the longed-for order by behaving as if it did, in fact, exist; as Oscar Wilde once remarked to André Gide,

> You must understand that there are two worlds – the one exists and is never talked about; it is called the real world because there is no need to talk about it in order to see it. The other is the world of Art; one must talk about it because otherwise it would not exist.[8]

Children's stories by authors such as Maria Edgeworth are shaped according to that aesthetic of enclosure in that they are about contained and structured societies, where each individual (and object) has its own function and place. Much of early children's fiction was set in the enclosed spaces of the schoolroom or the nursery, where the child could be kept safe and secure from the knowledge of the anxiety and doubt riddling the adult world. On the odd occasion where the child escapes from the nursery into the outside world, such as in *Us* (1885), Mrs Molesworth's tale about a pair of children who are stolen away by Gypsies, the child's youth and innocence act as a buffer, protecting him from the full horror of what is actually happening. The tone adopted in children's literature was most often one of authority intended not only to inculcate in the child a habit of obedience to the voice of authority, but also to impart reassurance. It was in this spirit that Leslie Stephen would write (*apropos* of Froude's life of Carlyle) that Carlyle's dogmatism was 'delightful and comforting and gave a sense of security';[9] in the same way, (to cite from a twentieth-century children's classic), it is Mary Poppins's sternness and resumption of her authoritative manner after a spell of softness that reassures the Banks children:

> At last Michael could bear it no longer.
> 'Oh do be cross, Mary Poppins! Do be cross again! It is not like you. Oh, I feel so anxious.' And indeed, his heart felt heavy with the thought that something, he did not know what, was about to happen at Number Seventeen, Cherry Tree Lane.
> 'Trouble trouble and it will trouble you!' retorted Mary Poppins crossly in her usual voice.
> And immediately he felt a little better.[10]

Here, Michael's feeling of insecurity and the fear that the world is in some way about to change is dispelled by the voice of authority – not just Mary Poppins's tone, but also the use of the adage which, as a piece of conventional wisdom, suggests a system of eternal and unchanging truth and which also reaches back to an earlier age of child governing, where the child was brought up swaddled in this kind of wisdom.

Though a good deal of fiction for girls and boys written in this period was ostensibly about growing up (breaking out) and preparing oneself for adulthood, it is worth remarking that the values which the adolescent protagonists were encouraged to carry with them into their adult lives were the simple and unadorned ones of childhood. Adulthood and sophistication are represented as corrupt states; in *Little Women*, when Meg goes among her contemporaries and temporarily adopts their values and manners, Laurie comments that she looks so 'grown-up and unlike herself' that he is quite afraid of her. Shirley Foster and Judy Simmons, in their recent feminist study of 'classic stories for girls', *What Katy Read* (1995), (quoting Catherine R. Stimpson), endorse her view of *Little Women* as '*the* American female myth, its subject the primordial one of the passage from childhood, from girl to woman'.[11] While this is true in the obvious sense, it may be argued that on the sub-textual level there is a reluctance and resistance to growing up; 'grown-up' is, in the passage above, as with Wordsworth, a pejorative term. If, at one level, it enacts a 'primordial myth', at another it may be construed as an attempt to rewrite or undo the myth of the Fall.

Not only was there thus a subtle undercutting of adulthood in children's literature, but, as U. C. Knoepflmacher notes, there was a desire in adults to become children again.[12] Repeatedly, one notes this. Mark Twain's Preface to *The Adventures of Tom Sawyer* maintains:

> Although my book is intended mainly for the entertainment of boys and girls, I hope it will not be shunned by men and women on that account, for part of my plan has been to try pleasantly to remind adults of what they once were themselves, and of how they felt and thought and talked, and what queer enterprises they sometimes engaged in.[13]

J. A. Froude, in *The Nemesis of Faith*, writes nostalgically of that 'Paradise, our own old childhood over which the old glories linger',[14] wistfully averring:

I would gladly give away all I am, and all I may ever become, all the years, every one of them, which may be given me to live, but for one week of my old child's faith, to go back to calm and peace again, and then to die in hope.[15]

To him and to others throughout the century, childhood and children's literature represented an enclosed space, a walled garden where doubt and anxiety were not allowed to intrude, a domain still ruled by authority. It was the form to which adults at the turn of the century chose to retreat, seeking simplicity, renewal and a temporary release from the pressures of adulthood. Claudia Nelson observes:

> ... one thinks of the turn of the century habit of writing children's books for adults [Grahame's *The Golden Age*, Nesbit's Bastable stories] and of the adult audience that first made *Peter Pan* a smash hit on stage.[16]

Besides those texts named by Nelson, one also thinks of the fairy tales (generally held to be a form or sub-genre of children's literature) of Oscar Wilde and Laurence Housman which were written for adults: *The Happy Prince and Other Stories* and *A Farm In Fairyland*, wherein again the adult can escape from adult forms and adult values. F. H. Burnett's *Little Lord Fauntleroy* was more popular with adults than children (it was especially unpopular with the male children), their parents signifying their approval of the book by dressing their hapless offspring in the velvet suits with Vandyke collars that Fauntleroy had worn. There was also F. Anstey's *The Brass Bottle* (1900), a story about an inefficient djinn and the difficulties he creates in the love-life of the protagonist, which provided the inspiration for Nesbit's *The Phoenix and the Carpet*. Anstey's story, however, was written for adults. In *Peter Pan*, which was incredibly popular with adults, Peter Pan is kept in a state of perpetual childhood, this being rather symbolic of adult wishful thinking, and in Anstey's *Vice Versa*, the father returns to being a child. The children's book, depicting the simple and protected world of childhood, became the adult's refuge where he could retreat from chaos into order, from the exposed world into the enclosed one.

The continuance of the authority and calmness woven into the fabric of children's books may perhaps have been one of the factors which helped to give birth to the fiction which is still generally current today, of the immense stability and security of eighteenth- and nineteenth-century societies. Superficially viewed, they appear as monuments of sublime strength, possessing definite purpose and clear-cut doctrines, societies structured and smoothly functioning. Yet, it is likely that these images were myths constructed by the nineteenth century out of its own need. Marilyn Butler, referring to the currency of this belief, also points to its erroneousness:

> Students of literature, even advanced ones, are apt to see late eighteenth century Western society as a serene and static world, rudely galvanised by the storming of the Bastille in 1789. But this is an old-fashioned and simplistic impression: more analytic recent scholarship suggests that in reality social and economic pressures were building up from the 1760s if not earlier ... It is a period of rapid change or expectation of change ....[17]

This is echoed by Houghton:

> Indeed, it was still common until very recently to draw a radical contrast between the Victorians and ourselves. One modern critic [D. Willoughby] thought that "a spirit of certitude, wonderful to us who live in an age which has taken the note of interrogation as its emblem, impregnated the great Victorians." [*The Great Victorians*, (ed. H. J. Massingham), (New York, 1932)], Another has claimed that it was only after 1900 that "the old certainties were certainties no longer ... the Victorians seemed to themselves to be living in a house built on unshakable foundations and established in perpetuity ... the Home, the Constitution, the Empire, the Christian religion – each of these ... was accepted as a final revelation.[18]

But although representative writers of the late eighteenth century, such as Maria Edgeworth and Jane Austen, would seem to present a smiling and untroubled face to the world, their novels and stories depicting a graciously ordered and assured world where 'change or expectation of change' seem not to operate, the reality was quite different. Tanner, in his introduction to *Jane Austen*, diagnoses such social order as being 'always precarious and insecure'.[19] 'Maria Edgeworth's heyday, from 1795 to 1817, coincide[d] more or less exactly (as does Jane Austen's) with the alarmist years,'[20] and the fiction of confidence was a veil hiding a growing insecurity and sense of disintegration, fuelled in the eighteenth century, as Butler has said, by social and economic pressures.

Fredric Bogel has also commented on feelings of insecurity in the late eighteenth century, making a convincing case for a fear of insubstantiality and a sense of ontological inadequacy having pervaded the late eighteenth century, and has also discussed the ensuing movement to reinvest meaning in things. What he describes as the Age of Sensibility rose out of the desire for the comfort of feeling: the need to feel that one could apprehend and approach the substance of things through the medium of the senses and the feelings, in this way reassuring oneself as to the actuality of the self and the world. Bogel sees the eighteenth-century interest in childhood as stemming from this ontological insecurity; the image of childhood symbolised not mere innocence but perpetuity and continuance, a means with which to affirm the future.[21] Because the future was vested in the child, that child had to be carefully taught and educated, not merely given a factual knowledge, but guided along a specific direction and moulded into a form most likely to help consolidate the future.

The emphasis on order and stability may be especially noted in Maria Edgeworth's work for children. Here, the noticeable concern with minutiae (especially concerning specific, and tiny, amounts of money) suggests in its fidelity to detail, a desire to lend substance to a world feared to be insubstantial. As mentioned earlier, insecurity could not be openly expressed, especially in works intended for the young, lest the expression of anxiety further undermine the society and perpetuate the mood of spiritual paralysis. However, in the work of Maria Edgeworth and Jane Austen, the reader will sense a concern with usefulness which is very much linked to a sense of insecurity and the individual's dependence upon the circle of the community, and his need to be recognised and sheltered by it. *Being* is tied to *doing*, and doing for others and for the community, rather than for oneself; in this way, being is made to bear the weight of social and functional associations. In their writings, there are models of an ideal society to be found, and ideas as to the kind of people there will have to be in order to make it work.

In *Mansfield Park* and *Persuasion*, for example, this is expressed in the persons of Fanny Price and Anne Elliot, both of whom feel a need to be thought useful to those around them and in this way to be validated by society.[22] Tanner has described Fanny as one of those characters in search of a place in society, in search of social being. She is unobtrusive, quiet, and so passive as to have the fact of her existence generally ignored or forgotten. As Tanner points out, not only is a fire not lit in her room, but the necessity of her taking exercise on the mare provided for her by Edmund is sacrificed to Mary Crawfurd's pleasure in riding, and she is excluded from taking part in outings and plays. The means by which she tries to create a place for herself in the wished-for environment is to stress her functionality:

> Fanny had *no share* in the festivities of the season; but she enjoyed being avowedly *useful* as her aunt's companion, when they called away the rest of the family; ... she naturally became *everything* to Lady Bertram during the night of a ball or party. She talked to her, listened to her, read to her... [23] [emphases mine]

Fanny succeeds in this in some sort by creating in Lady Bertram an awareness of her dependence on her. When she returns to her own home in Portsmouth, part of her unhappiness stems from the sense of becoming nobody or nothing again, of having no place and no being, no significance to her family and she tries to assuage this, again, by teaching her younger sister Susan, whose value, above that of the more idle members of the Prices, is intimated also by her usefulness:

> The first consolation that Fanny received ... was in a better knowledge of Susan, and a hope of *being of service to her* ... Susan tried to be useful ....[24] [emphases mine]

Fanny speaks of Mansfield as home; this passes unresented by the Prices, who do not think of her as part of the family. It is telling that at the point of this realisation, her thoughts run again on how useful she could have been at Mansfield:

> To be losing such pleasures as this was no trifle ... but even these incitements to regret were feeble compared with what arose from the conviction of being missed by her best friends, and the longing to be useful to those who were wanting her! ...
> Could she have been at home she could have been of service ... She felt that she must have been of use to all. She loved to fancy how she could have read to her aunt, how she could have talked to her, ... and how many walks up and down stairs she might have saved her, and how many messages she might have carried.[25]

Not only does this read as an expression of Fanny's undoubted goodheartedness; it is also how she attempts to reassure herself of her functionality – and hence of her place in society – and the actuality of her being which is in danger of being eroded when in her own home. The physical nature of drudgery is, ironically, a welcome testimony to the fact of her actual existence – she suffers, therefore she is.

Having a function, being of use, doing – all these are implicitly felt to be corollaries of being, for they help to ensure place. Anne Elliot, the heroine of *Persuasion*, is placed in similar straits. Early on, the reader is informed that she 'was *nobody* with either father or sister: *her word had no weight*; [emphasis mine] her convenience was always to give way; – she was only Anne.'[26] What Anne is has been to some extent determined by her partial isolation from the society of her own family. Upon the family deciding to remove to Bath, Anne's married sister, Mary, says,

'I cannot possibly do without Anne,' was Mary's reasoning; and Elizabeth's [the eldest sister] reply was, 'Then I am sure that Anne had better stay, for nobody will want her in Bath.'

To be claimed as a good, though in an improper style, is at least better than being rejected as no good at all; and Anne, glad to be thought of some use, glad to have anything *marked out* as a duty, ... readily agreed to stay.[27] [emphasis mine]

Boundaries, the 'musts' of duty, which present-day society delights in denouncing as inhibiting to notions of personal liberty, were welcome to the eighteenth- and nineteenth-century mind craving order. In the excerpt quoted above, Anne is said to be glad to 'have anything *marked out* [my italics] as a duty'. Ruth Danon has commented that duty and work, or what she calls the 'myth of vocation', become, in *David Copperfield* and *Great Expectations*, something approaching epistemology.[28] This is as true for the eighteenth-century denizen as for the inhabitants of the two novels named above, for industry and work rise above mere episodic relevance in their lives, becoming a system or way of organising experience and being.

The same current of thought runs through Maria Edgeworth's writings for children, works produced in the same era as Jane Austen's novels. Here, one finds a constant emphasis on the virtues of order and industriousness, and a strong condemnation of laziness, non-doing. This is an evil which, in Miss Edgeworth's stories, is the first step to further sinning, and on the path to hell. In 'Lazy Lawrence', a tale from the collection *The Parent's Assistant*, Lawrence says to Jem, the hard-working boy hero, '"I would not *be* you for all the world to have so much to *do* always"'[29] [emphases mine]. Jem's reply is that he would not be Lawrence for the world, to have nothing to do. Here, being is equated with doing; only those who do are counted as existing. In this context, the biblical Martha is the role model to be emulated, while her sister Mary would have received short shrift. Not *doing*, or making, means nothing earned, which in turn means nothing to eat, which must, practically speaking,[30] lead sometime to death: a state of effective non-being. The idle, as Miss Edgeworth makes clear, are people lacking definition; in the conversation leading up to the sentence above, Jem asks,

> 'What Lawrence! ... are you asleep?' 'Not quite,' 'Are you awake?' 'Not quite.' 'What are you doing there?' 'Nothing.' 'What are you thinking of?' 'Nothing.' 'What makes you lie there?' 'I don't know ...'[31]

Lawrence's responses mark him for what he is: a vacant shell, with no thoughts, no motives, no clarity of purpose, a non-actor in life's drama. The devil indeed finds work for idle hands, for Lawrence ends up stealing Jem's hard-earned money, and, as a result, is removed to Bridewell prison, like a drone from the hive, a non-entity as far as the village community is concerned.

For the aristocrat as for the working man, and for those feeling themselves to be dwelling on the margins, a sense of usefulness and contribution to the life of the community helps to shape the personal matrix of self. There is, for instance, Lady Catherine de Bourgh in *Pride and Prejudice*, who Elizabeth says should feel gratified by the circumstance of having been instrumental in bringing Darcy and herself together, as 'she loves to be of use'.[32] This is of course meant sarcastically, making fun of Darcy's aunt's habit of interfering and instructing those about her in the manner of conducting their lives. The sarcasm, however, has its root in the idea of patronage being a duty and function of the rich. The rich justify their place in the order of things by playing the role of 'moral overseer', one who rewards the industrious worker and punishes the miscreant on behalf of the Almighty, and whose work is to keep the frame of things from disjointing. As Defoe wrote in 1701,

> The country poor do by example live;
> The gentry lead them, and the clergy drive:
> What may we not from such examples hope?
> The landlord is their God, the priest their pope.[33]

The idea of the gentry having a function and thus earning or deserving their place within the shelter of the community repeatedly occurs in Edgeworth's writings for the young. In 'Lazy Lawrence' there is the unnamed lady who rewards Jem's industry and entrepreneurship, telling him, in the matter of the mat-weaving, that she will help him dispose of those he makes: by this she means that she will get her friends to buy them. In this manner, she strives to be of use both to Jem and also to her friends (who will benefit in terms of clean floors). This is paralleled at a lower level by Jem's selling of fossils for a man who is too busy working to sell them for himself. The intertwined nature of the community and the concept of mutual benefaction (generating income in the process) is emphasised.[34] 'Simple Susan' contains yet another instance of the 'usefulness' of the rich. Sir Arthur, the local squire, and his family exercise moral justice; and the sense which the reader gets of their function as God's deputies is strengthened by the use of the image of Susan's lamb. The lamb is used to recall the prophet Nathan's rebuke to David, delivered in the form of an allegory, where the rich man takes the sole, pet lamb of his poor neighbour and serves it to a guest. The crooked attorney, in Edgeworth's tale, has taken Susan's lamb, intending to present it to Sir Arthur in order to gain his favour and become his agent, and also gain his help in depriving Susan's father of a piece of land by claiming there is a flaw in the lease. The biblical stricture, condemning the guilty by 'bringing his conduct upon his own head and vindicating the righteous by rewarding him according to his righteousness' (1 Kings 8: 32) is the mandate by which the squire then operates, turning the attorney off his property by demonstrating a flaw in his own lease, and making Farmer Price his agent. Meanwhile his daughters order a new dress for Susan as a reward for her industriousness. Again, in 'The Orphans', the young ladies play their role of Lady Bountiful (though in the nicest way), by sending flax to Mary, who has finished her own supply, and also employing her and her brother, Edmund. Again, ingenuity in making things (rush candles and cloth shoes) is rewarded, and the finished products disposed of among the ladies' friends.

This encouragement of 'home industries' (though not of course described in these terms) places a value on the labour and creative ability of the worker, and also of his aristocratic patron and retailer. The Industrial Revolution, whose net result was to replace man with the machine, must, however, have severely weakened the bond between the concepts of being and usefulness. The substitution of mechanical for manual labour and personal creativity cut also at the worker's idea of self-worth, leading him to seek self-definition in other places. In consequence, dependence upon society for the validation of the individual was weakened. Carlyle commented in his essay, 'Signs of the Times',

> It is the age of Machinery ... Our old modes of exertion are all discredited and thrown aside. On every hand, the living artisan is driven from his workshop, to make room for a speedier, inanimate one ... wealth has more and more increased, and at the same time gathered itself more and more into masses, strangely altering old relations, and increasing the distance between the rich and the poor ... These things, which we state lightly enough here, are yet of deep import, and indicate a mighty change in our whole manner of existence. For the same habit regulates not our modes of action alone, but our modes of thought and feeling. Men ... have lost faith in individual endeavour .... [35]

Yet further on, he comments that the general feeling is that it is the ... 'force of circumstances that does everything; the force of one man can do nothing'. What Carlyle saw, and what was happening, was the gradual collapse of a perspective which grounded self-worth and being in ideas of personal output and contribution. Besides this, patterns of community and thus, of 'individuality', were in the process of being changed; as Carlyle said, 'old relations' were 'strangely altered' and rich and poor were becoming separated.[36] The cohesion of the social order was being threatened.

Edgeworth's tales describe duties of the individual to his community in terms of work. Children's literature of this period also went further in prescribing patterns of gender behaviour intended as ideals to be followed and realised in order to help stabilise the fragmenting order. The Prince's father in Tennyson's 'The Princess' put the case for this when he said,

> Man for the field and woman for the hearth;
> Man for the sword, and for the needle she;
> Man with the head and woman with the heart;
> Man to command and woman to obey;
> All else confusion.   (lines 437–41)

Ruskin, in his essay 'Of Queen's Gardens' (1865), claimed that woman's power was for rule, and her intellect for sweet ordering, arrangement and decision; having defined woman's role, Houghton comments that Ruskin goes on to 'describe the home, since it is women so conceived who make it a temple and a school of virtue. The more reason, therefore, to keep it in a walled garden.'[37] Men were there to guard the women within the holy of holies; women to guard the holy of holies itself.

Being and identity were intended to be understood mainly in terms of adherence to the patterns outlined above, and were dominated and shaped by an ethic of self-sacrifice, a paradox of being acquired through its sacrifice. Alan Sandison in *The Wheel of Empire* has noted this paradox, describing it in the following terms:

> The self in isolation is wholly vulnerable to the forces of disintegration ... So reassurance of integrity is sought in society and commitment ... But ... this involves sacrifice: for the creation of society inevitably means, for the individual, a partial surrender of integrity ... the great human paradox [is] that man can only exist in society which he alone can create out of his precious store of selfhood: thus every contribution to society is an erosion of the self which it is designed to identify and protect ... If ... too little is given to society, then the latter loses coherence, and the core of the self is once more left unprotected and wholly vulnerable.[38]

Thus, society was all-important, the symbol of order, and selfsacrifice was depicted as that which society needed in order to remain stable. Girls were encouraged to think of 'being' in terms of Ruskin's outline, in terms of wifehood and motherhood; their identity was made and formed in the environs of home, each home a small nucleus of stability.[39] The female role was especially important in the project of restabilizing the society, for hers was the work of caring for the child and inculcating it with the values that would help ensure the continuance of order and sanity. Hannah More, in strident tones, reminded women of this duty:

> On YOU depend, in no small degree, the principles of the whole rising generation. To your direction the daughters are almost exclusively committed; and until a certain age, to YOU also is consigned the mighty privilege of forming the hearts and minds of your infant sons. Your private exertions may at this moment be contributing to the future happiness; your domestic neglect, to the future ruin of your country.[40]

Mrs Beeton's *Book of Household Management* would have it that the woman

> ... ought always to remember that she is the first and the last, the Alpha and the Omega in the government of her establishment; and that it is by her conduct that its whole internal policy is regulated. She is therefore, a person of far more importance in a community than she thinks she is. On her pattern her daughters model themselves; by her counsels they are directed ....[41]

Boys were invited to devote themselves to the school team, the country, the empire. Individuals were asked to see themselves as part of the economic and social machine, *individual* or indivisible from the main body of the community, as opposed to being in the modern sense, discrete individuals separate from the masses.

Books for girls were thus being written with the intention of strengthening the threatened social order, preaching self-sacrifice, anti-individualism and voluntary enclosure within the home and submission to the role outlined for women of wife-and-mother.[42] Women, as the transmitters of values, had to be discouraged from making individualistic breaks for freedom, dissuaded from pursuing their own path in life and thus destabilizing society. This is demonstrated, for example, in Trollope's depiction of Mrs Proudie in the Barchester novels and Glencora, Duchess of Omnium in *The Prime Minister*, these two women stepping outside the roles allotted them to try to take over their respective husbands' jobs of Bishop and Prime Minister and threatening to plunge their communities into disorder. The role of homemaker was therefore glamourised in fiction for adolescent girls: hence the epithets of 'angel in the house' or 'home goddess',[43] which encouraged them to see and define themselves in these socially defined terms. Self-sacrifice[44] or self-denial was promoted, the ethos of individual development belittled; and these patterns of behaviour found their way into books like *Little Women* or Elizabeth Wetherell's *The Wide Wide World*.

The Daisy Chain by Charlotte Yonge also endorses these ethics. The 'daisy chain' of the title refers to the eleven children of Dr and Mrs May; two of these are named 'Margaret', hence the 'daisy' of the title. Published in 1856, the novel, became the prototype for the family chronicle, influencing works such as L. M. Alcott's *Little Women* trilogy,[45] Susan Coolidge's 'Katy' Books, Margaret Sidney's *Five Little Peppers* duology, and so forth. For anyone who has read *The Daisy*

Chain, its influence is immediately obvious, and 'Cousin Helen', the stable centre of the household, spreader of sweetness and light from the sick-bed, the bedridden Katy herself, and also Jill, of L. M. Alcott's *Jack and Jill*, are recognisably derived from the elder Margaret May of Charlotte Yonge's novel.

Charlotte Yonge was a firm believer in the inferiority of women, and the novel proclaims this doctrine, which shapes the path of the female characters, psychologically and physically limiting what they might become. Active women are potentially disruptive, but passivity is a virtue because it does not threaten to rock the domestic and social boat. Thus, Yonge's women are either passive to begin with or are taught to be passive and to conform; in *The Daisy Chain*, as in *Little Women*, there is also an undercurrent of authorial resistance to the idea of growing up and reaching adulthood. It is as though there is the desire on the part of the author to keep her female characters enclosed behind the threshold of adulthood in order to keep them away from the corruption of the adult world.[46] Margaret is hurt in the carriage accident that leaves the May family motherless, and is reduced to sofa-ridden invalidism all her days, passive and dependent on the men to move or lift her, and this, in a sense, partly symbolises the state of womanhood in the novel. Her impaired health acts as a halter, keeping her back from marriage, and the death of her fiancé deals the final blow that ultimately results in her early death. Ethel, likewise, is kept at the stage of perpetual girlhood, cloistered within the house, resigned to never being married and moving on. Of the three eldest girls, only Flora marries, and her marriage is seen to verge on disaster, with a lack of understanding between husband and wife and the death of her baby through neglect. Flora, it would seem, is being punished for insisting on adulthood when she should have remained in the circle of safety.

Ethel, to all intents and purposes the work's protagonist, is academically as good as her elder brother Norman. She keeps up with all his lessons, tries to found a Sunday school at Cocksmoor (the poor district), and helps to look after the younger children. Though she appears to cope reasonably well with the demands this makes on her, Margaret feels that she is attempting to do too much, and in consequence, not doing it well. Presented with the 'necessity' of giving up something, Ethel cries vehemently,

> 'You are not thinking of my not going to Cocksmoor? ... What would you have me do?' said Ethel in an injured, unconvinced voice. 'Not give up my children?'[47]

She need not have worried: Cocksmoor may be considered a legitimate sphere of female work. What Ethel is instead asked to surrender (and refusal is never a real option), is the intellectual life, the academic pursuits which distinguish her as an individual apart from the mass of female life around her. Individualism threatens the idea of social/communal being, and as such, is strongly discouraged. In the terms formulated by Sandison, she is asked to give of her store of individual 'selfhood' in order that social equilibrium and stability may be maintained. Margaret's response to the question above is:

'No ... but don't think me very unkind if I say, suppose you left off trying to keep up with Norman ... You see,' said Margaret kindly, 'we all know that men have more power than women, and I suppose the time is come for Norman to pass beyond you ... If you could keep up with him at all, you must give your whole time and thoughts to it, and when you had done so – if you could get all the honours in the University – what would it come to? You can't take a first class.'

'I don't want one,' said Ethel; 'I only can't bear not to do as Norman does, and I like Greek so much.'

'And for that would you give up being a useful steady *daughter* and *sister* at home? The sort of *woman that mamma wished to make you*, and a comfort to papa ... You own that is the first thing?'[48] [emphases mine]

Despite the fact that at the time of writing in 1856 university education for women on the same terms as men was unavailable,[49] and that taking a First is not, therefore, an option for Ethel, education is none the less a factor in her personal development, since the drive to achieve, the effort of wrestling with difficulty, can act as a stimulus to her growth. However, she is asked to renounce this and confine her ambitions to the established social roles of daughter and sister. Later, Ethel says:

'I suppose it is a wrong sort of ambition to want to learn more, in one's own way, when one is told it is not good for one. I was just going to say I hated being a woman, and having these tiresome little trifles – my duty – instead of learning, which is yours, Norman.'[50]

When Dr May is told of Margaret's attempt to dissuade Ethel from her studies, he heartily concurs in terms that seem to hint at a threat to Ethel's physical and mental being should Ethel not conform to the socially accepted formulation of femaleness:

> He was only surprised to hear that Ethel had kept up so long with Norman and thought it was quite right that she should not undertake so much, agreeing more entirely than Margaret had expected with Miss Winter's view, that it would be hurtful to body as well as mind.[51]

Ethel is asked not only to sacrifice her programme of self-development, but also to cede her right to rebellion. Her world is a shrinking and narrowing one, instead of an expanding universe, and the self that is in the process of being developed is likewise reduced. Later still, her choices to be are further narrowed when she renounces a prospective romance with Norman Ogilvie, a friend of her brother Norman May, in order to stay at home and look after her father. Nor is this a temporary measure; the implication is that the decision to be an old maid is a permanent one. While it is possible to view all this as an active choice on the part of Ethel to *be* an old maid, condemned to parish visiting and Doing Good, it is more probable that it is an act of compliance, resignation to the choices of others, to the lot imposed by society upon women of the period.

Nor is Ethel the only one in the family to be manoeuvred into the assumption of possibly uncongenial roles. Norman, becoming dissatisfied with a donnish Oxford existence, wishes to become a missionary, but feels he ought to train as a doctor to help his father out and, in time, take over from him, unless someone (that is, one of his brothers) should take this duty from him. His younger brother Tom is emotionally pressurised into feeling a vocation for medicine, and Norman is free to go forth and make disciples of the New Zealanders. Tom sighs, 'if I must, I must'; and though Norman responds in the expected manner –

> 'I have told you I do not mean to victimize you. If you have a distaste to it, there's an end to it – I am quite ready.'[52]

– one cannot help feeling that some degree of emotional blackmail is involved, and that Tom's acquiescence in the matter is a sacrifice of self arising out of devotion to his brother, rather than a development proceeding along natural lines. The point seems to be that it is not sexism that is at work here, women constrained and men emancipated, but that both are pressured by social expectations of them.

As time went by the fictional female stereotype would eventually undergo metamorphosis and become possessed of greater capabilities and a greater number of options, while her physical attributes also changed to reflect her increasing abilities. Judith Rowbotham writes that '[t]erms such as tall, well-grown, sturdy and resilient begin to be applied to the physical stature of modern maidens'.[53] But even so, the fate of the heroine was to be reabsorbed into the old order and the task of creating homes, enclaves of traditional values for children. Anne Shirley, heroine of L. M. Montgomery's 'Anne' series, is intelligent and wins a scholarship to University, but her life, after a brief spell of teaching (which, like the role of mother, is also involved in ordering the minds of the young within a closed environment), is devoted to producing a large brood of Blythes.

In the novels of Louisa May Alcott there is a very perceptible tension between what one senses to be a public acquiescence to popular ideals of womanhood or the necessary subservience to the needs of society,[54] and a private defiance and dislike of the domestic aesthetic which the author had felt driven to impose on most of the female characters in her novels. Both the author and the setting of her books are American, but the novels, clearly showing the influence of Charlotte Yonge, were absorbed quickly by the reading public on the other side of the Atlantic, rapidly becoming a classic on British shelves as well.

Writing to her uncle, Sam May, Louisa Alcott grumbled, '[p]ublishers are very perverse & wont let authors have their way so my little women must grow up and be married off in a very stupid style',[55] and expressed her exasperation with girls who wrote to enquire as to the matrimonial fates planned for the Marches, 'as if that was the only end and aim of a woman's life'. Here, she was stating her rebellion against the destiny of fictional girls, growing up only to be passively married off, and we may trace this rebelliousness regarding the destiny of women, even though conventional sentiments may often seem to prevail. Women authors, like the females they wrote about, had to assume docility so as not to rock the boat.

Even in the American tradition of nineteenth-century writing for girls, that succeeded, as it were, in loosening the social and intellectual corsets that had stunted the natural growth of girls in English fiction, it is amazing how many of the female protagonists (who are distinctive and vigorous, not to mention unconventional) grow up to become sweet young things who, on the whole, could stand in for each other without anyone noticing the difference. The March sisters are exempted from this criticism, for even when married they retain a good deal of their individuality. But Katy Carr, of Susan Coolidge's 'Katy' books, possessed of all the healthy animal spirits and childish inventiveness, her imaginative sister Clover, and even the buoyant Rose Red, pale into insipidity as they grow older, as the healthy tan of childhood fades into the alabaster skin fashionable for young ladies. Similar fates overtake Polly Pepper (*Five Little Peppers and How They Grew; Five Little Peppers Grown Up*), and Rose of *Eight Cousins; or The Aunt-Hill*, and Jill Pecq of *Jack and Jill*. There is a kind of anonymity about these fictional characters, a modesty and a surrender of individualism which mimes the message their books carry for the female reader, to join the throng and renounce the instinct to stand out.

Little Women opens upon a theatre of experience shaped by *The Pilgrim's Progress*, the Christian ethos of which, however, does not entail a sacrifice of self, but rather a discipline and tempering of the ideals that go into the making of the self which is conceived in social and moral terms. The Preface to *Little Women*, Part 1, is an adaptation of Christiana's speech at the beginning of the second part of *The Pilgrim's Progress* (1684). This sets the stage for the journey of the four pilgrims, the March sisters, a quest for self-definition that is overtly acknowledged to commence on the terms laid out by Bunyan: Meg goes to Vanity Fair, Jo meets Apollyon, Amy travels in the Valley of Humiliation, and Beth finds the Palace Beautiful. The adaptation, besides the omission of certain lines, also engages in the active alteration of others, reading, in its revised form:

> Go then, my little Book, and show to all
> That entertain, and bid thee welcome shall,
> *What thou dost keep close shut up in thy breast;*
> And wish *that* thou dost show them may be blest
> To them for good, may make them choose to be
> Pilgrims better, by far, than thee or me.
> *Tell them of Mercy,* she is one
> *Who early hath her pilgrimage begun.*
> *Yea, let young damsels learn of her to prize*
> The world which is to come, *and so be wise;*
> *For* little tripping maids may follow God
> *Along the ways which saintly feet have trod.*[56]

The italicisation indicates points where alterations to the wording of the original text have occurred (some of the original lines have also been lost in transit). There is a certain irony in the phrase 'tripping maids', the word 'tripping' conveying both the sense of lighthearted movement, and also that of 'erring'. The last line, not found in the original text at all, contributes to the sense of ambiguity in the text regarding the author's ideas and depiction of female identity and being, for it suggests again the image of grooves, a conformity to pre-defined paths, and following the example of others. Though the verse very properly speaks of this path as one trodden out by saints before, and the following of God, what becomes apparent if we examine the text of *Little Women*, is that the real example before the girls is 'Marmee', their mother. The March girls are attempting to mould themselves into versions of their mother, the book's female archetype. Jo exhorts Meg to 'shoulder our burdens and trudge along as cheer-fully as Marmee does'. In the talk she has with her mother about her bad temper after Amy's accident on the ice, Jo makes her mother the example she intends to follow, seeing her own attempt to conquer her temper in terms of her mother's struggle:

> The patience and humility of the face she loved so well, was a better lesson to Jo than the wisest lecture, the sharpest reproof ... the knowledge that her mother had a fault like hers, and tried to mend it, made her own easier to bear, and strengthened her resolution to cure it; though forty years seemed rather a long time to watch and pray ... .[57]

Her mother says that Mr March 'showed me that I must try to practise all the virtues I would have my little girls possess, for I was their example',[58] and that the 'love, respect and confidence' of her children was the 'sweetest reward I could receive' for her efforts 'to be the woman I would have them copy'.[59] The perpetuation of ideals is what Jo and her sisters are engaged in, as they move towards the fulfilment of their roles as women through the example of the women preceding them, in time becoming themselves the role-models for the next generation of girls.

   The result of the war in Louisa Alcott's books between the indi-vidual self of the girls and the perceived necessity of publicly upholding social conformity in women, was an uneasy compromise. For Jo and Amy at least, there is a side of being which has nothing to do with morality and social acceptability. This is their being as artists and creators, which is threatened by the pressures of being daughters of society. In this context, one is reminded of Robert Southey's letter

to Charlotte Brontë telling her that her social role as a woman super-
seded her artistic being as a writer: 'Literature cannot be the business
of a woman's life and it ought not to be. The more she is engaged in
her proper duties the less leisure she will have for it.'[60]
Jo fights the hardest against conventional usage, but gives in, albeit
reluctantly. In response to Laurie's wild plan to run away to
Washington, she sighs:

> 'If I was a boy, we'd run away together, and have a capital time; but
> as I'm a miserable girl, I must be proper, and stop at home.'[61]

The March sisters submit almost too gracefully to marriage and motherhood, Jo and Amy domesticating their personal aspirations of
becoming author and artist in order to do so, but the next generation,
while brought up to cherish the same Christian values and the sanc-
tuary of home, are left free to pursue the ambitions that their elders
renounced. Josie, Meg's younger daughter is allowed to train as the
actress her mother wanted to be but was not; Bess, Amy's daughter,
studies to be an artist; and Nan, one of Jo's protégées, goes to train as
a doctor and remains single:

> Bess and Josie won honours in their artistic careers, and in the
> course of time found worthy mates. Nan remained a busy, cheerful,
> independent spinster, and dedicated her life to her suffering sisters
> and their children.[62]

The 'worthy mates' found for the cousins are almost afterthoughts,
tacked on to the success of their careers, and this is a formal redressing
of the balance that led the previous generation into a betrayal, as it
were, of their artistic being and their other aspirations. Jo, who started
out at the beginning of the series as a tomboy, has, by the end of Part
1, been modified into a 'young lady', the androgynous side of her
nature quelled by the constant pressure to reform:

> 'In spite of the curly crop, I don't see the "son Jo" ... I see a young
> lady who ... neither whistles, talks slang ... her face is rather thin
> and pale ... it has grown gentler, and her voice is lower.'[63]

In the chapter 'Burdens', Jo says, 'I like good strong words, that
mean something.'[64] The suggestion is that language tamed to the
constraints of gender has ceased to signify fully. But as Jo is twitted

into ladylikeness, the dynamics of the personal voice and the power of language and expression, as indicated by whistling, slang and volume, are diminished, just as the forms of literary expression open to her are to shrink in the sequel. The low voice, that 'excellent thing in women' (in Book 2 we are also informed that only 'gentle words fall from her sharp tongue today') is soon to be reunited with the woman's 'crowning glory', as Jo's curly crop lengthens into a thick coil (another instance of ambiguous language, as 'coil' also suggests a sort of restraint). Though neither Cordelia's epitaph nor the biblical encomium is ever actually spoken, the resonances are present, implicit in the subsoil of the text. Thus, the frame of reference in which the development of Jo is seen to occur is by implication a clichéd one, where the dominating aesthetic is composed of inherited and traditional linguistic/ literary conventions, which are used to trap the evolving woman and leash her before her energy can disrupt the serene society about her. Jo belongs to an enclosed society, is forced into constricting roles which fail to accommodate the masculine side of her being, and is thus made to cut out this portion of self. This constitutes diminishment not only because its scope is limited to the social, moral and feminine, but because Jo is not only made to renounce part of what she is, but also to make what little remains into a totality, so that these parts of her become the sum of self: she ends with less than she began.

In the chapter entitled 'Castles in the Air', Jo voices her aspiration to write, Amy to be a great artist, and Laurie a great musician. Yet at the end of the book the 'great plans' that ferment in Jo's 'busy brain and ambitious mind' are played down as being:

> 'selfish, lonely and cold ... I haven't given up the hope that I may write a good book yet, but I can wait, and I'm sure it will be all the better for such experiences and illustrations such as these.' Jo pointed to the lively lads ... to her father ... and then to her mother sitting enthroned among her daughters with their children in her lap.[65]

The creative aspect of self is no longer seen in terms of literary creativity, but procreativity, a uniquely female privilege and form of power, and here, the mother subsumes the artist.[66] Many are the instances of equating the written work with the child and author with parent, for instance where we are told Jo 'feel[s] as a tender parent might on being asked to cut off her baby's legs in order that it might fit into a new cradle, she looked at the marked passages'[67] or where she says, 'An old maid –

that's what I'm to be. A literary spinster, with a pen for a spouse, a family of stories for children.'[68] But in the end, real children come to replace those of pen and paper, which she lays aside, at least for a time. Jo's early writings, like Louisa Alcott's, are scions of the Gothic house of fiction; titles such as *The Phantom Hand*, *The Duke's Daughter* and *The Curse of the Coventrys* can represent little else. Although the novel suggests that Jo's Gothic writings suffer from all the genre's potential weaknesses of style and plot, her writing remains a means of financial independence, and thus the means by which the physical aspect of her being may be indulged: Beth is sent to the seaside with the proceeds of Jo's novel, to regain health and strength, and the stories mentioned above pay the butcher's bill, and 'proved the blessing of the Marches in the way of groceries and gowns'.[69] Jo's writing is at once a part of her total identity, defining her, and a route towards self-discovery through literary expression that functions as a form of enactment, although Louisa Alcott puts this latter aspect in terms meant to convey condemnation:

> She thought she [Jo] was prospering finely, but unconsciously, she was beginning to desecrate some of the womanliest attributes of a woman's character ... She was beginning to feel rather than see this, for much describing of other people's passions and feelings set her to studying and speculating about her own – a morbid amusement in which healthy young do not voluntarily indulge.[70]

Jo's actions, the author implies, make her, and, in this instance, corrupt her moral and social being; being female carries a social responsibility, and in 'desecrating' her femininity, she transgresses against her social self. In the nineteenth century, introversion and self-analysis were quietly discouraged and considered unhealthy, as leading to indecision and paralysis; as Houghton says, 'Empedocles cannot act because he has become "nothing but a devouring flame of thought – but a naked, eternally restless mind".'[71] The process of self-questioning was thought to be inimical to belief in human value – 'we have learned to take to pieces all motives for actions' wrote Huxley – and without trust in others and in traditional beliefs, society was felt to be in danger of disintegration. Louisa Alcott's stricture against introversion recalls similar advice given by Elizabeth Gaskell to a young novelist:

> Besides, if you have thought the result of either introspection or experience – & the latter is the best & likely to be the most healthy

... you must observe what is out of you instead of examining what is *in* you. It is always an unhealthy sign when we are too conscious of any of the physical processes that go on within us; and I believe in a like manner that we ought not to be too cognizant of our mental proceedings, only taking note of the results. But certainly, whether introspection be morbid or not, – it is not training for a novelist....[72]

One may also recall also the words of J. C. Shairp, Matthew Arnold's successor at Oxford as Professor of Poetry, who spoke against the tendency of modern art and poetry towards subjectivity as 'so weakening, so morbidly self-conscious, so unhealthily introspective'. The keyword here is 'subjectivity', with its attendant notions of non-ascertainability and isolatedness of vision.

In *The Victorian Frame of Mind*, Houghton has well-documented the forces of pessimism and uncertainty prevalent in the Victorian world which the woman's cheerfulness might help to keep at bay, this cheerfulness having a functionality of its own. Mrs March's cheery manner, and the lifting feeling it inspires, are frequently described. Such functional cheer is also detectable in the opening of the novel, where the unhappiness of the sisters is making itself felt, and Beth spreads the gloss of contentment over the cracking lacquer:

'We've got father and mother, and each other, anyhow,' said Beth contentedly from her corner.
The four young faces on which the firelight shone brightened at the cheerful words, but darkened again, as Jo said sadly, —
'We haven't got father and shall not have him again for a long time.' She didn't say 'perhaps never', but each silently added it, thinking of father far away, where the fighting was.[73]

The Civil War is in the background, outside the circle of firelight; the function of the man is to fight, of the woman to be brave and cheerful, keeping things going at home, ensuring that there will be a home to come back to. In *An Old-Fashioned Girl*, another of Alcott's works, Polly, the eponymous 'old-fashioned girl', counsels cheerfulness in their new home as the way to hearten the menfolk when Fanny's father goes bankrupt. The 'glad game', played so enthusiastically by the heroine of Eleanor Porter's *Pollyanna*, is yet another study of, and exhortation to, the business of contentment recommended to the nineteenth-century girl.

The Gothic imagination, on the other hand, is tagged not to cheerfulness but its effective opposites: gloom and terror, relishing irrationality and madness over calm reason, the supernatural and the nebulous over the quotidian and concrete. Its denizens are not respectable members of society but society's marginalized. Since most of its aspects were therefore aligned with anti-social forces, it may be understood why it earned the disapproval of those committed to upholding the cause of social order. On the other hand, its qualities of imaginal and emotional intensity were what rendered the genre attractive to the likes of Jo March and Laura Rambotham, whose outer lives suffered from a lack of commodiousness. Jo's imagination is stopped from trespassing into Gothic domains by Professor Bhaer, and made to tread demurely in domesticated gardens. From the examples and illustrations she points to as the potentially enriching factor in her writing, namely, those involving her father, mother and children, one feels that the form of fiction Jo will turn her chastised and socialised imagination to is precisely that made popular by her favourite author, Charlotte Yonge, and her own creator, L. M. Alcott: that is, the family chronicle.

Amy, too, suffers a diminution of 'integrity', as the artistic side of her being, integral to her nature, is silenced, or only given voice in social/feminine terms. Her trip to Europe initially opens a wider world to Amy, and the cultural vistas of Europe feed her thirst for art. But Europe, instead of feeding the soul and expanding Amy's sense of individual and artistic being, becomes instead the stage for romantic experience; and after her marriage Amy comes home, symbolically reassimilated into the domestic myth. Art for her now becomes the limited vehicle for the expression of self-as-mother:

'I've begun to model a figure of baby ... and mean to do it in marble, so that whatever happens, I may at least keep the image of my little angel.'[74]

Laurie is the sole male lead in an all-female enclave; as Professor Elaine Showalter hints in her introduction to the Penguin edition of *Little Women*, he was originally rendered in such a way as to lay him open to charges of effeminacy, though this was later altered in accordance with current ideas of what male heroes should be like. However, though his physical attributes and mannerisms may have undergone literary plastic surgery, it is noticeable that in many ways his destiny is as limited as that of the girls around him, his musical ambitions castrated as he gives up his castle in the air to stay at home with his grandfather, and later, to be Amy's husband and Bess's father. As the next generation of girls achieve what was denied to their elders, Nat, one of their protégés, proceeds to musical fame in Laurie's place.

The tension between freedom and constraint, self and society, in Alcott's work is also perceptible in *Jack and Jill*, *Eight Cousins* and *Rose in Bloom*. Jill Pecq, in *Jack and Jill*, active and as spirited as the boys, has an accident, suffering back injuries that lay her up for a time. It is an enforced passivity, during which she learns the lessons of submission held to be necessary for girls. Henry James, reviewing *Eight Cousins* in *The Nation* (14 October 1875), spoke of the attempt to 'strip away the shams of life', but disapproved of the anti-authoritarian stance that this entailed:

> In this, her latest volume, she gives us an account of a little girl named Rose ... and a big burly uncle, an honest sea-man addicted to riding a tilt at the shams of life. He finds his little niece encompassed with a great many of these, and Miss Alcott's tale is chiefly devoted to relating how he plucked them successively away ... It is evidently written in good faith ... [but] it is unfortunate ... in its general tone ... [which] is the last one in the world to be used in describing to children their elders and betters and the social mysteries that surround them. Miss Alcott seems to have a private understanding with the youngsters she depicts at the expense of their pastors and masters ....[75]

The shams Rose's uncle tries to strip away are those surrounding the upbringing of young girls; 'We will show her [Aunt Myra] how to make constitutions and turn pale-faced little ghosts into rosy hearty girls'[76] says Uncle Alec, and he proceeds to take away her coffee, clothe her in dresses without frills and tight belts, and so on. There seems to be a genuine attempt to furnish a new image of girlhood, a healthy if not a fashionable one. 'Breathe,' he admonishes her, till 'your waist is more like that of Hebe, goddess of health than that of a fashion plate',[77] and sensible living is enforced throughout the book. Yet, in the sequel, we find again the curtailment of the expected new freedom. The promise of a new image of girlhood ceases; the courtship and marriage of Rose seems to be all that her early training has prepared her for, and while this causes no great consternation in the breast of the reader, who finds her insipid and coy, the fate of Phebe, the servant girl who the family has sent for voice training, leaves the reader stamping with vexation. Phebe does well, and is in the process of becoming famous, but comes home instead to marry Archie, Rose's cousin; here we have another artist lost to the world,

> 'Think of what she gives up for me – fame and fortune … You don't know what a splendid prospect she has of becoming one of the sweet singers who are loved and honoured everywhere, and all this she puts away for my sake, content to sing for me alone, with no reward but love' … Phebe bent toward him a look and gesture which plainly showed how willingly she offered up all ambitious hopes upon the altar of a woman's happy love.[78]

As we have seen, when the claims of art come into conflict with those of society, art loses. Art and music, according to the Utilitarians,[79] did not have any perceptible and measurable use. Not till the *fin de siècle*, with the rise of aestheticism, did the motto 'art for art's sake' gain any currency. But until that time, women would have had little 'legitimate' access to their artistic selves, encircled by the narrow definition of wife and mother.

Towards the end of the nineteenth century signs of change began to be visible. It was at about this time that the mind and its workings emerged as the literary medium itself, the 'stream of consciousness' the means through which experience was freed from the straitjacket of formal narrative and linguistic progressions and from the artificiality of the conventions that interpreted and constructed thought and consciousness in terms of a linear rather than tangential causality. Emancipated from such binds as these, narrative is made as the mind roams and transcribes these wanderings onto paper, alighting on the natural and on the arbitrary instead of the contrivances of traditional or obvious associations. The literary experience became infused with a new vitality because of the new permutational possibilities arising out of the fluidity of the medium, and the creation of new species through the 'irregular' union of ideas. (By 'irregular', I mean 'not traditionally associated' rather than 'illicit'.) The new fluidity of the medium led to the depiction of fluid experience, nor can it be coincidence, I think, that the 'stream of consciousness' is so named, or that novels by Joyce and Virginia Woolf, pioneers in the medium, contain inbuilt references to water. *Ulysses* contains the reference to the voyages of the Greek hero, and titles like *The Waves*, *The Voyage Out*, and *To the Lighthouse*, require no explanation. More significantly, the fluidity of experience and of the medium were used to free the female self; *The Voyage Out*, for instance, is the voyage of the girl out of safe harbours. As Dusinberre writes,

> Helen Ambrose, forty and wise, takes Rachel out of a Victorian story-book childhood with two maiden aunts, in which she trails around Richmond Park like Mary Lennox at Misselthwaite Manor, into a room of her own peopled by Meredith's *Diana of the Crossways* and Ibsen's Nora in *A Doll's House*.[80]

The newer freedoms of the female in this wider world may be evaluated in *The Getting of Wisdom*, published in 1910 in England by the Australian writer Henry Handel Richardson (psuedonym of Florence Richardson), which continues from where Jo March left off. Born and brought up within a society as enclosed and narrow as Ethel May's, Laura is more fortunate than either Ethel or Jo, for in the end she manages to depart from the constraining social part that girls are expected to play, and to gain a sense of being that stems from herself as artist in the expanded world outside school. As Jo in some sense represents the author's artistic submission, Laura's story is that of her creator's escape into the freedom of a fiction not bound by cultural strategies. She is an enigma; the reader finds it hard to penetrate the text's meaning and cannot discover *what* she is, but in this very puzzle lies the integrity of the character. This is to say that she cannot be compartmentalised, and it is not easy to define Laura either socially or morally, though both these aspects are fully treated of in the novel. They are linked and inseparable from all else that goes into making up Laura, and as this integrated being, she resists and eludes the category-makers and the would-be enclosers, symbolically running out of school and the pages of the novel, beyond the reader's following, into a future not determined by either her femaleness or a conventional moral and social vision. When her schoolfriends Mary and Cupid declare their intentions of becoming a surgeon and journalist respectively, it emerges that Laura has no fixed idea of what she wants to become or what she will be:

> 'Wish? ... oh, I've tons of wishes ... I want to see things – yes, that most of all. Hundreds and thousands of things. People and places ... and China, and Japan ...' ... In Laura's case no kindly Atropos snipped the thread of her aspirations: these, large, vague, extemporary, one and all achieved fulfilment; then withered off to make room for more.[81]

Yet, it is those with fixed notions who end by becoming stifled within traditional roles: Mary gets married and Cupid becomes a governess. Laura, as the excerpt says, with large, 'exposed' visions of places outside her narrow orbit, with no firm ideas, achieves fulfilment of her wishes.

The novel details the experiences of adolescent school life based on the author's own schooldays at the Melbourne Presbyterian Ladies College. Laura Rambotham is twelve when she is first sent away to school, to 'get wisdom', and with wisdom, get understanding (Proverbs 4: 7), and also to have her wildness and individuality eradicated that she may take her place in society. The nature of the wisdom and understanding she acquires is not the narrow intellectual wisdom that school life provides her with; this wisdom is the comprehension of humanity, its inner, not its outer forms.

The story of Laura's time at school is balanced between two notions of being. One such conception is that which society at large finds acceptable, an existence within the confines of a peer group, which dictates a set pattern of behaviour and thought, and where one prepares a face to meet the faces that one meets. One is Laura's private consciousness that rebels against the *modus vivendi* espoused by those around her, and which every so often breaks out in a display of personal opinions and imaginative fireworks. When this happens it results in ostracism for Laura, forcing her into periods of hibernation; the structure of the text thus comes to resemble birth-pangs of a sort, the constrictions alternating with the assertions of self, and culminating in Laura's release from school into a wider world:

> ... many a day came and went before she grasped that oftentimes, just those mortals who feel cramped and unsure in the conduct of everyday life, will find themselves to rights, with astounding ease, in that freer, more spacious world where no practical considerations hamper, and where the creatures that inhabit dance to their tune: the world where are stored up men's best thoughts, the hopes, and fancies; where the shadow is the substance, and the multitude of business pales before the dream.[82]

The gestating self thus spewed out into the world is a novelist in the making. Like Jo March, Laura, the fictional representation of the author herself, is destined to write; at least, it is so implied though the text leaves the ending open, this itself constituting recognition of the ultimate freedom to choose one's own ends, a release from both the constriction of narrative fixity/closure and the narrowing vistas of an end foreknown. At the outset, Laura is first glimpsed telling stories to her siblings. These are constructed in the fairy-tale mode; they are symbolic of the enclosed world of childhood she speaks of and speaks from:

> 'And there he saw a lady, a beautiful lady ... She was lying on the sward – a sward, you know, is grass as smooth as velvet, just like green velvet ... The bottom of the lovely silk dress was all dirty –'
>
> 'Wondrous Fair, if you don't mind you'll make that sheet dirty, too,' said Pin.
>
> 'Shut up, will you!' answered her sister, who, carried away by her narrative, had approached her boots to some linen that was bleaching ... 'Well, as I said, the edge of her robe was muddy – no, I don't think I will say that; it sounds prettier if it's clean. So it hung in long straight beautiful folds to her ankles ... '.[83]

However, they contain a certain mobility and flexibility, for although Laura employs the tropes of the fairy tale, the details change and are embroidered according to her imagination, true to the vision of each isolated moment. For instance, the statement 'And there he saw a lady' is presented as a bare narrative fact: she is thinking of sequence; this is then qualified with an adjective: 'a beautiful lady'. Again, 'She was lying on a sward' is elaborated into 'grass as smooth as velvet' and then, finally, in a further accretion of detail and texture, 'just like green velvet'. Then again, she exchanges her initial idea of travel-stained garments for the more conventional, Pre-Raphaelite drapery. The style of her narrative, like Jo's, is initially Romantic, though as will be seen, this will change.

The path of the artist and the path of the self are so closely linked as to be inseparable. Laura, being shy, is incapable of doing what the other girls naturally accomplish in terms of attracting members of the opposite sex. In the eyes of her classmates, this is tantamount to failure as a 'woman', and she is written off as a nobody. The ultimate achievement, the purpose of being, for the many, is marriage. One of the scholars is engaged, the author writes, as from the girls' point of view, 'You could not really treat her as a comrade – her, who had reached the goal. For this was the goal.'[84] Laura is moved by this dismissal to develop a crush on Mr Shepherd, the curate, as if to prove to herself that she is as other girls are – capable of being caught up and enclosed in the same way. When the crush has worn off, however, she is forced to continue not only with the pretence of passion, but also to concoct a tale of reciprocated love and various other tarradiddles. This she is goaded into doing when Tilly, one of the girls, says, 'I bet you there's nothing to tell', implying that Laura is incapable of holding any man's interest, and by this statement threatening to move Laura back into the ranks of those who do not signify.

Laura then tells 'all', in a style and mode recalling her earlier narrative creations for the benefit of her siblings:

> 'And what about his old sketch of a wife?'
> 'Her? Oh' – and Laura squeezed herself desperately for the details that would not come – 'oh, why she's a perfect old ... old cat. And twenty years older than him.'...
> '... Well, why in the name of all that's holy did he take her?'
> Laura cast a mysterious glance round, and lowered her voice. 'Well ... she had *lots* of money and he had none. He was ever so poor. And she paid for him to be a clergyman.'
> 'Go on! As poor as all that?'
> 'As poor as a church mouse. – But oh,' she hastened to add, at the visible cooling off of the four faces, 'he comes of a most distinguished family. His father was a lord or baronet or something like that, but he married a beautiful girl who hadn't a penny ... '.[85]

Naturally, she is discovered to be telling lies. Her fabrications are certainly untruths, and of a tall order, and her classmates ostracise her out of vaunted scorn for her mendacity, and also out of anger at having been so gulled. They fail to see that her intention in lying is not to give expression to simple wickedness, but that, somewhere along the way, lying has become indistinguishable in her own consciousness from the other kind of storytelling, carrying her further than was originally intended.

Later she is accepted back into the fold and becomes a member of the literary society. Her reading at this stage, it is indicated, is instrumental in helping her formulate an approach to writing, although till that time, her creative efforts have been oral rather than written. Reading through Ibsen's *A Doll's House* (whose predominant idea is, after all, female emancipation), instead of finding the children's story she expects, she is confronted by the 'queerest stuff she had ever seen in print'. Her expectations of literature and its contents are thus overturned:

> It seemed to her amazingly unreal ... and yet again so true, in the way it dragged in every day happenings ... Her young romantic

soul rose in arms against this, its first bluff contact with realism, against such a dispiriting sobriety of outlook.[86]

As a consequence, her first literary attempt for the Society is entrenched firmly in the extravaganza of Romantic idiom, and falls flat:

> 'Here,' Cupid chimed in. 'Look here, Infant, I want to ask you something. Have you ever been in Venice?'
> 'No.'
> 'Ever seen a gondola?'
> 'No.'
> 'Or the Doge's palace? – or a black cloaked assassin? – or a masked lady?'
> 'You know I haven't,' murmured Laura, humbled to the dust.[87]

As with Jo before her, the Gothic has to be renounced, but in Laura's case it is not necessarily to withdraw into the circumscriptions of the domestic realms of fiction. Laura's authorship will be of the kind of book that *The Getting of Wisdom* is about: the emancipation of the individual from a claustrophobic, enclosed world.

Nina Auerbach, in *Communities of Women*, says that though a community of women 'may suggest less the honour of fellowship than an anti-society, an austere banishment from both social power and biological rewards',[88] 'initiation into a band of brothers is a traditional privilege'. The desire for social stability also demanded that men give of themselves, but whereas girls were trained to fill roles, giving a portion of their individuality in order to fill the confines of a given role, the sense of individual being for the male was generated, paradoxically, by being subsumed and absorbed into a larger group identity, 'groups' which were units of order, structure and enclosure that society aspired towards. There were honourable models and precedents; the fellowship of the Round Table[89] was one such, where self was ennobled by its partaking of the larger identity of the Order which existed to defy chaos and establish order and stability. The nineteenth-century adolescent male was encouraged to think of himself in terms of membership within a larger entity, whether of the cricket or rugby teams, school house, school, university, or nation, and this was reflected in the fiction penned for him.

This is patently the case in Thomas Hughes's *Tom Brown's Schooldays* (1857), which was the novel to give impetus to the genre of school stories, though it was not the first to contain a school setting. In so far as the theme of development is concerned, the establishment of the school novel was an important step forward, the world of school being largely one where the student is the measure of things, and where he has to shoulder responsibility for himself as a 'full citizen'.[90] This decontextualization of the child or adolescent, forcing it to stand on its own feet, also encourages it towards the formation of identity and character in an environment given to cliquism and factions, and, generally speaking, a degree of greater absolutism in ideas. The individual has to make and stand by his decisions, or else, should he abrogate this responsibility, he runs the risk of being rated by the school body as a non-leader, a 'nothing'. However, the formation of identity is complicated in *Tom Brown's Schooldays* by the group ethic spoken of earlier. Tom Brown's initiation into school life begins with the rugby match between School house (his house) and the School. East says that no School House boy would cut the match; if he did, he would soon be cut by the rest of the house. The kind of social pressure exerted by this statement encourages Tom, the new boy, to quickly develop in terms of loyalty to side, to see himself as one of *them*. The preservation of self is unimportant, weighed against the preservation and glory of the group, and this is shown in the author's condemnation of Speedicut and Flashman:

> You don't really want to drive that ball through that scrummage, chancing all hurt for the glory of the School house, but to make us think that's what you want ....[91]

Or again, as Tom does what the two seniors shirk from, and throws himself on the ball, and is promptly jumped on by the leaders, he is rewarded with, 'Well, he's a plucky youngster, and will make a player.'

School stories of the twentieth century appear much less concerned about fanatical loyalty to house and school; *vide* the following extract from Antonia Forest's *End of Term* (1959), where Nicola Marlow, tricked out of a place in the netball team, states her intention of watching the match none the less:

> Nicola looked sympathetic. But she added, 'And anyway... you've got to come and watch with me.'
> 'Oh? Have I?' Tim tilted forward with a thud. 'Why? D'you have to be a terribly sporting type, with a stiff upper lip, cheering Our School to victory?'
> Nicola flushed. It wasn't that in the least and Tim ought to have

known. It was simply that if she didn't watch, everyone would go round saying how much poor old Nick minded.[92]

This passage continues to debunk the nineteenth-century school ethic, a process which Kipling had begun in *Stalky and Co*. Terms once used in all seriousness, like 'stiff upper lip' and the capitalised 'Our School', function here as gentle mockery of the ethos found in works like *Tom Brown's Schooldays*, and Nicola is not worried about being 'cut' by her schoolmates, but rather of losing her personal dignity. The individual has replaced the group in the twentieth-century consciousness.

Tom Brown's Schooldays is prefaced with a quotation taken from the *Rugby Magazine*, which reads, tellingly,

> As on the one hand it should ever be remembered that we are boys, and boys at school, so on the other hand we must bear in mind that we form a complete social body ... a society, in which, by the nature of the case we must not only learn, but act and live; and act and live not only as boys, but as boys who will be men.

The emphasis here is both on the evolution of the youth and on the social body in the company of which the youth develops. The opening chapter tends to confirm one in the suspicion that the reader is intended to see Tom Brown, not so much as an individual, but as a representative of English boyhood, belonging to the house of Brown whose members are themselves used by the author to represent good, uncompromising English citizenry:

> Notwithstanding the well-merited but late fame which has now fallen upon them, anyone at all acquainted with the family must feel that much has yet to be written and said before the British nation will be properly sensible of how much of its greatness it owes to the Browns. For centuries, in their quiet, dogged, home-spun way, they have been subduing the earth in most English counties, and leaving their mark in American forests and Australian uplands. Wherever the fleets and armies of England have won renown, there stalwart sons of the Browns have done yeoman's work. With the yew bow and cloth-yard shaft at Cressy and Agincourt ... under Rodney and St. Vincent, Wolfe and Moore, Nelson and Wellington, they have carried their lives in their hands ....[93]

Group loyalty was another form of social cement; its inculcation was undertaken with the aim of providing a common view of things among its members. Group athletics was encouraged as likely to help instill team spirit, an inspiration that was to be sublimated towards the building and establishment of empire. The connection is one that is easy to make; the rugby match mentioned above sports many combat metaphors, as seen in the following two extracts:

> His face [Brooke's] is earnest and careful ... but full of pluck and hope, the sort of look I hope to see in my general when I go out to fight.[94]

> You say you don't see much in it all, nothing but a struggling mass of boys, and a leather ball ... My dear sir, a battle would look much the same to you, except that the boys would be men, and the balls iron ....[95]

One may also recall in this context Sir Henry Newbolt's 'Vitai Lampada', where the trumpet call of 'Play up, play up and play the game!' is first used on the cricket field, and – Pavlovian group-responses having once been established – the individual graduates to the battlefield, plays up, plays the game and helps to win the war.

Ironically, perhaps, this illustrates how little change or develop-ment really takes place in fictional characters (and maybe even real persons) subjected first to cricket balls and then to real artillery. The boy's scholastic and athletic training was to allow the heroic man to take form; Hughes spoke in the preface of it enabling them to 'lose nothing of the boy that is worth keeping', while building 'the man upon it'. But one might well argue that what was in the process of being built here was a rather larger edition of the schoolboy trans-planted into the adult world, and that the Buchan thrillers, for instance, spoken of as appealing so much to 'man and boy', did so precisely because there was scant difference in the mental and emotional framework of both sets of readers. The quasi-schoolboy antics of Sir Edward Leithen, Lord Lamancha, Palliser-Yeates and Sir Archibald Roylance in Buchan's *John MacNab*, where these heroes worm their way through the heather, daring the owners of the estates they trespass upon to stop them from poaching either a salmon or a deer, emerge as a big-boy edition of Stalky, Beetle and M'Turk crawling onto Colonel Dabney's estate to escape the schoolmasters Prout and King.

The identity of the boy and man was bound up with that of the nation, his personal development marching side by side with the development of empire. This strain of nationalism was in turn fuelled by the forces of classicism sweeping through Britain in the nineteenth century. Richard Jenkyns, author of *The Victorians and Ancient Greece*, argues that the Victorian genre of school stories, and in particular *Tom Brown's Schooldays* and F. W. Farrar's *Eric, or Little by Little*, were infused with Homeric ideals. Hughes, he says, 'saw adolescence in a Homeric light'.[96] The ideal youth for Hughes, he says, was a 'speaker of words and a doer of deeds', and Arthur is held up as an example to Tom: 'Arthur there has taken in Greek and cricket too.' The intellectual and emotional influences of Hellenism were used to deepen the sense of a shared national identity, taking the classical culture as part of the national heritage. In *The Heroes*, Charles Kingsley emphasises this:

> And as you grow up, and read more and more, you will find that we owe to these old Greeks the beginnings of all our mathematics and geometry – that is, the science and knowledge of numbers, and of the shapes of things, and of the forces which make things move and stand at rest; and the beginnings of our geography and astronomy; and of our laws, and freedom, and politics ... And we owe to them, too, the beginning of our logic ... and of our metaphysics – that is, the study of our own thoughts and souls ....[97]

The last-mentioned link with the Greeks is especially significant, for from them, according to Kingsley, was inherited the framework of living within which the Victorian self was studied and defined. The Greeks were considered responsible for the elements of formal culture inherited by the British, and these elements, interestingly, are what give order, structure and stability.

In the person of Tom Brown, representing the youth of England, Hughes fuses the impulses of Homeric belligerence and English nationalism. His fight with Slogger Williams occurs after a class reading of Homer, where Helen mourns the passing of Hector; Arthur is moved to tears, Williams to insult, and Tom to fight, upholding not only Arthur but also the Homeric ideal, for the wrestling match recalls that between Odysseus and the Telamonian Aias at Patroclus' funeral. Pickard-Cambridge, in *Demosthenes and the Last Days of Greek Freedom* (1914), underlined even further the fact that British imperialism was viewed in terms of Athenian empire building, saying that it was not an 'absurd contention that the life of the individual [is] ennobled by membership of an Imperial nation', adding a footnote asserting 'that British imperialism contained nobility beyond the Athenian range of conception'.[98] Here, too, the group identity that Pickard-Cambridge sees as having given greater meaning to the life of the individual Athenian reinforces the ideology of the immersion of self in the nation spoken of earlier.

Less obviously gendered in that its apparent audience consists of Dan and Una (although it is suggested that the construction of history is a male activity) are Kipling's *Puck of Pook's Hill* and *Rewards and Fairies*, whose main enterprise appears to be rooting the youth of England firmly in its soil, feeding it with a sense of a great history and culture so as to allow the flourishing of a national identity. *Puck of Pook's Hill* has assimilation as its basic theme, the assimilation of the invader, the assimilation of the individual;[99] and its secondary theme is the ordering and structuring of society. The frame story, if story it may be called, is the introduction of Dan and Una, through the agency of Puck (the Oldest of the Old Things in England), to characters out of England's past. After each episode they forget what they have seen till the next time they see Puck, and are rendered in this manner unable to tell what they have seen and experienced. Dusinberre contends that this means that they are not

> ... improved or educated by their experiences. The enriching of consciousness is the reader's not the fictional character's. The children grow out of one pair of boots into another but their minds show no such expansion.[100]

However, another reading may be possible. Tolstoy in *War and Peace* writes:

> Nowhere is the commandment not to taste the fruit of the tree of knowledge so clearly written as in the course of history. Only unconscious activity bears fruit, and the individual who plays a part in historical events never understands their significance. If he attempts to understand them, he is struck with sterility.[101]

It is likely that forgetfulness in the 'Puck' books may be a literary device to indicate the deeper assimilation of experience, where experience becomes a part of the person, ingrown and thus part of his unconscious though not bubbling on the surface of his mind, in the same way that the Saxons and Normans can only grow into a single people, the English, as the idea of unity gradually permeates the unconscious.

In this manner, the children are made part of the land; Puck cuts a clod of earth and gives it to the children: 'Now you are lawfully seised and possessed of all Old England',[102] he says, and in so doing symbolically makes over to them a part of their spiritual and physical heritage. The law cuts both ways, for the rights (and rites) of passage to their past entail responsibilities to the land and country itself; when Dan says, 'I'm planting a lot of acorns this autumn too',[103] he is stating a commitment to the land and the continuance of a tradition. The acorns are part of Kipling's triune emblematisation of Old England in the Oak and Ash and Thorn that Puck speaks of.

Within the framework arc individual encounters with folk from days long past. The tale they all tell is the same. It is the story of how they came to England to conquer her, only to be absorbed into the life of the country, ultimately reconfiguring their identities in her, but also forming a part of her identity – that is to say, the heritage in fact enjoyed by Dan and Una is composed of Roman, Norman, Angle and Saxon elements. The first of those to be introduced to Dan and Una is Sir Richard, in 'Young Men at the Manor', whose narrative details how he followed De Aquila and William of Normandy in the conquest of England. After being gifted with the manor he has won from the Saxons, news comes of Norman thieves with intent to steal the swine belonging to the manor. 'Norman or Saxon,' says Sir Richard, 'they must be beaten back'; and in finding common cause against the pig rustlers, his men of both races move one step closer to being welded into a single people. Hugh, the Saxon to whom the manor originally belonged, becomes friends with Richard; though he has not sworn fealty to De Aquila, he is made lord of Dallington, a nearby manor. 'I am a Saxon,' says Hugh, 'and ... have not sworn fealty to any Norman.' De Aquila's answer is the point towards which the narrative is moving: 'In God's good time ... there will be neither Saxon nor Norman in England.'[104] Later, in 'Old Men at Pevensey', he is to sound this claim again: 'In fifty years there will be neither Saxon nor Norman, but all English'; 'I think for England, for whom neither king nor baron thinks. I am not Norman, Sir Richard, nor Saxon, Sir Hugh. English I am.' The refrain to Sir Richard's song, which concludes the episode, 'Young Men at the Manor', claims that England has taken him. Parnesius, the centurion out of Roman Britain, is British born, and counselled by his father to think for Britain, as Rome is past saving. The song that rounds off this chapter is a good example of the classical, though not Greek, influence regarding the viewing of empire:

> *Strong heart with triple armour bound,*
> *Beat strongly for thy lifeblood runs,*
> *Age after Age, the Empire round –*
> *In us Thy Sons.*

> *Who, distant from the Seven Hills,*
> *Loving and serving much, require*
> *Thee –* thee *to guard 'gainst home born ills*
> *The Imperial fire!*

Omit the reference to Rome's seven hills, and the two verses might well refer to the British empire, but even so the strength of the Roman empire that went into the making of England is being invoked here to strengthen the Imperial spirit of the (then) present British empire. The counter-tensions of conquering and being conquered, possessing and belonging, structure the entire book. *Puck of Pook's Hill* is a dialogue between times past and present, where the citizens of both times engage each other in conversation and proceed to share things that are common, and also to learn from each other.

Puck of Pook's Hill and *Rewards and Fairies* have the same preoccupation with order as Kipling's other work. As with Kim, who in the end becomes part of the forces of social control, and the wolf pack in the *Jungle Book*, who cry for Akela to lead them when they have grown sick of 'lawlessness', Sir Richard and Hugh, Parnesius and Pertinax and Gloriana are engaged in creating order and enclosure out of disorder. They are about the business of restoring a sense of homogeneity to societies which are uneasy and restless, lacking a sense of cohesive identity.[105] After Hastings, they are busy with fighting off robbers, and in the 'Knights of the Joyous Venture' they are fighting apes, which may represent the bestial and the untamed, uncivilised side of man. The gold they bring back from this adventure eventually goes to 'bring the law', being used to exert economic pressure upon King John in order to make him sign the Magna Carta, the document of law and human rights. Parnesius and Pertinax, Roman centurions, are posted to Hadrian's Wall (another image of ordering and structure) to keep out the tribes and Saxon invaders, to fight the threat to their ordered society. Gloriana, Elizabeth I, has a similar task: to keep out the Spanish and keep England safe.

Rudyard Kipling's writing for young people both supported and challenged the doctrines found in the chronicles of Tom Brown at school. On the one hand, the rights of the individual go to war with the forces of group mentality, and this shows up quite clearly in *Stalky and Co.* (1899); yet on the other hand it would be difficult to find a more ardent imperialist and believer in British nationalism – and thus, the 'group' structure – than Kipling; imperialism was the inspiration behind *Puck of Pook's Hill* and *Rewards and Fairies*, and is detectable in *Stalky* itself. *Kim*, though set in British India, and superficially concerned with the maintenance of empire against unscrupulous Russians and other comers, is again about the individual rather than group consciousness, and is in fact, more than Kipling's other books, about self-discovery. Paradoxically, however, *Kim* was the novel most often used to fuel the imperialist ideal. The Scout movement was started by Lord Baden-Powell to toughen up British youth, inculcating patriotic sentiment and teaching physical fitness, in order to prepare these youths for participation in empire-building and empire-holding. In the manual prepared for the use of scoutmasters Baden-Powell holds Kim up as the Scout *par excellence*, who it would well behove the general boy populace to imitate. To this day 'Kim's game', the memorisation and description of sundry objects, is still a feature of the Scout and Guide movements.

Stalky and Co. is a school story constructed along very different principles from those found in either *Eric* or *Tom Brown*. Stalky, Beetle and M'Turk are upholders of land and nation, but also firm believers in individual rights and the necessity of a private space where they can exist outside the regimen imposed by the officious housemasters, King and Prout. The three are unpopular with Prout for flaunting their independence, for refusing to subscribe even nominally to school 'doctrines' of house loyalty, enthusiasm for sports (especially cricket), and agreement with the Powers That Be. Prout feels that their lack of social fusion with the rest of the school body betokens something fundamentally wrong with them:

> Boys that he understood attended house matches and could be accounted for at any moment. But he had heard M'Turk openly deride cricket – even house matches; Beetle's views on the honour of the house were incendiary ....[106]

This is corroborated by M'Turk:

> 'If we attended the matches an' yelled, "Well hit, sir," an' stood on one leg an' grinned every time Heffy said, "So ho, my sons. Is it

thus?" an' said, "Yes sir," an' "No, sir," and "Oh, sir," an' "Please, sir," like a lot of filthy fa-ags, Heffy 'ud think no end of us'.[107]

What Kipling appears to be attacking in *Stalky & Co.* is not the *esprit de corps* of any particular unit, schoolhouse, team or country, but the mass of cliché, fossilised language without personal meaning attached to it, that has grown up to surround the various units. It is up to the individual to act so as to give significance to ideas and ideals. Phrases like 'the honour of the house' are treated with contempt by Stalky and Co. not because they are completely devoid of any feelings of partisanship, but because of the lack of real thought and meaning with which they are thrown about. Though Stalky and his friends do not invest as much of themselves in the business of the school house as some of the other members consider proper, they are stung when King's house insults theirs with regard to the matter of hygiene. Besieged by indignant house members to help do something about the situation, the trio express their scorn of their fellow students' rhetoric and language, which is not only meaningless and powerless, but hamstrung by bad grammar:

> They read ungrammatical resolutions, and made speeches beginning, 'Gentlemen, we have met on this occasion', and ending with 'It's a beastly shame'... M'Turk ... delivered himself: 'You jabber and jaw and burble, and that's about all you can do. Besides, that resolution of Orrin's is full of bad grammar, and King'll gloat over *that.*[108]

'Jabber', 'jaw', 'burble' – the words used by M'Turk to describe the efficacy of Orrin's language are telling. Stalky and Co. are men of action, not utterers of worn-out platitudes, and the way in which they do something for the honour of the house is not to prate about it, but to put a dead cat between the floorboards of the rival houses, to stink them out. For them, action *is* language; this is made evident in the way that their exploits become for them the inspiration for their own meanings in words. 'Cat', for instance, becomes in their vocabulary not merely a naming word, but a verb, a doing word: 'Besides, we shall cat ... It's a regular Pomposo Stinkadore.' Action and not empty words is the route that the three take, and this is what defines them.

In the episode entitled 'The Flag of their Country' Stalky and other members of the school set up a cadet corps, training for the time when they will, they hope, enter Sandhurst and the army. During the period of their training a Member of Parliament is invited to speak to the school, with the intention of encouraging and inculcating the growth of the patriotic spirit. But the words he uses, in his address to the 'boys of today' who are going to be the 'men of tomorrow', again belong to an empty rhetoric that debases the private dreams and aspirations of his adolescent hearers:

> Some of those now present ... he had no doubt – some of them anxiously looked forward to leading their men against the bullets of England's foes; to confronting the stricken field in all the pride of their youthful manhood ... In a raucous voice, he cried aloud little matters, like the hope of Honour and the dream of Glory, that boys do not discuss even with their most intimate equals ...
> He pointed them to shining goals, with fingers that smudged out all radiance on all horizons ...[109]

This man, who M'Turk is convinced is the Gadarene Swine, speaks a storybook language out of boys' books, not real experience, and thus not only fails to inspire but embarrasses the boys, who recognise the inherent falseness of his terms of reference. In speaking as he does of honour and glory, he causes them to wince, for in his mouth their private aspirations are trivialised into so much cant, and he damages their private sense of personal identification with the 'national' ideals.

Kipling's work, while attentive to the question of how self may be constructed out of the negotiations with approved social codes, works with the question of how these are internalised and refined by the private consciousness. *Kim* (1901), a novel about an Irish orphan in the Punjab, is no exception. More than any other of Kipling's books for younger readers, it is a work attempting to grapple with the enigma of arrival, a story that, on one level at least, investigates the question of who and what Kim is. As an orphan Kim has no special ties with anyone, and when the book begins all that may safely be established is that he is 'white', or Caucasian. This is a 'surface' truth about Kim, not the whole truth, for, English or not, he neither behaves like an English child would nor thinks of himself as a European; he is accepted by the Indians, Hindu and Muslim alike, as one of themselves. Meeting a Tibetan lama, in search of the river which is said to have sprung up where an arrow of Buddha touched the earth, he leaves Lahore, where he lives, to travel with his new friend, whom he protects and begs food for. Kim is a free agent; with no one by to keep him chained to a fixed way of life and home, he decontextualises himself to set off his journey towards self-understanding, though this is not a conscious motivation.

In the course of his travels he encounters his father's old regiment, who, on discovering his identity through the agency of the birth certificate worn in a case around his neck, promptly hold fast to him, refusing to let him return to his peripatetic existence. He is sent to school at Lucknow, and after his time there is done, he goes to rejoin the lama. On his way he is struck with a sudden sense of aloneness, which acts as a catalyst to trigger off his question, 'Who is Kim – Kim – Kim?' Kipling writes:

> A very few white people, but many Asiatics, can throw themselves into amazement as it were by repeating their own names over and over again to themselves, letting the mind go free upon speculation as to personal identity ... 'Who is Kim – Kim – Kim?' ... In a minute – in another half-second he felt he would arrive at the solution of the tremendous puzzle ...[110]

The search for being preoccupies Kim; poised as he is between worlds, finding a satisfactory answer to the question of what he is, and where he belongs, is more difficult than for most. In the world of the Great Game, of spying between nations, identity is fluid and fluctuates rapidly. Disguise is the way of life, and occasionally the only way to preserve it. Kim, early in the book, happily switches from European child to Hindu beggar brat to lama's *chela* (disciple), and the question is whether he is one, or none, or all of these. Later, he helps to disguise E23, a fellow player in the game, on the run from hostile elements. Yet all the identities Kim moves into are but temporary houses, surface identities. Kim tries to span all worlds: India and Europe, the Great Game, and the different religions as well. In Kim's universe, these last are many: there is Christianity and its sub-divisions (both Catholic and Anglican padres fight over him), and Muslim (Mahbub Ali), Hindu, Sikh, Jain, and Buddhist (Teshoo Lama), and he is equally at home with all, though, from what one can make out, not particularly devoted to any one creed. But in not having a formal place in a society and thus not contributing of himself in any deep way, there is a vulnerability. Without the safety of enclosure and place he is rootless and isolated, and needs to commit himself to some greater body in order to draw new validation. As Sandison comments:

> So Kim chooses involvement, and significantly it is with the Secret service – the force for law, order and control, the force above all others which can bring against the insidious powers of disruption

and disintegration an equally insidious weapon cast from stealth, dissimulation and all-knowingness.[111]

While he represents freedom and fluidity in himself, he realises that fluidity without some kind of container means shapelessness, and it is in dedication of his freedom to a cause that will give him meaning. Finally, Kim finds or comes to understand his place in the larger scheme of things. After having wrested certain documents from Russian spies, he collapses with exhaustion, and, during his recovery,

> look[s] with strange eyes unable to take up the size and proportion and use of things ... All that while he felt, though he could not put it into words, that his soul was out of gear with its surroundings ... 'I am Kim. I am Kim. And what is Kim?' His soul repeated it again and again.
> He did not want to cry ... but of a sudden easy, stupid tears trickled down his nose, and with an almost audible click he felt the wheels of his being lock up anew on the world without. Things that rode meaningless on the eyeball an instant before slid into proper proportion. Roads were meant to be walked upon, houses to be lived in, cattle to be driven, fields to be tilled, and men and women to be talked to ....[112]

Here there is the sudden dawning of an understanding that his place in the order of things is a simple matter, merely requiring the rendering up of smaller classifications – for example, 'European' or 'Indian', that impede his acceptance of that simplest and yet most profound of great truths: that what Kim is, Kim is, and that he has a part in mankind, that largest grouping, which renders all the lesser definitions meaningless. He is a 'cog wheel', part of the total sum of machinery that makes the world move, and he finds a sense of self and identity in the human context, in that he no longer feels impelled by a feeling of displacement to ask what he is. The definition which he achieves is partly a social one, a sense of place within community. But to a large extent, what Kim has accomplished is the integrating not merely of himself into the world, but of the world and its elements within himself. Being, for Kim, is a sense of wholeness, of corporeality and spirituality, a welding together of diverse things. The simplicity of finding the self parallels the simplicity with which spiritual enlightenment is found. The lama's quest for the river follows a similar path, for after traversing the larger part of India to find a river that will, he says, cleanse him of his sins and cut the ties of illusion that bind him to the world, he finds it in a tiny streamlet that runs through the lands of the talkative maharanee, by tumbling into it. He has been seeking non-being, rather than being, the attempt to apprehend the real through the loosing of ties and feelings. Symbolically, enlightenment for the lama comes in a way that indicates links of affection in humanity, rather than a cutting-off of relationships, for he comes to it through the agency of his care and affection for Kim and even for the old woman and the people he has learned to care for.

In Kipling's work, therefore, one finds evidence of more than one code or governing ethos. Many aspects of enclosure may be detected here, in the value accorded to law, order, social vision as well as to the reinforcement of tradition, and so forth, while at the same time, the spaces inhabited by Kipling's characters are generous, and dionysian energy of play is also permitted a proper degree of license. And while his works tend to argue at one level the fulfilment of the male individual as taking place within a larger scheme of things, none the less, there is also the attempt to balance this against the claims of the private imaginal and emotional self. In this context, *Kim* may be seen as a work that, like *Jane Eyre* and *Alice's Adventures in Wonderland*, broke new ground, for it aspired to move beyond categorisation. For Kim, race, religion and nationality are no longer seen as sufficient terms to define the self by but have, on the contrary, become that which hinder the process of naming the self.

The real blow to the teaching of self-sacrifice upon the altar of duty to country and community came with the First World War. The generation that fought the war was one brought up on Homeric skirmishes, the history of the Peloponnesian war, the last stand of the heroic Spartans at Thermopylae,[113] and the dictum of returning with the shield, or else on it. This classical inheritance, as was earlier argued, provided the basis for much of nineteenth-century culture. The poetry of the war generation bears the hallmarks of a long dalliance with the Greek heroes and mores, that of the early part of the war, at least, approves the tag *Dulce et decorum est pro patria mori*, that later, under the pen of Wilfred Owen, was to become the bitter epitaph for the generation. The war changed the way in which that generation felt about the society that had promoted that code, promised a stability in return for acquiescence, a promise unfulfilled. The society for whose stability they were giving themselves was under threat, its ineffectuality all too visible, this failure of order making nonsense of their sacrifice. Models of masculinity and group manliness which they had been given to follow were seen to be impotent ones. As Fred Inglis comments:

> That picture of manliness suffered terribly, particularly on the Somme, not because men were unable to embody it in those dreadful circumstances, but because they did so pointlessly. The courage was available in awful plenty, but it was betrayed by the institutions which demanded it as a duty. Consequently that manliness has played an increasingly ambiguous part in growing up in Britain ... since 1917.[114]

What is also noticeable in the body of First World War poetry is the manner in which the war eroded the sense of a group idea, and the isolated and occasionally alienated consciousness began to re-emerge. From poems like Brooke's 'If I should die, think only this of me: / That there's some corner of a foreign field that is forever England', which still express self in terms of nation, one detects a growing sense of introspection and brooding – very natural in the circumstances – and a perspective of things seen from the 'I' rather than the 'we' point of view. The images one finds are those of disintegration, disintegration not only of material things in the bombardment of war, but also of ideals and in the identification with the doctrines of establishment and social unity. The loss of faith in the classical and imperial ideals that had been implanted in the war generation and which had failed them was to lead to the re-emergence of the individual consciousness, but this consciousness was not necessarily to be a happy or healthy one.

Children's literature did not immediately show the effects of the First World War – at least not in terms of overt cynicism and anti-establishmentarianism: that was to come later. Though the kind of literature that stressed gender-based roles slowly disappeared, one form of enclosure fading away, it is noticeable that the literature written between the two world wars is characterised by a sense of protectiveness – the positive face of enclosure. It was as though the war, while sowing disillusion and sorrow in the older generations, had instilled in that same generation a passionate desire to shield the child from that same grief. From this sense of love and protection came the immortal children's classics dating from the period between the wars: *Winnie-the-Pooh*, the Martin Pippin books, the Mary Poppins books and many more.

3
Of Rabbit-Holes and Secret Gardens

> A genuine work of art must mean many things: the truer its
> art, the more things it will mean.
>
> George MacDonald, 'The Fantastic Imagination'

The century reaching forward from about the 1850s marked a golden
age in children's literature, an age in which we see the child's world
first begin to truly widen and the parameters of both space and being
redefined. This period would also see a literature for children in
which a fruitful balance between enclosure and exposure would eventually emerge after long resistance. Gertrude Stein observes that '[f]or
a very long time everybody refuses and then almost without a pause
almost everybody accepts. In the history of the refused in the arts and
literature the rapidity of the change is always startling.'[1] This is
perhaps nowhere more true than with reference to the history of the
fantastic in children's literature. Before the advent of *Alice in
Wonderland* fantasy was an uneasy guest in the house of children's
reading. 1865, however, marked the beginning of a shift in attitude
towards it. Alice, in falling down the rabbit hole, had discovered the
way into the empire of the imagination where the notion of boundaries itself would unravel. Through this route, the child (both
fictional and reader) was enabled to escape out of the enclosures of
nursery and schoolroom into the realm of Wonderland where 'being'
could find an added dimensionality. Where much of early children's
literature may be seen as authoritarian in its emphasis on moral
didacticism and factuality – didacticism working upon the presump-
tion of its own certitude – the incursion of the fantastic into literature for children was to disrupt and subvert all that. As Rosemary
Jackson has argued in *Fantasy: the Literature of Subversion*, through its

'misrule', fantasy ultimately questions social order, refusing to ratify 'closed, unified or omniscient vision'.[2] Fantasy, a mode in which the strictly mimetic impulse has been abandoned, permits a playfulness which deconstructs the world of stable meanings. As it is manifested in nineteenth- and early twentieth-century children's literature, fantasy is located in space that has been 'framed' in one way or another: Wonderland, for example, exists in a dreamspace and time framed by the real world, and Griselda's adventures with the fairy cuckoo are also framed or contained, within cabinets, cuckoo clocks, and so forth. Yet, it is possible to understand the unease that might be felt, for these frames are often fluid, their boundaries, as Garner's *Red Shift* states, 'undefined'. It is here that the sharpness of division between 'closed' and 'open' first begins to give way.

Most early responses to the fantastic ranged from the cautious to the outright hostile, and the reasons for this were legion; indeed, the distrust felt by many in the eighteenth and nineteenth centuries for fantasy has been well-documented. John Locke, for example, dismissed them as 'perfectly useless trumpery'.[3] Sarah Trimmer condemned *Mother Goose* and her kind as filling 'the minds of children with confused notions of wonderful and supernatural events'.[4] Yet, though critics today have noted the disapproval meted out to fairy tales, the reasons they find for this disapproval are either unclear or, at least, incomplete. Jack Zipes, author of *Fairy Tales and the Art of Subversion, Breaking the Magic Spell* (1979) suggests that:

> The resistance at first to the fairy tale during the Enlightenment stemmed from the tales' implicit and explicit critique of utilitarianism. The emphasis on play, alternative forms of living, pursuing dreams and daydreams, experimentation, striving for the golden age – this stuff of which fairy tales were [and are] made challenged the rationalistic purpose and regimentation of life to produce for profits and the expansion of the capitalist industry. Therefore the bourgeois establishment had to make it seem that fairy tales were immoral, trivial, useless and harmful if an affirmative culture of commodity values supportive of élite interests were to take root in the public sphere.[5]

This is certainly an interesting angle from which to view resistance to the fairy tale. Apropos of Zipes's view, it might be usefully noted that developments in education in Victorian England were linked not only to the evangelical movement that sought to teach children to read their Bibles, but also to the Industrial Revolution. It was a programme undertaken not simply for the sake of education in and of itself, but one that espoused eminently pragmatic aims, seeing the child as a potential cog in the industrial machine. The Newcastle Report on Popular Education (1861) complained about inferior schools where the education given was 'ill-calculated to give to the children an education which sh[ould] be servicable to them in adult life'.[6] Concerned with the need to keep up the momentum gained by the Industrial Revolution, W. E. Forster, in the Taunton Report on Endowed Schools (1867–8), urged:

we must not delay. Upon the speedy provision of elementary education depends our industrial prosperity. ... if we leave our workfolk any longer unskilled, notwithstanding their strong sinews and determined energy, we will become overmatched in the competition of the world.[7]

For the Utilitarians, the fantastical had no overt use, and that was sufficient reason to ban it from the canon of acceptable children's literature.

Angela Bull, writing in conjunction with Gillian Avery in *Nineteenth Century Children*, offers a different reason:

Moralists, educationalists and those concerned with the religious teaching of children found it hard to reconcile their consciences to offering ... fictitious enormities ... to innocent boys and girls.[8]

The problem, as she presents it, was a twofold one: the question was, first, whether or not children exposed to fantasy would subsequently be able to distinguish between fiction and reality, and second, whether time spent on the perusal of fairy tales could not more profitably have been spent in assimilating factual knowledge.

To the list of reasons already cited above might be added the fear or dislike of the irrational and its presumably deleterious effect on the mind. Edmund Burke had posited in his *Philosophical Enquiry into the Origin of our Ideas on the Sublime and the Beautiful* (1757) that terror, or '[w]hatever is fitted in any sort to excite the ideas of pain, and danger, ... [was] the source of the *sublime*',[9] which to Burke meant not only that it was delightful, but also that it was expansionary in its effects. However, Sarah Trimmer, reviewing the *Histories and Tales of Past Times told by Mother Goose*, in fact objected to fairy tales precisely on the grounds that they would terrify, pointing to 'the terrific images, which tales of this nature present to the imagination, [which would] ... make deep impressions and injure the tender minds of children, by exciting unreasonable and groundless fears'.[10] These were views similar to those held by Hannah More, who in *Mr. Worthy and Mr. Bragwell*, commenting on another branch of fantastic literature (in this case, Gothic novels), had argued that too frequent a perusal of these could lead to madness. The anonymous author of *The History of Little Goody Two Shoes* spoke of 'Tales of *Ghosts*, *Witches*, and *Fairies*' as being the 'Frolicks of a distempered [ill] Brain', '[g]ood sense' [the author's italics] in conjunction with a good conscience, however, being the remedy for 'these imaginary ills'.[11]

Harvey Darton might, however, be closest to articulating the real cause of uneasiness, describing, in *Children's Books in England*, the opposition to fairy tales as:

> a manifestation, in England, of a deep-rooted sin-complex. It involves the belief that anything fantastical on the one hand, or anything primitive on the other, is inherently noxious; or at least so void of good as to be actively dangerous.[12]

The fear of 'noxiousness', that the fairy tale would have injurious effects, had a religious bias to it, insinuating an inability to discern between spiritual truth and fictitious/fictional creations, both being located in noumenal, rather than phenomenal frames of reference. William Caldwell Roscoe (1753–1831), that Victorian man of many parts – banker, botanist, Member of Parliament for Liverpool, and also the author of a book of children's verse, *The Butterfly's Ball and The Grasshopper's Feast* – had this to say on this score:

> It is possible to fill their [children's] minds with a confused medley of ideas, the chaotic residuum of all that has passed through their apprehensions, where Aladdin and the Little Naturalist, Captain Cook and Cinderella, Moral Tales and the Habits of Monkeys play their shifting parts and mingle in inextricable entanglement.[13]

Leaving aside the question whether this is a just or flattering assessment of the child's power of discernment, Roscoe's view generally agrees with Isaac Watts's notion of the way in which the child's mind synthesises ideas. Watts, the eighteenth-century composer of the *Divine Songs* for children, contended that:

These Stories have made such a deep and frightful Impression on their [children's] tender Fancies, that it hath enervated their Souls, it hath broken their Spirits early, it hath grown up with them, and mingled with their Religion, it hath laid a wretched Foundation for Melancholy and distracting Sorrows.[14]

And in speaking as he does on the enervation of spirit and tendency to melancholia, he again adduces the idea of mental illness already noted above, suggesting injury to the child's psyche resulting from the imprint of 'terrible' images (melancholy was traditionally seen as the first stage of madness, as Nicholas Robinson noted in 1729 in his *New Systems of the Spleen*. However, the point to be emphasised here is the sense of misgiving regarding the adulteration of religious truth, by its commingling with the elements of magic and the psuedo-miraculous in the mind of the child. Such a misapprehension would have been a mortal danger in the eyes of the nineteenth-century guardians of childhood, seen as paving the road to hell. Ruskin, however, argued to the contrary, saying that a child was 'never so impressed with ... supernatural phantasies as to be in danger of retaining them as any part of its religious faith'.[15]

As suggested earlier, the Romantic movement, not merely through its (re)visioning of the child, but also in its valorisation of the imagination and its works, helped in time to influence and shape attitudes in children's literature. In the 1820s the main flood of opposition to fairy tales in the nurseries began to subside. 1823 saw the appearance of the first English edition of the collected fairy tales of the Grimm brothers, while the 1840s witnessed the first translations into English of Andersen's fairy tales. It is possible that one of the reasons for the new-found acceptability of fairy tales as reading matter for the child was the respect garnered by the philological work of Jacob Grimm (the first volume of the *Deutsche Grammatik* had been published in 1819, just a few years previously). A certain attempt to cover the fairy tales with the dignity of academia may in fact be detected; in the 1885 edition of *Aunt Judy's Magazine*, a children's magazine edited by Mrs Ewing, an article by the Reverend S. Goldney states:

But thanks to the labour of of an indefatigable German, Jacob Grimm ... these legends, which were usually looked on as merely affording amusement for children, have been made to help in throwing light upon various problems of the world's history. He is better known as the means of tracing the connexion of all nations descended from Japhet by their language. He has, however, made fables and fairy tales contribute to the same result by his method of comparison, and he brings them in as witnesses in support of truths which he proves by his comparative grammar.[16]

The philological work is given pre-eminence as 'proving' truths which fairy tales only suggest,[17] and Goldney holds that Grimm is better known for his work with words. It is of course ironic that today more people may be found who are familiar with the fairy tales, while the *Grammatik* is the concern of people mainly concerned with linguistics. Other collections of fairy tales were soon to follow; the most well known of these today are the collections in the colour fairy books edited at the turn of the century by Andrew Lang (and later by his wife), whose main interest in fairy tales was an anthropological one. There was the rough idea that folk and fairy tales, developed in the 'childhood' of the race (that is, in its more primitive times), might well be suitable for children.

However, the greater tolerance for fairy tales did not signify complete capitulation on the part of the educationalists and the majority of writers of children's books, who considered themselves the guardians of juvenile morality. It was reluctantly conceded that the tales might be pleasant light reading, but, by and large, the true role played by the tales in extending the imagination and enriching the spiritual being of the child remained misunderstood. Writers of children's books began to employ the tropes of the fairy tale, or the fantastic mode, in order to disguise the moral teaching they still felt to be essential. Mrs Sherwood, editor of the second edition of Sarah Fielding's *The Governess, or The Little Female Academy* (1820), for instance, realised that '[i]nstruction when conveyed through the medium of some beautiful story or pleasant tale more easily insinuates itself into the youthful mind than anything of a drier nature'. Meanwhile, Andrew Lang's complaints were uttered to the opposite effect; he argued that the 'new fairy tales, as a rule, ha[d] no human interest', dealing in 'allegory and little episodic sermons' in place of unobtrusive morals arising naturally.[18]

Didactic fairy tales, fantasies restricted to a teaching purpose, had their heyday during the period from 1844 to about the middle of the 1860s. These were tales that might be described as monosemous works, by which is meant that they are only capable of generating a single reading, that reading being the specific teaching message which the author desired to communicate; such writing intentionally sets limits on the play of meaning in a text. It is this principle that dictates, for example, the choice of names in didactic fairy tales such as the story of the 'cruel Giant BARBARICO, the good giant BENEFICO, and the pretty little dwarf MIGNON' found in Sarah Fielding's *The Governess*. Catharine Sinclair's 'Uncle David's Nonsensical Story about Giants and Fairies', from *Holiday House*, has fairy Do-nothing, Master No-book and Giant Snap-em-up, and the eponymous 'hope of the Katzekopfs' in the story by the Rev. Paget is the spoiled Eigenwilig, ridden by the imp Selbst, and aided by the old man Discipline. The names by which we understand the nature of the character are in part the legacy of allegorical tradition, perhaps in particular of *The Pilgrim's Progress*; they guide the reader along the straight and narrow path of meaning. This is not to say that flat characters are a sign of monologism, but that naming is indicative of the limited meaning-making allowed the reader by the author in the text. The characters are defined and characterised by a single function and rarely grow beyond their given role, and thus occupy a world which is morally two-dimensional.

With the exception of one or two of the longer tales, like *The Water Babies*, Victorian fairy tales tended to explain themselves rather than allow the reader to read his own meanings into and from the text. Symbols are immediately and ponderously elucidated, thus fixing and imprisoning their meaning. For example, Charles Lamb, in the preface to *The Adventures of Ulysses* (1808), writes that 'the agents in this tale besides men and women are giants, enchanters, sirens: *things which denote external force or internal temptations*' [my italics]. This may indicate Lamb's private understanding of the mythic shape of the *Odyssey*, but nonetheless also represents an attempt to guide the child into a specific reading of the text.

Often, too, the symbols or other associative devices used in didactic fantasy are generally of a sort that suggests an underlying matrix of Christian/moral ideas. For instance, in *The Hope of the Katzekopfs* (generally reckoned to be the first of the literary, albeit didactic, fantasies written for children), the clothes worn by Eigenwilig's fairy godmother, Abracadabra, change colour in a way indicative of her mood. They are ugly and violent in composition when she is angry, but more to the point is the description given of her when she appears after the two instances of Eigenwilig's especial naughtiness:

... her eyes gleamed like *coals of fire*, her wrinkles were deeper than ever, and gave her face a most harsh and severe expression, – nay, her black jacket had acquired a most ominous sort of intensity, and the yellow petticoat seemed shot with a lurid *flame colour*.[19] [emphases mine]

And, on the second occasion, her robe is described as seeming to glow with living fire'.[20] The resonances here are those of a hell that awaits the unrepentant and wicked; if the latter seems too strong a word to be applied with justification to the naughtiness of the child, Abracadabra none the less speaks a reminder that his actions will eventually tend that way, as his parents are doing all they can 'to make him wicked and miserable, a bad man and a bad king'. She then takes him off to fairyland, where he first has to learn to obey orders, and then to govern himself. The second part of the regime which he undergoes is shaped like a child's *Pilgrim's Progress*, with all that that book stands for; these resonances serve to reinforce the frame of reference the author wishes to establish. The word 'pilgrimage' is in fact used at the outset, when the old man, Discipline, appears:

'I have set out upon pilgrimage with multitudes such as you are,' answered the stranger with a sigh, 'and some,' he added, 'have I accompanied to their journey's end …'.[21]

Nor is the figure of the burden lacking: Selbst the imp, representing (as his name in German suggests) the self, and whom Eigenwilig chooses as companion instead of Discipline, climbs onto his back and refuses, like the Old Man of the Sea, to release his hold.

The emancipation or 'exposure' of the imagination cannot be said to have occurred until *Alice's Adventures in Wonderland* appeared in 1865, but two decades before this (the same year, incidentally, that saw the publication of *The Hope of the Katzekopfs*), the critical debate on the subject of the mind's activity was beginning to gain momentum. Elizabeth Rigby, Lady Eastlake, writing anonymously on 'Children's Books' in 1844 for *The Quarterly Review*, thought it:

one thing to stock the mind like a dead thing, and another to make it forage for itself; and of incalculably more value is one voluntary act of acquirement, combination or conclusion, than hundreds of passively accepted facts … Nature … has decreed that unless a child be permitted to acquire *beyond what it positively understands*, its intellectual progress shall be slow, if any.[22] [my italics]

She was asking for an end to boundaries or limitations on what the child should read, and also finding a place for suggestion and imaginative activity in children's literature. As noted in Chapter 1, 1847 saw the establishment of one the landmarks both of adult and children's literature in the publication of *Jane Eyre*, the first adult novel to portray the workings of the child's mind and nature in any depth. At the start of the book, kept indoors by the bad weather, Jane sits down with Bewick's *History of British Birds* and muses:

> the *suggestion* [my italics] of the bleak shores of Lapland ... with the vast sweep of the Arctic Zone, and those forlorn regions of dreary *space*–that reservoir of frost and snow ... Of these death-white realms I formed an idea of my own, shadowy, like all the half-comprehended notions that float dim through children's brains, but impressive. The words in those introductory pages connected themselves with the succeeding vignettes, and gave significance to the rock standing up alone in a sea of billow and spray ... each picture told a story.[23]

There is a quality of absorption in the writing of this piece, from the time Jane takes *Bewick* on her knee to the time John Reed breaks into her idyll; for her, time and space do not stand still, but expand during the exercise of the mind. While she retires into the window seat and draws the curtain, creating the illusion of a private space (which in the Reed household she does not have), this space is seen as painfully cramped, but with the opening of *Bewick* the 'enlargement of mental territory' referred to by Cardinal Newman in his *Idea of a University* begins. The book sweeps her out to places that are only names to her, outlines to be filled in in time according to increasing knowledge or thought. The places mentioned (Lapland, Nova Zembla, Greenland and so on) are, interestingly enough, places with a sparsely populated, and hence a greater symbolic, spaciousness. The book is about birds: the regions of the air are added to the space claimed by the child in the name of its imagination. Here the child Jane has managed to depart for a while from the enclosed world of the repressive present, and in that wider world her cramped being is allowed to expand.

With the writing of *Alice's Adventures in Wonderland* in 1865, the mental landscape of children's fiction began to undergo a significant metamorphosis. The *Alice* books are important not only because of their underlying assumption of the imagination's importance but also because they betray in many ways a strong resistance to the fixity or stasis of form and classification, thereby displaying a quality of anti-authoritarianism important to the undermining of enclosure. As a 'dream' work, the text subverts the claims of the real world. Though apparently framed by that 'real' world, the boundaries between both realms are fluid: Alice moves within the space of one sentence between wakefulness and dream, the real and the imaginary:

> So she was considering in her own mind (as well as she could, for the hot day made her feel very sleepy and stupid), whether the pleasure of making a daisy-chain would be worth the trouble of getting up and picking the daisies, when suddenly a White Rabbit with pink eyes ran close to her.

In Wonderland, babies turn into pigs, white roses are painted red, children shrink and stretch; the stuff of the imagination defies the attempt to fix it, remaining fluid and expansive. But most importantly, by loosening the bonds on imagination, Wonderland implants in the child's mind the ability to create new ideas which are perhaps iconoclastic in the sense that they tear down habits of thought, routine perception, fossilized assumptions, and in this way may be said to extend the range of thought and spirit of the child.

The extension of territory is first signified by the expanded possibilities of language in the text, where words' functions multiply, and meaning is fluid. For example, the significance of *Wonder*land is manifold: 'wonder' can be adjectival, describing a 'a land of wonders', but more interestingly, it signifies active imaginative investigation, if we consider 'wonder' to be also a verb. In re-reading the text, the preponderance of varying forms of the verb *to wonder* becomes apparent. In the course of a mere twenty pages we encounter the following:

> 'she ought to have wondered at this' (2)[24]; 'to wonder what was going to happen next' (3); 'I wonder how many miles I've fallen by this time?' (4); 'but then I wonder what Latitude or Longitude I've fallen to by this time?' (4); 'I wonder if I shall fall right *through* the earth?' (5); 'But do bats eat cats I wonder?' (6); 'wondering how she was ever to get out again' (7); 'I wonder what I should like then?' (12); 'I wonder who will ever put on your shoes and stockings for you now (15-16); 'I wonder if I've been changed in the night?'(19).

The pattern of 'wondering' continues. It is as though the word 'wonder', when given utterance, sets Alice free into an enlarged imaginative territory not limited by matter (as she falls through the earth), longitudes, latitudes or platitudes. Virginia Woolf was to write in an article on Lewis Carroll, of that 'terrifying, wildly inconsequential, yet perfectly logical world where time races, then stands still, where *space* stretches then contracts . . .'. [emphases mine].[25] She, too, was noting the way in which physical laws as we know them, when touched by the imagination, cease to obtain. In Lewis's world, the metaphysical takes precedence over the physical.

In order to help bring about mental enlargement, Carroll has first, however, to rid the child's mind of its 'Gradgrindian' heritage. As Alice falls down the rabbit hole, the facts she has had to learn as part of her formal schooling also fall away from her; the Antipodes become the Antipathies (surely apt, in the context of this argument), and later, reading and writing are changed to 'reeling and writhing', from denoting forms of written meaning to connoting chaotic movement, from being merely fixed words on a printed page to being live movement. In an act of unfixing where the word has become unstable, denotation, it may be argued, yields to connotation. Alice has to release the security of the single denoted meaning, but in return, is admitted to the world of free-ranging associations, a wider universe. Didactic and turgid writing for children is gently satirised in *Alice*; some of what started out as 'improving rhymes' for children are lightly parodied: the moral one is intended to draw from the industry of the busy bee is swallowed forever between the gently smiling jaws of the crocodile.

As mentioned earlier, fantasy is subversive of authority, and in *Alice*, other forms of social authority than the educational are also undermined. Work and study give place to play: *Alice's Adventures in Wonderland* is a book about games, even though these games know no recognisable structure or logic, in fulfillment of the work's predominant principle of flux. In the caucus race, the race-course is marked out in 'a sort of circle, (the exact shape doesn't matter', it said)', and there is no starting signal: ' . . . they began running when they liked, and left off when they liked, so that it was not easy to know when the race was over'. In the croquet game, the players all play at once without waiting for turns, and the hoops get up and walk away. The figures of authority, the King and Queen of Hearts, who also preside over the trial at the end, are a pack of cards, and it may be argued that the conflation of social hierachy, judicial system and games, by mutually undercutting each others' premises, serves to deconstruct the world of social authority and institutions. (The Mad Hatter's Tea-Party had earlier in the work begun this by making nonsense of social etiquette and procedure.) It has even been argued that religious practice, is (in *Alice*) also subjected to the subversions of fantasy: Humphrey Carpenter suggests in *Secret Gardens* that 'the story's very structure [is] a parody of religion',[26] and that its dream-mode recalls the medieval dream poem whose promise of a vision (Carpenter implies this is religious) is then undercut by its less-than-serious narrative. (This latter point regarding medieval dream poetry could also be read as Carroll's undercutting of the authority of literary tradition.) According to Carpenter, the 'Drink me' and 'Eat me' sequences are parodies of the Eucharist. The plausibility of such a reading of the text as anti-religious must remain open to question, but may none the less be seen to demonstrate how the fantastic may operate to dismantle authoritarian structures. It might be added that the dream sequence as a whole stands as an alternative world to the real one, thereby challenging it.

Thus, it is with *Alice* that children's literature really begins to develop as a literature to be taken seriously. With *Alice*, it began to have a depth and richness, to cease to be only didactic, to acknowledge the place of play in childhood. Furthermore, the kind of fiction written after *Alice* would invite the active participation of the child: he would be required to think, invited to interpret. The encouragement to imaginative and intellectual activity was the beginning of autonomy, both for the fictional child and the child reader.[27] Surveys began to be conducted among children regarding the literature they perused,[28] and thus children were for the first time given a voice with which to express their needs and wants. With the institution of such surveys and the development (albeit a small one) of criticism concerning children's literature, the quality of literature for children had to improve as authors became to a certain extent dependent upon the goodwill of their child readers and adult critics. This dependence was partly economic: without the approval of the child, the sales of the author would go down.

With the imagination having gained the *entrée* into children's literature and the new respect being given to the child, the concepts of space and freedom became invested with new power; also, with the new emphasis on space, the text quickly became redefined as an area shared by author and reader, adult and child. In some cases the sharing or collaboration might be a literal one, as with Stevenson and his stepson, Lloyd Osbourne (the 'S. L. O.' to whom *Treasure Island* (1883) was dedicated). Together they wrote comic verse which they printed, embellished with woodcuts by Stevenson on a hand press, who drew the map that led to the creation of *Treasure Island*, in which lack of female characters, apart from Jim's mother, was due to 'Lloyd's orders', as Stevenson revealed in his letter to W. E. Henley.[29] Further sharing of the text occurred, for example, in terms of allowing the child to have a hand in determining meaning and inter-pretation. This is especially obvious in a text like *Peter and Wendy* (1911)[30] where the geography of Neverland, configured according to childish desire and imagination, is created by the author with the outlines and particulars left vague for the children to fill in:

> Neverland is always *more or less* an island, with astonishing splashes of colour *here and there*, and coral reefs and rakish-looking craft in the offing, and savages and lonely lairs.[31] [emphases mine]

For this purpose, the language is left loose and flexible – 'more or less', 'here and there' allow for expansion or change according to the child's imagination. The child is allowed an individual play of creative desires, in a space of his own:

> John's [island] for instance, had a lagoon with flamingoes flying over it ... while Michael ... had a flamingo with lagoons flying over it. John lived in a boat turned upside down on the sands, Michael in a wigwam, Wendy in a house of leaves.[32]

Here, something quite significant is being indicated, for we have a recognition that the child is not a generalisable entity, but an indi-vidual with different likes and dislikes, a different personality with different needs from other child individuals. Stevenson attempts to cater for these differences and in the imaginative space there exists room for opposite and alternative realities: John has a lagoon with flamingoes flying over it and Michael has the reverse – a flamingo with lagoons flying over it. In this space reconfigured by the imagi-nation, power is shared between characters, between author and reader, adult and child. Nor is it only the meanings of things that children share with the author and with each other, but also the ability to create. The Neverland that the children finally visit with Peter Pan is the amalgamation of all their thoughts and something more than that. It is also a playground in another sense, combining the most frequent games of make-believe that real children play – Red Indians, pirates, keeping house (where the girls are given equal place with boys for play) – and a text into which these desires may be corporately written.

Imaginative literature was capable of carrying the child outside the enclosure of nursery and schoolroom in yet other ways, magic making anything possible. After *Alice*, fantasy fiction for the young made good use of the notion of entering a magical space unbounded either by adult authority or normal rules. In Frances Hodgson Burnett's *A Little Princess* (1905), magic truly becomes a metaphor for the imagination, for it is through the power of the imagination that the heroine, Sara Crewe, transcends the dreariness of her life after her father loses all his money and she is reduced to drudgery in order to live. Imagination is the 'Magic' whose agency 'won't ever let the worst things quite happen'. In the beginning, when Sara is a rich and privileged child, her imagination is emancipatory in that it opens the doors which shut out people from each other: it is through the stories that she imagines and relates that Ermengarde, the plain dull child, and later Becky, the school drudge, both so different from herself, are drawn to her. Through the medium of the tales she dreamingly tells, the various children are enabled to live in a separate space where all are equal. Later, when Sara herself has become dependent upon the scanty mercies of Miss Minchin, relegated to a tiny vermin-ridden attic and starved of sustenance, the activity of her imagination takes on a greater importance in keeping her alive: though her room is without a fire, her imagination becomes a fire at which she and Becky are warmed. More importantly, Sara can escape from the confining and oppressive reality of the garret by imagining it to be the Bastille, a prison to which she alone holds the key. When scolded by Miss Minchin, she retreats into her role which she has created for herself: that of a princess whose noble moral qualities preserve her in the face of tribulation. Thus, the imagination is also seen to function as a tool which may be used to sculpt the inner shape of self.

Sara manages to free herself from the unhappiness that threatens to overwhelm her, and which itself acts as an enclosing force, through that part of her imagination which treats life as a story. When first introduced to Miss Minchin who says what a lovely child she is, she thinks, 'Why does she say I am a beautiful child? ... She [Miss Minchin] is telling a story.'[33] With reference to Miss Minchin, 'story-telling' is a form of lying, whereas with Sara it is an expression of creativity. Miss Minchin's repressive 'stories' about Sara the Slave are challenged by Sara's stories about Sara the princess, whose positive imagination enables her to prevail against the malevolent power of the teacher and remain herself, unhumbled, undiminished. On the other hand, Sara's imagination can work to reshape her friend Ermengarde, because hers is a benevolent and expansionary power. Ermengarde's name, she tells her, sounds like a story book. Here, the reference to story-telling and imagination provides a new way for Ermengarde to think of herself. From thinking of herself as a dull stodgy child, the 'story-book' name enables her to reconceptualise herself as a more romantic being and this, too, constitutes a breaking out of the prison of image.

When at one point Sara is locked in her attic, Ermengarde exclaims:

'... it is like a story!'
'It *is* a story,' said Sara. '*Everything*'s a story. You are a story – I am a story. Miss Minchin's is a story.'[34]

Like Alice, who claims power over the dream by exclaiming that her persecutors are nothing but a pack of cards, Sara is claiming power as creator to banish the stories she does not like. She may be a story, but she is also the teller of the tale and if what is happening to her is a fiction, then, by implication, a wider world outside the covers of the book exists and can be reached.

The wariness felt towards fantasy and the imagination, while lessened, did not straightaway disappear altogether, and discreet supervision of the child in this regard was for a while maintained. Mrs Molesworth's *The Tapestry Room* (1879) and her more famous *The Cuckoo Clock* (1877), for instance, are tales of escape from mundane reality into magical space, though it is noticeable that the child never quite goes unaccompanied by an adult in disguise. In the *Cuckoo Clock*, for example, in Griselda's visits to Butterfly Land, the Land of the Nodding Mandarins and other places, where there is respite from the daily tedium of her lessons, and where the elements of delight and companionship help her to settle and put down roots in her new home, the fairy cuckoo is constant companion, guide – and overseer. By the time one gets to E. Nesbit, however, this vestige of control has practically disappeared. Nesbit's books show the child rampaging joyously through time and space unchecked: the Psammead, Phoenix and Mouldiwarp stay at the sidelines for the most part, and these magical beings are as vulnerable as the child (the Psammead is, for instance, susceptible to water), no longer figures of unquestioned power and authority.

If one sees magic as a metaphor for the imagination, then one finds in Nesbit's work a perfect image of the child coming to a wholeness of being in gaining access to the imaginative part of himself in *Harding's Luck* (1909). Its hero, Dickie Harding, is a badly treated and crippled orphan, whose true background is as wreathed in mystery as Oliver Twist's. Dickie lives with his so-called aunt in a cramped and poky house, and because of his infirmity he cannot escape from her but is kept dependent and powerless. Magic and the imagination change all this. Through the text run various images and instances of breakage and imperfection which magic (imagination) makes it possible to heal. Making friends with a man who runs a pawn shop, Dickie is given a gift of a broken seal whose insignia matches that of a rattle he possesses, which he calls 'Tinkler'. With this man he talks happily, practising on him all the words he derives from his reading, though at the outset he has only an imperfect grasp of their meaning and pronunciation. The abstract meaning of the words he uses initially lies outside his sphere of comprehension; the separation of language from experience is indicated by his broken words, 'I'm in Lux Ury and Af Fluence.'[35]

Language is part of becoming and necessary to the acquisition of being. Not only is it a system mediating between abstract and concrete, word and thing, but also a means of translating and generating meaning in human terms between person and person, a means by which the child learns to define the world and his experience, and which, in turn, helps to define him. Thus, in the fractured language he speaks, we have an indication of many things: for example imperfect social relations, of fissured understanding that require mending. Dickie grows towards linguistic maturity, and this may be seen as an index of his increasing sense of identity and wholeness. Through the magical journeys he makes back to the time of King James I with the aid of Tinkler and the seal, he finds an identity for himself as Richard Arden, the sixteenth-century analogue of Dickie himself, except that in this time, he is no longer lame. In the past, he leads a happy existence, learning to read, write, ride and carve. More importantly, in this time, he has a family who love him and whom he loves in return.

Dickie learns that his father was kidnapped as a baby, and that his surname, 'Harding', is actually a corruption of 'Arden', just as 'Dickie' is of 'Richard' – this is one instance where the growing purity of language may be seen as concretely leading him towards his identity and birthright. He is torn between his life in the past and that in the present, where he finds relatives and has established a close relationship with Beale, a former thief, this tearing being the ultimate fissure. The book contains the recognition that 'being' necessitates integrity, and his half-and-half existence will only impede his search for being, though it has helped enrich his life in giving him a sense of personal and general history. Finally faking his death (like Huck Finn) in the twentieth century, he lives out his life in the sixteenth; the integration of his dual existence and his final achievement of wholeness in his sense of self are eventually symbolised in his having left his crippled state behind for ever. The story winds up in the present continuous tense: 'I see the roots of his being take hold.'[36] Dickie, or Richard, has escaped his constrained and maimed existence and has gained home, family and a cure, becoming a whole person through the agency of magic. All this has been made possible by the entrance of the imagination into children's literature.

In this century, imaginative writing has made possible even further enlargement of the child's territory. As John Rowe Townsend writes in *Written for Children*:

> The obvious genre to which we may look for a re-expansion of the far horizons is science fiction. It allows the writer to get around the limits of physical possibility, to invent not only fascinating gadgets but new forms of life, and above all to display human nature in contexts of his own devising.[37]

Though science is generally held to be antithetical to the imagination, science fiction exists at the frontier where science has not yet hardened into concrete reality, but maintains itself as a world of infinite possibility and potential. Not just other times and countries, but other planets are laid open to the child, and this is seen, for example, in L'Engle's *A Wrinkle in Time*, where the Murry family go to the planet Camazotz to rescue their physicist father. But finally, if the imagination and its fictions have been responsible for the emancipation of the child in a number of ways, the most important of these is perhaps that referred to by the Victorian, W. E. H. Lecky, who spoke of the value of the imagination as residing in its power to take one out of oneself:

> Often, the power of dreaming comes to our aid ... the mere fact of placing [ourselves] in other circumstances and investing [ourselves] with the imaginative powers and functions sometimes suggests possible remedies for great human ills.[38]

This sounds escapist, but what Lecky is saying is that the imagination, in allowing us to step into the shoes of other people, provides us with a clearer perspective on ourselves and our own situations, teaches us about 'otherness' – that which is not-the-self – and human possibility, as Coleridge had also suggested, saying,

> For this object is much effected by works of the imagination; – that they carry the mind out of self and show the possible of the good and the great in human character.[39]

This is the most important freedom that has been gained by the imagination: that it takes one out of oneself: it is not so much space but self that has been expanded.

While we see children's literature in the later half of the nineteenth century having its boundaries extended through the agency of the imagination, we may also note that the new aesthetic of freedom was not allowed to reign absolute. A different system, where childish liberty and privacy could coexist with positive adult control, may be seen to be at work in the golden age of children's literature. To provide the child with guidance, moral authority to lean upon and draw strength from, useful rules to structure one's life by, is to provide them with laudable forms of 'enclosure', and when combined with equally positive forms of 'exposure', such as removing the barriers to imaginative experience and freedom of movement, the two forces can work beneficially for the child.

Absolute liberty is a potentially dangerous thing. Despite the fact that *Alice's Adventures in Wonderland* depicts imaginative enlargement in all its positive forms, the flipside of all this is also evident for those who would see it. The marvellously free-wheeling narrative which inspires and encourages mental agility and freedom is at the same time edged with peril, and the lack of signposting in Wonderland puts the wandering and wondering child at risk. As discussed earlier, law is a suspended principle in Wonderland: natural laws, game rules and legal systems have all ceased to operate. And while it is possible, of course, to view this as the realisation of the principle of play and hence as a tacit valorisation of the non-utilitarian, to see it as intentionally disruptive of systems which have fossilized, it may equally be argued that play and games can benefit from structure or even that the meaning of a game is generated *by* its structure. In this alternative viewing of the suspension of rules, Wonderland is not playful but threateningly chaotic, for in the loss of governing structures, the activities supposed to take place within those structures become meaningless. For example, the time, according to the Mad Hatter, is always teatime: one may see this as a giving way of temporal distinctions to allow teatime (presumably perceived by the Victorian child as a treat) to exist in perpetuity. But that destruction of temporal syntax, if one takes de Saussure's point about meaning as a thing generated by its ability to be distinguished from other things, leads to the loss of the 'specialness' of teatime, and in fact, the lack of a governing etiquette at table is felt by Alice to be irritating rather than liberating. In the trial scene no proper judicial system is in operation, and this puts the defendant (in this case, Alice) at the mercy of the court's whims and fancies.

The failure of definition, as Alice falls down the rabbit hole, moving away from the hedged-in world of received conventions and upbringing, can result in a disorienting loss of sense of identity and place which that world had to give her.[40] This loss of formal identity can both threaten the destruction of self, or constitute the beginning of a greater freedom of being, as we saw with Huckleberry Finn, whose pretended death marks such a loss, and who then moves, exploring, from identity to identity. The loss of identity is pointed as Alice, fanning herself with the White Rabbit's fan, says:

> 'I'm sure I'm not Ada ... and I'm sure I can't be Mabel ... Besides *she's* she and *I'm* I ... It'll be no use their putting their heads down and saying, 'Come up again dear!' I shall only look up and say 'Who am I then? Tell me that first, and then, if I like being that person I'll come up: if not, I'll stay here until I'm somebody else.'[41]

In a world without strict definitions, she has ceased to be certain of who and what she is. 'Serpent!' screams the pigeon at a later point in the tale, fearing that Alice is about to steal its eggs; Alice indignantly denies this, but upon being asked *what* she is, she can only reply, as the author writes, 'doubtfully', that she is a little girl. In Wonderland, systems of classification[42] and definition are flexible – *so* flexible that self-knowledge is a state difficult to enter upon. The state of being is seen to fluctuate madly, as when babies change to pigs, cats can disappear, leaving their grins behind them, while size is a property of being that is neither stable nor remains the same for any length of time.

Wonderland is generously commodious, and in its freedom from rules and regulations, is a holiday from the schoolroom. But despite the numbers of dictatorial people to be found in the story: 'Everybody says "come on!" here,' thought Alice, as she went slowly after it: 'I was never so ordered about before in all my life, never!'[43] there is an absence of true supervision, an absence which has been commented on at length by critics.[44] The failure to signpost the world adequately finds its visible symbol in the confusion regarding the actual whereabouts of the Mad Hatter and March Hare's residences. The absence of direction can be a worrying thing: Alice has little certainty while in Wonderland of what, where, or even *if*, she will be. She may have the freedom to act as she will, but there is nothing, no one and no walls, to stop her running into danger or situations that could put an end to her existence (which, indeed, almost occurs at the hands of the Queen of Hearts).

Alice attempts to wrest self-definition from the frightening fluidity of her world, but this in itself is seen to be a tortuous and far from painless process. Her progress towards definition may be understood as a metaphorical or symbolic approach to concreteness and self-control. At first, her growing and shrinking happens not of her own volition, but appears to be arbitrary; later, armed with bits of mushroom and the advice of the caterpillar, she learns to control her size according to the dictates of will. Being is very much linked to control, whether exerted from within or without, and where there are no rules or directions, the child is apt to become lost, or sink in moral or situational quicksands.

A balance between the two forces of control and freedom represents, then, an ideal, and this ideal to some extent is realised in children's literature from the middle of the nineteenth century to about the 1950s. Here, the child and the adult are allies; the adult represents neither a repressive force to be overthrown nor an overly solicitous one whose existence might protect but also diminish the child, never allowing it to develop, but instead forcing it to remain a default Peter Pan. In works written during this period, such as those by E. Nesbit, Eleanor Farjeon's *Martin Pippin in the Daisy Field*, A. A. Milne's immortal *Winnie-The-Pooh*, Arthur Ransome's delightful Swallows and Amazons series, there is a respect and trust between adult and child. The child trusts the adult to be there when needed, to put things right when necessary and respects his right to exert discipline over his young life. The adult in turn trusts the child to be sensible and not to stray past the boundaries erected for his safety.

The stories are only made possible by this alliance, created out of the freedom enjoyed by the child, and framed by the adult. *Winnie-the-Pooh* is created out of the relationship between father and child. The father tells the stories, in that sense framing them, but the content of those tales is dictated by Christopher Robin, and the

Hundred Aker Wood in those tales remains his private domain. Within these 'enchanted spaces' in which 'expotitions' to the North Pole can be mounted, the child is lord, Pooh and Piglet and friends deferring to his greater wisdom. His father's narrative power acts as a force-field keeping out the *real* uglies, even while the inhabitants of the Hundred Aker Wood can still enjoy the thrill of imagined dangers, as when Pooh and Piglet fall into the trap for Heffalumps. A similar relationship may be seen at work in *Martin Pippin in the Daisy Field*, where the raconteuse, Martin Pippin, authority's representative in the child's world, the enforcer of the child's bedtime, meets the seven children in the limitless, unenclosed, daisy field and tells them stories which, interestingly enough, also hold in balance tenets of enclosure and exposure, order and chaos. In 'Tom Cobble and Ooney', for example, the advocates of magic's randomness and of the routines of everyday living are at first opposed to each other's *modus operandi*, but then strike up a creative partnership later.

Where the pressures of enclosure are too powerful the claims of self may often be denied, but without the benefit of guidance and regulation the child may also fail to acquire identity because of the absence of shaping forces at work in its life. Paradoxically, the spoiled and undisciplined child at one level lacks a sense of defined self, while on another level possessing too great a sense of himself. Initially Mary and Colin of Frances Hodgson Burnett's *The Secret Garden* (1911) have only this overweening sense of self-importance and self-conscious-ness, an obsession with self-image though that very image is presented as misshapen. To Mrs Medlock, the housekeeper of Misselthwaite Manor, for instance, Mary is 'quite an old woman'.[45] Here, the distortion and representation of the child-image as old-woman-image is a sign of the distorted self. Colin, too, is seen to have a 'young rajah' persona, a self-image which appears to be undesirable, bringing with it arrogance and discourtesy towards those around him. The two spoiled cousins, Mary and Colin, presented at the outset as ailing and fretful, move towards a physical and moral health which is only seen to be attained when the forces of discipline and self-expression are in balance. The preoccupation with self is seen to be linked to the ill-health of the children:

'I don't want to remember,' interrupted the rajah, appearing again. 'When I lie by myself and remember I begin to have pains every-where ... It is because my cousin makes me forget that she makes me better.'[46]

When left with nothing to focus on but himself and his health he remains ill, but in abjuring this narcissistic outlook he begins to get better.

This selfishness appears to be a state for which parental neglect is in part responsible. Mary, for instance, is an orphan, her parents having died of the plague in India, and she is dislocated, taken from her home in India to that of her uncle in Yorkshire. Some of the most significant defining and enclosing forces at work in the life of the child are its parents and its home, and Mary's parents are represented as having been remiss in their attention to her, with the result that she grows up with her manners and temper unchecked, and, never having been the recipient of love, with no idea of how to give or show it. That parental shaping has never come Mary's way is recognised early on by Mr Crawford with whom Mary is temporarily sent to stay. His wife remarks what a pity it is that Mary has inherited none of her mother's beauty or pretty manners, only to be drily answered by her husband that if Mary's mother had taken her pretty face and manners into the nursery more often, perhaps the child might have learned some of those manners.

'It is the child nobody ever saw'[47] is what the army officer who discovers Mary in the abandoned bungalow says, and this comment stands as a measure of her loneliness and non-identity. Being known, recognised and named is a measure of being and a hold on identity, but at the outset the reader is made aware of how tenuous Mary's hold upon identity is, for the people who knew her have either died or run away, and, as evidenced by the officer's remark, her name is not common knowledge; she is 'the child', anonymous and forgotten, who might have died if she had not been found. Some were unaware even of her existence. Her cousin Colin is a sickly child, who, like Mary, has been effectively invisible from a young age, kept out of his father's sight as he reminds his father too painfully of his dead mother. Like Mary, he lacks the benefits of discipline and attention, and as with her, this manifests as a lack of self-definition and self-control. Colin enters the book as 'a cry in the corridor', this being symbolic of his state of being when the reader and Mary first encounter him. He is represented as a sound without corporeal existence, a sound which is not even a word, an inchoate and formless utterance, and this is analogous to the way in which he is himself seen to lack definition.

Whereas in early children's literature 'being' is seen in terms of spiritual health, the physical domain is here shown to be important in any consideration of self. In *The Secret Garden* health is an index of being, the body the concrete sign for the state of the interior life. Colin's early inability to walk is a sign of his inability to act and exert self meaningfully in the world. When Mary's skipping exercises are observed by her to have developed muscles in her legs which were formerly and unflatteringly compared to sticks, the physical shaping may be understood as correlating to what is happening to Mary on other planes.

The movement towards acquiring physical being is seen to happen in tandem with the movement towards social being. The children gradually become aware of themselves as at once shut in and shut out, too much kept indoors as well as not part of their societies, and begin to desire absorption and acceptance into the community, aware that on their own, they are, in some measure, unfulfilled. This may be seen in the following exchange between Mary and Colin:

> 'Am I queer?' he demanded.
> 'Yes,' answered Mary, 'very. But you needn't be cross,' she added impartially, 'because so am I queer – and so is Ben Weatherstaff. But I am not as queer as I was before I began to like people and before I found the garden.'
> 'I don't want to be queer,' said Colin.[48]

As Roderick McGillis says in 'Secrets and Sequence in Children's Stories', 'This desire not to be queer is a desire to join community, a desire to shed difference and eccentricity as well as illness and irritability.'[49]

Robert Elbaz has commented that '[l]anguage is a vacuous structure in which every speaker engages to assert the existence of the Other, the world and himself'.[50] Certainly, language is another of the various indices within the text against which the changing relationships between characters may be marked, and through these changing relationships, the alterations in individual conceptions of self. Not only does language assert the things which Elbaz claims, but, more importantly, it serves to indicate the speaker's view of the relationship existing between world, Other and self. With Elbaz's statement in mind, the impression conveyed by the early speeches of Mary and Colin is that language for them is a structure in which they do indeed assert not merely their own existence, but the primary position of their selves in relation to that of others.

'What *I* want is your duty,'[51] Colin says grandly to Martha on one occasion. As yet without control over himself, his desires operate as constraints, hedging in the lives of his subordinates, and Mary, to begin with, is no better, screaming when enraged, 'You – you daughter of a pig!'[52] at Martha Sowerby, the housemaid assigned to dress her in the mornings. The cousins betray a view of the world that is shockingly imbalanced, their swollen egos impeding their view of others, relegating them to the plane of lesser, scarcely human beings, as Mary's insult suggests.

If language may be said to mark self-control and thus self-definition, then a good part of the book presents the children as not yet fully in control of language and words. When the cousins quarrel a great deal of sound and fury is generated. The rule of the day to them appears to be 'the greater the volume, the greater the assertion of being', as when Mary, awakened by Colin's tantrum in the middle of the night, says fiercely, 'If you scream another scream, ... I'll scream, too – and I can scream louder than you can, and I'll frighten you, I'll frighten you!'[53] Affection and warmth, however, are defining forces as much as is discipline, and it is through the exercise of these things that the unhealthily bloated selves of the children are properly shaped and directed. In the gardens Mary meets Ben Weatherstaff the gardener, Dickon (Martha's brother), and a friendly robin, and first begins to thaw out of her frozen, uncommunicative state. Interaction with other people for both children is a means of having their corners rubbed off, and also of learning to give. As Mary becomes more affectionate her language changes, for she begins to use the speech and Yorkshire dialect of those around her, even making cheeping noises back at the robin. The alteration of language indicates a modification of identity, for it shows Mary in the process of being absorbed into the lives of the inhabitants of Misselthwaite (though not being at the same time diminished by this) and adapting herself to them.

The process of growth involving the children is not only stimulated by contact with other people, but especially so by the secret garden to which Mary discovers the key and the entrance into the secret garden, which is the text's primary symbol, one which represents that ideal state of enclosure and exposure in balance. Interestingly enough, there are walls here as well, real edifices of brick, not merely metaphorical structures. It is possible, however, that these as well as the garden carry symbolic significance. Victorian walled gardens were places where gardeners grew young plants,[54] away from direct exposure to wind; certain of these gardens had concentric walls, between which small fires were lit so as to heat the brick, imparting warmth to the young plants growing next to the inner wall. The children are warmed by their activities within the garden, both physically, by their exertions, and spiritually, by the sense of helping to give life to the plants. Physically and spiritually, they are stimulated into development; as was mentioned in the Introduction, Mary and Colin are brought into fullness of being by their interaction with nature.

After eradicating the negative effects of both enclosure and exposure the positive aspects of these forces may then be set up in their place. If Mary and Colin have lacked restraint in self-expression, they have, however, been too greatly confined in physical terms, always indoors and 'kept out of the way', a situation that demands remedy. The novel at one level is about opening to them the external and natural world of plants, animals and people, and the garden is at once a symbol of enclosure and emancipation, for in it they are protected from the intrusions of those who, like Mrs Medlock, would otherwise tell them what to do and limit their freedom of action; in it they are at liberty to follow their own pursuits.[55] Although seemingly held within a confined space, the children are in reality freed to be themselves in the secret garden.

Writing at about the same time as Frances Hodgson Burnett was Edith Nesbit, who, along with her husband Hubert Bland and George Bernard Shaw, was a founder member of the Fabian society. Her books for children also show the child at liberty; adults stay on the periphery, guardians at a distance. In Nesbit's novels, children are the narrators, the makers of the tale and of the rules which govern their societies, and as the legislators and narrators they are the wielders of power. Where to be 'grown-up' is what most children aspire to be, here, instead, childhood is the standard. The adult has to be, in a sense, reconfigured as a child before it can enter the world of magic,[56] and then is let in only by kindness of the children, as when, in *The Story of the Amulet*, Anthea persuades her siblings to let the childlike 'learned gentleman' accompany them to Atlantis because it will be a change of air for him. This reverses the pattern of adult/child relationships where the child is the one to be told what is good for him. When the Lamb, their baby brother, becomes suddenly, magically and horribly grown-up in *Five Children and It*, we in fact see this theme of reclaiming the adult for the world of childhood that is so much a part of Nesbit's governing 'ideology'. This pattern of reversal where child and adult is concerned are often found in Nesbit's 'Bastable' stories. In *The New Treasure Seekers*, for instance, Mrs Bax, who is supposed to be looking after them, thinks up new entertainments for their enjoyment: 'she had ... taught us eleven new games that we had not known before; and only four of the new games were rotters'.[57] The child has become the judge of the adult's capacity rather than the adult of the child's.

The balance of enclosure and exposure is maintained in Nesbit's works, however, by 'a carefully conceived moral structure beneath the surface'[58] which has been implanted in the children by their guardians or parents and strengthened by their peers. The need for external forms of enclosure has vanished with the internalisation of regulatory structures. This code of moral beliefs and behaviour functions to prevent the children from wrongdoing, internally policing and protecting them when the adult is out of sight. Promises, for example, are sacred to the motherless Bastable Children, just as the children of *Five Children and It* and its sequels have their private laws and standards which they consider to be as unalterable and unbreakable as the 'law of the Medes and Persians'.

Although the moral and ethical structure within which the children function within may be built on good, old-fashioned concepts of honour and truth, the children in Nesbit's books none the less do not mindlessly imitate examples of virtue and heroism found in early children's books. A measure of their freedom comes from the trust which is invested in them by the adults; they use their initiative and common sense rather than docilely follow precepts laid out by the would-be guardians of child morality. For instance, in *The Phoenix and the Carpet*, when the Phoenix has set fire to the theatre, Anthea thinks they should stay put because their father had said to stay there. Her brothers, however, reject enclosure when it threatens to become fatal:

> 'He didn't mean to stay and be roasted,' said Robert. 'No boys on burning decks for me, thank you.'
> 'Not much,' said Cyril, and he opened the door of the box.[59]

This marks the point of the child's release from literary heroics; like Jane Eyre before them, they do not aspire to the status of exemplary children in fiction, but are real, and preserve this reality through the rejection of what is pointlessly restrictive, refusing to die the deaths ordained for noble, saintly children in books. Cyril opens the door of the box, this being in itself an image of emancipation, one of many to be found in Nesbit's fiction. What is being escaped from are the parameters of textual existence itself and the limitations imposed upon hapless fictional characters.

Arthur Ransome's twelve novels, written between 1930 and 1947, are another highlight of the golden age of children's literature, and like those already mentioned, emerge out of the alliance between child and adult, and between the forces of enclosure and exposure. The children in Ransome's books for children are the direct inheritors of the tradition begun by Nesbit, of granting the child independence from adult interference, in a space in which to learn to cope on his own. As with Nesbit's children, those in Ransome's novels enjoy the trust of their guardian figures. In the famous telegram from Captain Walker that opens *Swallows and Amazons*: 'BETTER DROWNED THAN DUFFERS IF NOT DUFFERS WON'T DROWN', Captain Walker expresses his belief that if his children cannot cope for a brief spell without the safety of their parents' protection, then they are 'in deep trouble'. For children will eventually have to grow up and leave the family circle and survive on their own, and they may as well learn to do so early on. But Captain Walker also expresses his trust that in their not being 'duffers', they can safely be exposed to the open spaces and benefit from the experience; he also trusts them sufficiently to let them begin growing up. This principle is something which they, in turn, have to learn to adopt with regard to others. In *Secret Water*, the first adventure of Bridget, the ship's baby, and the Swallows and Amazons, the Eels play at sacrificing Bridget. Her brothers and sisters are worried that she will be afraid, and keep trying to protect and reassure her:

> 'All right Bridget!' cried Susan. 'It's all right. We'll cut you free. You're going to be rescued.'
> 'Oh go AWAY,' shrieked Bridget. 'Go AWAY. They're just in the middle of it. I don't WANT to be rescued.'[60]

Bridget is making it clear to her loving but over-protective siblings that she can be as independent as they, and can deal with exposure to mock-violence as well as to outdoor life without the protective supervision of her parents. Play is here seen to function as an interesting space where the child can be simultaneously exposed to various forms of 'danger' while still being protected.

'Being' in Ransome's novels is not conceptualised under particular headings; Wordsworth's densely significant phrase 'the being that we are' – which knows no discrimination between aspects of self, speaking instead of being in language pertaining to a unified whole – here comes into its own. The enlargement of self is seen in how the child's hidden identity or potential emerges and becomes a concrete and accepted part of self-identity. Titty in *Pigeon Post*, for example, discovers that she possesses the gift of dowsing, of finding water, a talent that frightens her initially as it renders her temporarily strange to herself. The roles which the children create for themselves, such as those of pirates and eels, are also means of exploring aspects of self or potentialities.

Victor Watson has noted in his article 'Poetry and Pirates – Swallows and Amazons at Sea' the essentially poetic qualities of Ransome's writing in the Swallows and Amazons books.[61] In Ransome's books may be found the poetry of discovery that sets the child free from the prosaic and quotidian, and here we may note a modern example of imaginative enlargement. While Ransome's novels (except for *Peter Duck* and *Missee Lee*) are ostensibly about ordinary, un-magical holidays in the Lake District and on the Norfolk Broads, the children, by virtue of their imagination, escape out of a merely three-dimensional world into an imaginative fourth dimension. For instance, the hill that they climb has a double existence not only as a real hill in the Lake District, but also as 'Kanchenjunga' (for the Blackett parents and Uncle Jim in their youth, the same hill was the 'Matterhorn'). Their activities take place simultaneously on two planes, and this enriches their experience, exercising their imagination while strengthening their bodies. This kind of literature lets the child escape from enclosed spaces on both the real and the imaginary planes. Yet there is a balance between the elements of enclosure and exposure: the children are free of parental control, but parents or helpful adults are seldom too far away to be of help when necessary. And if the children are allowed their own space, Ransome points out that adult space should be equally sacrosanct: in *Winter Holiday*, when Nancy and Peggy invite the two Ds to camp on their Uncle Jim's houseboat the *Fram*, they are met the next morning by a notice:

> A big piece of board had been fixed on the side of the *Fram*, close by the ladder. On it, in big black letters, was printed the word 'TRESS-PASSERS'. As the skaters came nearer they were able to read the second line, which was in rather smaller letters 'WILL BE HANGED', and when they were already close to the *Fram* they could read a third line, of letters smaller still, 'LIKE THE LAST'.[62]

Here the adult makes his point, albeit humorously and kindly, that the boundaries which do exist to protect the child's rights also protect those of the adult.

The rhythm of the children's holiday life is dictated by the child, but at the same time there *is* a formal structure to this flexible life.

There are signposts to guide the child; in *Peter Duck*, for instance, the lightships and buoys of the Channel are described as the 'signposts of the sea',[63] and in *Secret Water* posts are hammered into the ground to create a strict schedule for mealtimes. Exposure at its best stimulates the mental, spiritual and physical growth of the child, while structure helps the child to direct this growth. In the Ransome corpus both these forces work in constructive unison, with the result that the children in his stories emerge strong, independent and well-balanced.

In twentieth-century children's literature the child has fallen heir both to the advantages and disadvantages of the spaces opened by Alice. The early part of the century, especially, saw the creation of enchanted places that were both free from adult interference and yet protected enclaves, like Milne's Hundred Acre Wood and Farjeon's Daisy Field, where the child reigned supreme. Another aspect of the child's new freedom came in the form of admittance to the adult world, but along with the privilege of staying up to dinner, metaphorically speaking, came with adult uneasiness of dwelling in a world of ever-increasing uncertainties.

Another interesting form of emancipation which has been dealt with in children's fiction may be found in Alan Garner's *The Owl Service*, in which imprisonment is troped both as psychological and cultural, from which the individual must be freed. 'Cultural' here refers to the mythic structure that underlies the work, a recurring pattern that, unless stopped, will destroy every generation. *The Owl Service* features three adolescents, Alison, Roger and Gwyn, and is set in Wales, supposedly in that valley where the fourth branch of the Mabinogion took place. The myth of Math ap Mathonwy which structures the work tells how Blodeuwedd was created out of flowers to be the wife of Lleu Llaw Gyffes, and how she subsequently betrayed her husband with Gronw Pebyr and, as a consequence of this betrayal, was turned into an owl. In the valley, once in every generation, the myth surfaces, taking hold of three people and turning them to its patterns until the tragedy is worked out and the psychological master power exhausted for a time.

The story is one of psychological enclosure, a spiritual bondage that must be broken and its victims freed if they, the protagonists, are to survive and be made whole. As Neil Philip notes, 'At its best, the book is suffocatingly claustrophobic and intense.'[64] Alison, Roger and Gwyn are dominated and thus defined by their parents and also by the power of the valley which seeks to channel itself through them. When the book opens Alison hears a scratching in the loft, and she remarks that it sounds like something trying to get out. Upon investigation there proves to be a china service decorated all over with a motif that could be either owls or flowers, depending on the perception of the person looking at it. A wall in the billiards room, previously pebble-dashed, suddenly cracks open to expose a picture painted on the wall, of a woman, surrounded by either owls or flowers, again. This is the mythic power trying to free itself from the holding measures which previous generations have tried to keep it in check, by inscribing it on china and in painting, thus seeking to cut it out of themselves and so contain it.

The pattern itself acknowledges the dual possibilities of being; one can be either owls or flowers, cruel or kind, but thus far all the Blodeuwedds have become 'owls'. This is perhaps born of psychological imprisonment: a despair of holding on to one's better nature, a despair of being forgiven, of managing to break the ingrained pattern of things. The entrenchment is part of the problem, for all the mental and spiritual hurts lie deeply buried below the surface of relationships, and need to be exposed before they can be excised. Roger, Gwyn and Alison are each stunted or handicapped in some way by their parents. Alison's mother, who never directly enters the book, desires to create her daughter in her own image and imbue her with her own notions of class and being.[65] It is she who is responsible at a later point in the book for Alison's betrayal of Gwyn, thus setting in motion the pattern of the myth. This domination is the more frightening for never being seen, for that which is not totally apprehended cannot be properly combated; that which is not thoroughly known cannot be named and so banished. Alison's mother represents the unseen power of the myth which cannot be fought because of its elusiveness: the ways in which it works are confusing and not clear-cut.

Roger, who is Alison's step-brother (his father has married her mother), is weighted down and controlled by his parents: his mother, the 'Birmingham Belle' as Alison's mother sneeringly calls her, has run off, leaving his father as the sole dominating influence on his life. Nancy, Gwyn's mother, was the Blodeuwedd of her generation, and tries to constrain Gwyn within her narrow framework of life: all she wants is social upgrading, and she has no thought for what he wants and desires to be. As the pattern is set in motion Alison, who can only see the owls and not the flowers in the pattern on the plates, betrays to Roger all of Gwyn's secrets regarding his ambitions, and Roger uses this information to hurt Gwyn. What Alison sees is only a partial iden-tity ('owls' is contained in 'flowers') and she despairs and falls into a trance-like state, where long red scratch marks, as from the talons of owls rending her, appear under her skin, symbolic of the psychological pressure she is under and is as yet unable to externalise and so be free of. Gwyn refuses to forgive Alison and Roger, condemning her to being and remaining 'owls'. Ultimately, it is Roger who finds enough grace to stand and be hurt in return in order to find the power to restore Alison to herself. Gwyn taunts him about the 'Birmingham Belle', of whom he has never spoken, and whom he has rejected. He takes the pain of the taunt as Gronw Pebyr finally turned to take the spear cast at him by Lleu, accepting the reminder that he is his mother's as well as his father's son, and with the coming of wholeness through the acknowledgement, exposure and expulsion of personal bitterness, he is able to say to Alison, 'You've got it back to front, you silly gubbins; you're flowers, not owls,' words of re-naming, fresh definition, forgiveness, that help her excise the mental anguish and become 'flowers'. Having found the strength to break that which that bound them to the tragic pattern, Roger has found freedom for himself and Alison and hope for coming generations in his affirmation of will over predestination.

In this chapter so far, 'emancipation' has been a term of approval; but the validity or wisdom of permitting the child to be exposed to the painful realities of the adult world, and the question of the function of what might be called 'disturbance' or pain in children's fiction, has long been debated. Julius Lester, in his article 'The Kinds of Books We Give Children: Whose Nonsense?', notes:

> Too many of us feel that children are to be protected and sheltered from pain. Yet they live close to it and perceive it every day. And not to acknowledge its existence is to leave them unprotected and unsheltered.[66]

Lester speaks of how the knowledge of pain is necessary in order to know how (in Tess of the d'Urberville's phrase) to 'fend hands against it'. Patricia Meyer Spacks, however, speaks with even more force in *The Adolescent Idea* of pain as a necessary correlative to growth, a stimulus to becoming, an idea given concrete form in the first of Rilke's *Duino Elegies*, where he writes of the arrow 'enduring the string so as to become something more than itself in the gathering out-leap'. Yet, though pain can be a stimulus, a goad which drives the individual to deeper perception and internal spiritual formation, it can also be the rack upon which the individual is broken beyond mending, and writers for children require judiciousness in their handling of exposure lest the child be blighted, not stirred.

Rumer Godden is one of those who introduces the child to the problematic adult state with some gentleness, screening the child from an excessive degree of trauma. This is positive exposure, where horizons are broadened without what some see as gratuitous soul-shaking and shock tactics that a good many children's authors today seem to think of as necessary ingredients in the making of a good children's book. This is true both of *The Greengage Summer* and *The Peacock Spring*, where the children (both readers and fictional characters) are not shielded from the facts of life, but are brought into contact with emotions and experiences which the nursery has sheltered them from.

The Greengage Summer is about a family, the Greys, who live in Southstone, a small insular town. With the intention of educating them in matters of the spirit, in matters of 'otherness', their mother takes them to France:

> 'You never think of anyone but yourselves.'
> We stared. Whom else should we think of? ...
> Mother took a deep breath. 'I shall take you to the battlefields of France ... So that you can see what other people will do in sacrifice ... You need to learn ... what I cannot teach you.'[67]

The Greys have hitherto led an uneventful life, shut up, as Cecil (short for Cecilia) says, in a 'private child's world'. This private world does not necessarily stand for a negative form of enclosure, being created out of their mother's desire to give the children, whose father is away a good deal of the time, a life that is sheltered from storms and unpleasantness. But the children feel a sense of claustrophobia even under this kindly dispensation, a sense of their world being too small and limiting: 'We were never quite comfortable in Southstone and the rudeness came from the discontent; it was as if a pattern-mould were being pressed down on us into which we could not fit.'[68] Because of this they are focused inwards upon themselves, developing a tendency towards selfishness in the fight for space to be and to grow within a limited place, without room to spare for others.

Cecil, the 14-year-old narrator, says,

> We were odd, belonging and yet not belonging, and odd is an uncomfortable thing to be; we did not want to belong but were humiliated that we did not. I know now it was not good for us to

live in Southstone. We should not have been as odd somewhere bigger, in London, perhaps.

'In London,' said Joss dreamily, 'you can be anyone ....'[69]

The effects of being kept enclosed – though this is benevolently done – are painfully felt; they are unable to get away from who and what they are, yearning instead after space and *possibility*, the ability to be 'anyone', to move outside the sphere of fixity into areas where they can become acquainted with other things and become other people. For the Greys, language and the lack of it are limited and limiting things. Their mother sets a barrier between them and experience by keeping the words of naming away from them; for example, when Cecil experiences menstruation (what she has been taught to call 'Eve's curse') for the first time, she says, 'Mother had not taught us any of the words.' She is given a euphemism in place of a naming word, in the hope of keeping her innocent of adult knowledge, and thus of keeping experience private and shrouded. The inability of the children to name things, and their paucity of words, work in the same way that Orwell's 'Newspeak' does, limiting concepts by limiting access to the words that define them. 'Words,' as Rosemary Sutcliff writes, 'are man's means, not only of communicating, but of giving shape and manageability to his own thoughts and ideas,'[70] and removing language hinders any attempt at self-government and self-definition.

In Vieux-Moutiers the Greys find themselves suddenly unprotected, set adrift in strange waters. When their mother becomes ill and has to be moved to a hospital and they go to a hotel on their own they are removed from the circles of safety and security, her forms of censorship becoming temporarily de-activated. Cecil and her siblings are then let loose in the world of Les Oeillets, the hotel, and its inhabitants, amongst whom is Paul the kitchen boy, who is a complete stranger to the kind of upbringing which the Grey children have enjoyed. His mother, we are told, was a camp follower, and he never knew his father ; he is the antithesis of the Greys, representing all that is exposed just as they have hitherto stood for all that is enclosed. Their coming, 'so unaware, so pink and protected, gave Paul a smart he had not known before',[71] and it is thus suggested that Paul too, in his own way, has led an enclosed life, albeit enclosed within a 'fallen' world, and is now being exposed to the knowledge of another world outside his own. 'Fallen', because the shape of the narrative follows the myth of the Fall: Cecil refers to the first greengage as an 'Eden apple' which had suddenly rendered her 'older and wiser'.[72] The movement towards awareness and adult knowledge comes packaged with a sense of transgression; for example, the growing sexual awareness is felt by Cecil to be a 'badness' in herself: 'I could not help it; it was a stain spreading through my bones.'[73] This says less about the author's position on sexuality *per se* than it says about the narrator's perception of her own loss of innocence – that to grow up is, mythically, to enter the world of sin.

Through their acquaintance with Paul their capacity for naming expands as their experience – both innocent and not-so-innocent – increases with the widening of their world. The novel broadcasts the intense freshness of first-time experiences: their first time abroad, the first time they meet people from the outside world, their first champagne, and so forth. Upon first encountering Eliot they are less concerned with the man than the fact that '[i]t was the first time we had seen anyone in "tails"'.[74] Words are themselves an experience, generating *frisson* with their newness, and the text shows many instances of word and reality, signifier and signifed, coming together to illumine fresh understanding in the children. For instance, upon first stepping into the hall of Les Oeillets, Cecil tells the reader:

> The hall was elegant too. It was odd that we, who had never seen elegance before – though it was our favourite word – immediately recognized it ...[75]

Cecil is 'the one who likes words', as Joss says in the beginning, and the reader is made aware of the narrator's excitement in using new words such as, *sucette* (lollipop) and *bouillon*, the acquisition of language bestowing symbolic power over the real world. Even Paul is spurred on to use the new words which his interaction with the Greys has brought him: 'He swore at me with his new word. 'Shut up!'[76] Interestingly enough (though of course this is unintentional on the author's part), the 'new word' picked up from the sheltered English children *is* one of enclosure: shutting up. There is an irony here, words both liberating expression but also codifying thought.

Paul, however, also introduces them to less innocent pleasures, such as smoking and drinking. Cecil is at first oblivious to any danger that such activities might represent, for at the outset they appear merely as new things to be sampled, as are the rest of the new sensations of Vieux-Moutiers. It is partly the excitement of the word that she tastes as well as the flavour of cigarette smoke when she says to Joss, 'It's a Gauloise, a French cigarette.'[77] Later, set on by Joss's unhappy recklessness, Joss, Cecil and Paul get drunk on wine taken illicitly, like the apple in Eden. Colours are symbolic in Godden's novel, and their progression from white to red, from blanc de blanc to Bouzy Rouge, charts a pathway from innocence to experience, where the spilled red wine and gashed table suggest ritual and initiation. The white wine, blanc de blanc, conjures up for Cecil the things of innocence, things which belong to the enclosed world of childhood: bubbles, 'a mountain, a pudding, shoe polish, a white poodle'.[78] Forced to drink the red wine poured by Paul, Cecil says,

> When I looked at the walls, they moved inwards a little, while the stairs went sideways. It was no longer blanc de blanc, that happy time; the red was terrible, and I began to cry again.[79]

The danger of their entry into the exposed world which this episode marks is later shown when, suddenly aware of Joss as adult rather than child, Paul attempts to climb a ladder into her room and (presumably) rape her. This last irrevocable step out of childhood is, however, prevented by Eliot, who despite his own criminality (he is a thief) has always looked after them. Happening to pass by at that point, Eliot catches Paul and murders him; in so doing he maintains the sanctity of their world, though at the cost of Paul's life.

In *The Greengage Summer* exposure, even to painful things, is presented as enrichment, pain bringing about a deepening of self-awareness and contemplativeness. But unlike a good many books penned for teenagers today (such as the books written in what Michele Landsberg in *The World of Children's Books* calls the 'Blumziger' tradition, in reference to Judy Blume and Paula Danziger), Godden does not traffic in facile (and rather unbelievable) sudden enlightenments that take one from a state of muddled and unformed adolescence to complete and assured selfhood. *The Greengage Summer* is about process and becoming, and it acknowledges that the notion that self can crystallise once and for all is a myth; there is no single rite of passage or baptism of fire that one emerges from into a final version of self. Perfection and finality are not achievable, but only visions to travel towards.

This is made evident in the text. The family grows more conversant with 'real' and 'adult' things, but their own sense of their new 'adultness' which they get through their fleeting contact with champagne and cigarettes and other things they associate with being grown-up is shown to be, in fact, largely illusory. The Greys have been witness to adult passion, tangled motives, hurt, murder and seduction and jealousy of different kinds, but there none the less remain areas of textual opacity, things which the narrator muses on but as yet cannot see clearly into or understand. At the end of the novel they are still 'simple people'.[80] The children are journeying towards knowledge and deeper being, not towards mere adulthood, for the text suggests that adults have not themselves arrived at the point of final wisdom and omniscience, are not themselves fully crystallized selves: Mother 'could look very like Hester [Cecil's younger sister]'; Joss 'crumpled like a little girl'; 'Zizi [the proprietress of Les Oeillets] was a little girl's name'. And when, after Paul's murder and Eliot's disappearance, the situation becomes too difficult for the Greys to handle, their Uncle William arrives on the scene to take them home, allowing a return to childhood. The path to adulthood is not necessarily linear, nor is adulthood a terminal, but only a transition–point.

While exposure to that which is painful and disturbing is portrayed as being, within limits, necessary to development, pain can also be seen as a psychologically imprisoning thing, and this is another form of constraint which is addressed in many modern works of literature for children. A philosophy involving the reading of children's books which has particular interest in the context of this discussion on literature governed both by the exposing and enclosing impulses is that of 'bibliotherapy', which is based on the theory of the book's ability to provide therapy for the child in pain. Pining over one's parents' divorce, or other family problems, experiencing bewilderment over the mechanics of growing up and bodily change – situations and issues such as these which contain the potential for pain form the content of many 'problem novels' for the young which are used in the service of bibliotherapy. Such books are a species of 'designer' literature tailored to specific problems and presumably intended to doctor the reading patient out of his or her private trauma or angst into psychological wholeness by articulating and giving a name to one's hurts and formulating ways of understanding one's own situation, thus enabling one to grapple with the problem and so exorcise the hurt. It may provide solutions, comfort and reassurance through its message that there *are* other people in the same boat, sharing the same experience, and that the child is not alone in its pain and bewilderment. What it tries to do is to help the child towards the accommodation, acceptance and coping that the protagonists in the novel have reached. The text, as analyst, performs its own kind of transference. It is an attractive idea, especially to those who believe in the value of reading and love books; none the less there is a degree to which the assumption that texts can heal all hurts, accomplishing what real psychoanalysts may not manage to do, is over-facile, over-simplistic. What is interesting is the way in which the thinking involved in bibliotherapy might be seen as embodying the dual principle which this chapter has been examining. The text's exposure of both fictional child and child reader to the painful and the problematic is undertaken with the intent of eradicating psychological constraints, and thus has a protective impulse at its heart.

Having said that, it is also true that, despite its beneficient motivations, much of the 'problem' literature produced for therapeutic purposes goes no deeper than the surface, and it is doubtful whether its avowed mission is accomplished after these books have been read. This kind of fiction is, as Joan Aiken says,

> intended to show teenagers how to adjust to the colour problem and keep calm through parents' divorce and the death of poor Fido ... And how insulting they are! Adults are not expected to buy books called *Mrs Sue Jones – Alcoholic's Wife*, or *A Hundred and One Ways to Lose Your Job and Keep Calm*.[81]

It might even be argued that with the best intentions in the world, desiring to free the child from psychological imprisonment, the kind of work castigated by Aiken, herself one of the most imaginative of writers for the young today, in fact brings about a different kind of imprisonment of the self. The constant exposure of the child to his problems in literary form in an attempt to make him face up to them may not so much eradicate the scars as render the child narcissistic and self-centred, in that he is not being allowed to move away from the contemplation of his own problems, but is required to read about them instead. This is arguably unhealthy, for it is in the contemplation of 'otherness' that one acquires perspective and wisdom, the wherewithal to rise above the crippling griefs and worries of the self. As suggested earlier in this chapter, the ability to move out of the self is important, and, as Landsberg notes:

> The special quality of self-forgetfulness that we cherish in reading the best fiction has been lovingly and painstakingly described by many critics over the years. T. S. Eliot called it the 'radical innocence' of the person who is amused and entertained, and thus wonderfully distracted from self-concern. Gertrude Stein wrote

about the shocking discovery of immutable otherness which yanks us permanently, disillusioningly but liberatingly out of our egocentricity. Helen Gardner drew our attention to the mother reading to the child: both mother and child, she said, have 'thrown open the doors of the prison of the present' and the child is temporarily distracted from the claimant needs and desires of childhood.[82]

This is the insight of Jean Little's *Mama's Going to Buy You a Mockingbird*. Unlike other modern novels which try to frame a response to death and separation, and other difficult experiences, this novel takes a distancing stance, refusing to get sucked into the latent emotionalism of the situation. Jeremy's father who is dying of cancer does not try to distract his son from the fact, but asks him to read *Kim*, not with the idea of its being bibliotherapy or didactic (although reading about an orphan who is independent and joyously courageous may well be helpful to Jeremy), but as a means of re-directing his attention to the fact that there is still joy to be found, value to be gained out of life beyond the shadows of his father's passing. Literature is seen as the means to the emancipation both *of* and *from* the self, rather than a mirror which, by reflecting a situation, effectively locks one into it.

In this age of children's literature, the meanings of 'enclosed' and 'exposed' have been seen to expand their range of associations and significance. Generally, however, the widening of the child's world has been welcomed as a movement in the right direction. As the next chapter discusses, however, the removal of boundaries may often leave the child threatened, with the twentieth-century child needing more than ever a stable sense of self so as to withstand the absence of external stabilities.

4
'Shivering in the Midst of Chaos'

All the previous ages ... had something we could take for granted ... We can be sure of nothing; our civilization is threatened ... In our present confusion, our only hope is to be scrupulously honest with ourselves ... Most of us have ceased to believe, except provisionally, in truths.

Bonamy Dobrée

I can see that in such an increasingly threatened and frightening world as ours now is, children, probably more than ever before, need to be given real values and sustaining ideas and memories that they can hold on to and cherish.

Joan Aiken

In *The Greengage Summer*, Cecil Grey, the narrator says,

We had, too, been chiefly with girls and women, and had been ruled by Mother, who had made a private child's world for us; now suddenly we were surrounded by a public and almost rude life ...[1]

Her remark might well be representative of the child in the twentieth century looking back at a previous existence. The individual's quest for being would be set no longer in those enchanted places – daisy fields and secret gardens – but in an exposed context of 'death, war, [and] ... psychological crises'.[2] What this reflected was a radical shift in assumptions governing literature for children. The philosophy behind nineteenth-century texts for children was a protective one, in favour of sheltering the child as far as possible from things that would make unhappy reading, in the belief that it was during the 'blessed season of unconsciousness and delight' that 'strength for the future contest'[3] was being absorbed, and that shielding the young from unhappiness was necessary in order to cultivate cheerfulness, in which sunny climate character and moral strength were most likely to develop. Louisa M. Alcott noted this general attitude in *Jack and Jill*, writing, 'It is often said that there should be no death or grief in children's stories. It is not wise to dwell on the dark side of these things.'[4] However, in the twentieth century, sentiment on the subject may be seen to have suffered a dramatic about-turn, critics as distinguished as C. S. Lewis saying that, after all, 'there [was] something ludicrous' in the idea of protecting from the horror of real life, 'a generation which is born to the Ogpu and the atomic bomb'.[5] Russell Hoban, in 'Thoughts on Being and Writing' agreed, saying: 'Today's children do not live in an expurgated world. With their elders they must endure sudden deaths and slow ones, bombs and fire falling from the sky ... They must endure the reality of mortal man.'[6]

Hoban's own classic work for children, *The Mouse and his Child* (1967), which, perhaps more than any other work examined in this chapter, embodies and considers all the ideas to be discussed in it, explores a world blatantly 'unexpurgated', in which the mouse child, who 'doesn't want to go out into the world', is forced out into it. This is a work whose symbols are resonant, powerful and perturbing, which not only surveys the world on both sides of the barrier that marks off 'protected' from 'unprotected', but combines this with charting a movement towards autonomy: the Mouse and his Child, together forming a composite clockwork toy, want to be 'self-winding', independent of external control, and to an extent, independent of each other as well. From the shop in which the story opens, and in which the Child first speaks of 'wanting a mama' and 'liv[ing] in the house where the party is, and not go[ing] out into the world',[7] the Mouse and his Child are sold, and have to 'work', entertaining others for their living; for them, playtime is over. But this 'emergence' into the real world is seen to be only a prelude to 'real' exposure, for when the mechanism gives way and breaks, they are thrown out.

At this point, Hoban's work begins to manifest intense symbolic activity, generating a great deal of energy. The Mouse and his Child have been originally configured so as to move circularly when wound up, the father swinging his child up and down, this leading them to question the 'futility of dancing in an endless circle that led nowhere'.[8] Their time inside the safe spaces of shop and home is therefore associated with this movement; it is in this way suggested that safety within the house where the party is going on in perpetuity is also a limitation upon the self and a hindrance along the route to autonomy. When the mechanism breaks and they are set going again by the tramp, however, their movements are found to have been altered: they are no longer caught in movements of repeating circularity, but can move forward, albeit with the Mouse's child forever facing him, and, perforce, always looking back in the direction from which they have come. As their adventures continue, the Mouse and his Child meet with danger and disaster, becoming ever more ragged and tattered, this marking their passage through the world which reveals itself as absurd, painful and bleak. The Mouse and Child find at the end of their journey not merely the ability to be self-winding, but also the other toys from the shop, and the doll's house, now battered and broken; these broken things come together as family. This work is a powerful and poignant revisiting – indeed rewriting – of the myth of the Fall, where the fall into experience and knowledge, seen to entail pain and damage, and which knows no return to innocence, may yet find itself able to bring forth, out of the ashes, something of grace and courage. There is, as Yeats wrote, a gaiety capable of transfiguring dread. Self refined in this fire, if it survives, will be the stronger for it. *The Mouse and his Child* does not valorise 'exposure' as an undoubtedly good thing, but seems to acknowledge the exit from Eden as a necessary thing which needs to be negotiated and which can be survived.

The ever-present danger found in *The Mouse and his Child* is a hallmark of much twentieth-century children's literature, and we may also perceive here a sense of threat to the being and identity of the child which has arisen from his newfound access to the world outside the Hundred Acre Woods and secret gardens.[9] According to Sheila Egoff, in modern children's literature, especially that written since the 1960s, '[p]ressure on the Individual is intense and the feeling of being threatened is very real. The age of faith has passed and what is to fill the void?'[10] Another critic, Jason Epstein, has written that the concept that 'organized society is hostile to growth and freedom and defeats the individual ... is a dominant idea in the literary tradition'[11] both in works for children and adults. Yet, in this century at least, the defeat of the individual comes as much at the hands of the *dis*organized society as the organized one, because, with society in ferment, the pull on the individual and his loyalties comes from many different directions; the individual is disconcerted because society itself is disconcerted, no longer pulling together. Holden

Caulfield in Salinger's *Catcher in the Rye* is not a victim of 'organized society', but suffers as a result of his exposure to a world which has quietly rotted away underneath the façade of organization and stable structure. Into children's literature, especially in the later half of this century, has gradually crept a mood of discontent and melancholy, and sometimes even of despair and defeatism, and even in those environments portrayed in children's literature which still contain stability and security there may still be seen to come, now and then, a sense of threat.

A more subtle evil, however, which may threaten the integration of self in the modern world as a result of the decline of authority and responsibility, is the philosophy of moral relativism, where the notion of absolute values of right and wrong has either become muddied or has been abolished altogether. Absolute morality might seem to be too rigid a frame through which to view the world; however, where distinctions are blurred, and where there is no clear moral light to see by, the self is in danger of losing its way. Instead of being able to form an identity around the nuclei of beliefs and certainties, the individual becomes less sure, more hesitant in committing the self to definition according to any one principle, and is thus in danger of remaining morally formless.

The weed of moral relativism which has fully flowered in our time first began to take root in the nineteenth century. The growth of relativist philosophy and pluralist thinking was encouraged, *inter alia*, by scientific and anthropological developments during the nineteenth century and in the early years of the twentieth century. The impact of Charles Darwin's theories are well-known, especially in the implicit challenge they posed to the 'truth' of the Biblical narrative of creation, and thus to the moral authority of the church. Einstein, of course, would further aid the cause of relativistic thinking when, in 1905, he came out with his Special Theory of Relativity, which demonstrated that time and space are relative to the place of the observer and that, *ergo*, absolute time and absolute space are non-existent and no absolute frame of reference exists. Even in the domain of archaeology, events like the digging up of the library of the Assyrian king Ashurbanipal at Nineveh revealed the *Epic of Gilgamesh*, whose similarity to the story of Noah in the Bible helped add to the uneasiness, even as the question of whether the Old Testament was God-given truth (and therefore morally authoritative) or merely an alternative version of Middle Eastern mythology helped to call into question the moral absolutism of Christianity.

Without the great moral and spiritual authority of Christianity established firmly at the centre, relativism naturally gained in strength. As B. J. Craige has said in *Literary Relativity*:

> If the universe has no center, then no one individual or event is of intrinsically greater significance than any other. Correspondingly, if the world has no God, then no one individual or event is of intrinsically greater significance than any other for there is no transcendent source of meaning to bestow meaning selectively on individuals and events. Since the sources of meaning are plural and non-transcendent, meaning is relative rather than absolute. The world comes to appear homogenous, isotropic, decentered.[12]

In the 1860s (interestingly enough, the decade marking the appearance of Alice in an environment characterised by fluctuation and lack of fixity), Matthew Arnold had noted the rise of the 'baneful notion that there is no such thing as a high, correct standard in intellectual matters; that everyone might as well take his own way'.[13] Humpty Dumpty in Lewis Carroll's *Through the Looking Glass* exemplifies, ironically, this idea of individualism. With his lofty, 'When *I* use a word ... it means just what I choose it to mean', he may claim authority over meaning, but if such a claim were to be found admissible, language would cease to carry out its primary directive of facilitating communication. To relativise language to the self would either urge it towards meaninglessness or over-abundant meaning. In a world where individualist and relativist principles hold sway, no 'high, correct standard' of language can truly exist; and where the individual has no standards of objective meaning to work with, even where power over language is exerted the means with which to communicate meaning or to receive it may not exist. The individual is thus effectively isolated through the assertion of his or her individualistic 'rights'.

Whereas nineteenth-century literature for adults may have embodied the relativist principle in action, writers for children, motivated by the wish to protect the child from the anguish of doubt for as long as possible, maintained the stand that

> the principle of authority is not a thing to be talked about to a child ... It should be taken for granted ... a book in which the grounds of obedience are discussed ... causes him to regard as an open question that on which his own nature, if it were not for

an over-careful and meddlesome education, would never lead him to doubt.[14]

These writers constructed their texts accordingly, so as to shield the child from the knowledge of diluted good and evil.

In Arnold's *Culture and Anarchy* the whole issue of emancipation is discussed and the movement from the enclaves or enclosures of certainty to the 'emancipation' of the individual from authority examined. The conclusion that Arnold arrives at is that emancipation can go too far, that the worship of liberty or freedom for its own sake is a dangerous delusion, and that there is a crying need for 'standards of perfection that are real'.[15] Arnold's poems as well as his prose writings betray his unslumbering awareness of doubt as a spiritual malaise, speaking of the isolation of the individual that has arisen from the 'lack of certitude', the end of mass affirmation of a single creed, and the mortal millions who live alone. What was required was a reinstitution of authority, of certainty – but none was to be forthcoming. As Walter Houghton in *The Victorian Frame of Mind* writes:

> When old beliefs are being questioned, and no new ones have been established, the modest man doubts, and the presumptuous man dogmatizes.[16]

A few stood out to affirm beliefs and standards, but they were cried down as presumptuous, and the majority did not 'dare disturb the universe' with firm and uncompromising views, which, perhaps, in their secret heart of hearts they were no longer altogether sure of. Farmer Price, in Maria Edgeworth's 'Simple Susan' (1796), had refused to blur the clarity of his values, ('To say that black is white, which I won't do'), but the time of men like him was passing, and with them, the simplicity of the morally homogeneous world. Hence the ease of the slide towards relativism and the culture of private perception in place of a publicly avowed creed accepted by all.

The release from 'enclosing' principles, with the disappearance of clearly defined moral guidelines in the present age, has not made it impossible for the child in modern children's fiction to attain selfhood and integrity, but it has certainly made this a more difficult state to attain. Sheila Egoff has written, 'A society where rules and standards are clear and consistently supported offers a form of security for children,' and that '[a]utonomy, though stimulating, can bring with it insecurity',[17] present-day society being no longer as united as it once was in its support of consistent doctrines. 'The difficulty,' then, as Fred Inglis comments, 'is dialectical: how shall you make a soul which is faithful to a lost yesterday and strong enough to meet a discontinuous tomorrow?'[18] How is one to ensure that the child has enough selfhood to stand firm and be true to itself in the context of a chaotic and morally ambiguous world? Is the implanting in its mind of principles from a non-relativist age sufficient to stabilize the child working within an unstable frame of things?

Being 'enough', generating sufficient moral substance, wresting control of it and consciously directing one's own growth – these are issues increasingly found in children's books today. Fanny Price, in Jane Austen's *Mansfield Park*, Oliver Twist and Jane Eyre are characters of a bygone age who exemplify this concept of sufficient being, moral solidity, and whose possession of these attributes allow them to emerge unscathed from the corruption of their respective environments. This is of course less clear in the case of Oliver Twist than that of Fanny and Jane, for Oliver appears to be less conscious than Fanny that there is actually a moral battle going on, but Dickens intended him, as he mentions in his introduction to the novel, to represent the undefeatable principle of Good.

The children's author today most conscious of this issue of 'being enough' in the exposed and morally ambiguous waters of the present age – of the need, as Bonamy Dobrée puts it, of being 'scrupulously honest with ourselves' in order to survive the eroding seas of uncertainty – is Antonia Forest. Through a gross critical oversight her literary achievement has been ignored, her contribution to children's literature written off as stories about 'firmly upper-class' children, and 'conventional girls' boarding school[s]'.[19] The quality of her writing, however, is in my view unsurpassed by any, and the subtle depiction of the growth of her characters towards self-knowledge and 'enoughness' over a series of ten books has nothing to do with the rather embarrassing American 'problem' novel, whose characters, one supposes, reach a form of selfhood after a sudden gaining of profound 'insights', which Professor Egoff equates with 'soft and flabby answers'.[20]

The ten novels are about a family of eight, the Marlows, their neighbour Patrick Merrick, and various people at school. Four of these novels are, technically speaking, school stories, and the other six, which deal with the home life of the Marlows, conform to no specific genre of children's fiction, being not quite adventure literature and not 'problem novels', though elements of each are certainly present.[21] The environment which contextualises them is one where personal standards of honesty and integrity are the only ropes to hold on to, and though the Marlow parents affirm moral and ethical standards which are there to guide their children, the moral ambiguity of the outside world creeps in to corrupt their perception with the idea that as there is no objective measure of truth, no right and wrong, decisions essentially of a moral nature are unimportant and may be arbitrarily solved. This is so because in a relativist universe, moral choice no longer signifies something greater than itself, and the chooser has nothing to gain or lose in noumenal terms by his or her choice. Lawrie, for instance, when her sister Karen lets it be known that she intends to marry a widower more than twice her age, with three young children, says:

> 'Well, I suppose she can always get a divorce if it doesn't work out,' said Lawrie in a worldly way which didn't quite sort with her damp, upended hair and tent-like bath towel.
> 'That's an atrocious thing to say,' said her mother sharply. 'I know you don't really know what you're talking about, but don't say or think it again. To get married with *that* idea in your head is the blackest possible sort of cheating.'[22]

Here, we encounter the idea of enclosure versus emancipation all over again. Perception has indeed become enlarged, moral vision attained breadth in that it has stretched, but emancipation can stretch morality till its former shape has utterly disappeared, its former nature distorted beyond recognition. Lawrie is speaking of a philosophy which claims individual desire as the sole arbiter in moral matters, that the enclosure of marriage and the rules constructed to surround it are not sacrosanct, and that the individual may leave the enclosure any time just by claiming the rights of the emancipated. By saying that neither marriage nor divorce matters, she puts them on the same plane of non-significant being.

In another conversation with her family it is made obvious that the traditional authority of the church's teachings has not merely degenerated in the present time to the status of a relative truth, but that even this particular species of 'relative truth' has worn so thin in some places as to be reduced to the level of myth or legend. The family is speaking of a portrait of Our Lady said to have been painted from memory by St Luke after her death. Lawrie interrupts to say:

> 'But ... people who aren't real can't paint portraits of other people who aren't real, can they?'

Everyone looked at her, trying to disentangle this, her mother as if she hoped Lawrie didn't mean what she thought she did. Her grandmother said, 'What do you mean, Lawrence?'
'Well, I mean – well, it's just a story, isn't it? Like Hercules and those people. So how can you have a portrait, that's what I mean. It's like saying that a statue of Athene was done by Jupiter, isn't it?'
'Lawrie!' said her mother.
Lawrie, suddenly aware of an odd quality in her listeners' attention, shied. 'Why? What have I said? ... I never thought I was supposed to think it as *real*. I mean, people don't, not now, do they?'
'Just a fairy tale,' suggested Rowan politely.
'Not a fairy tale. More like a legend. *You* know.'
'Heroes of Asgard?' said Rowan contemplating her. 'Well, well. Sometimes I wonder, I do really.'[23]

The frailty and tenuousness of self and self-image in the modern world, where not even the stereotypes discussed in Chapter 2 exist to aid in the shaping of being, are shown in the figure of Ginty Marlow. In the first two novels, *Autumn Term* and *The Marlows and the Traitor*, she appears ordinary enough, but in *Falconer's Lure*, it appears that the events of *The Marlows and the Traitor*, in which she, Nicola and Peter are abducted by a traitor in the navy, have made her, in her mother's words, 'worked up and weepy'. In this state, she has fallen under the influence of a girl in school called Unity Logan. Ginty emerges as a person whose moral being is plastic and who lacks self-knowledge, this allowing her to become a pale echo of Unity Logan, a copy of an image, and as such, insincere and false but without even the capacity to know this. It is this quality of plasticity and lack of self-awareness in a world without moral guideropes that will put Ginty at risk of having her self annihilated. Unity is described by Rowan as

'a dreadful child ... One's always falling over her and the current friend of the bosom sitting on short flights of stairs, looking intense ... '[24]

and by Karen, as the kind of child who flatters her friends, 'wag[ging] round saying, "I know I'm nothing: but aren't you wonderful? Let me tell you about you."' Unity 'tells' her friends about themselves, and manages to convince them that they *do* actually exist in the new image she has formed of them; rather than peeling down the onion of self to expose the inner layers of people, however, she is adding on a false layer of self, blurring the true identity of the individual beneath. This is apparently what has happened with a previous 'friend of the bosom'; as Karen relates, grinning,

> 'I sat behind her on a bus once, coming home from a match. I don't quite know what it was all about – I think a staff had been harsh to My Pal about running in a corridor – and she knew, she just *knew*, how dreadfully My Pal was feeling about it. And after a bit, My Pal stopped protesting she couldn't care less and agreed she was heartbroken. It was fascinating.'[25]

This, too, apparently is the fate which has overtaken Ginty: to have the self reconstructed along the lines of another's imaging. Unity obviously thinks of herself as a poet (she has written a poem 'All about Beauty and how she didn't know what it was'), and her mental image of the 'poet' makes her cultivate intensity as a mode of being, as she attempts to convey the impression of possessing great perception, great sensitivity and great capacity for experiencing hurt and intense emotions. It is the same kind of dishonest self-imaging which is analysed in *Peter's Room*, with reference to Branwell Brontë:

> 'You know where Charlotte describes the Angrians and she says Young Soult, the poet, is wild-haired and dishevelled and drunk and all that? And Young Soult was Branwell's person and that's what happened to Branwell himself in real life? Well, don't you think it wasn't so much Charlotte being prophetic as both times it was Branwell being the kind of person he thought a poet ought to be? I mean, even when he grew up, because he thought of himself as a poet, he thought he had to be a Young Soult?'[26]

The image of the poet (as a rarefied aesthete) becomes the model for both Unity and Ginty, but the falseness both of the image itself and also of attempting this kind of self-construction is lost on them. In *Peter's Room*, Ginty argues with Karen, saying, 'If you're a poet, you're a different *kind* of person –'; Karen replies, 'But you're not. You have a different kind of talent, that's all. Branwell thought what you think and it ruined him.'[27] Karen also adds that wickedness or silliness is just as much wickedness or silliness whether one is a 'poet or an admiral or a – a city gent' – an affirmation of objective standards which Ginty refuses to accept.

In *Falconer's Lure* Ginty, depicted by the light of these observations, is shown to be a second-hand version of Unity-the-poet, having taken on the veneer of her mannerisms, as when, during a family conversation on hawking, she falls into the mode of the eighteenth-century heroine, quivering with sensibility:

> 'And poor Mrs. Bertie's cat too, I suppose,' said Ginty in a strangled voice. Then she gave a haughty trembling look round the table, said in the same strangled voice, 'I've finished, thanks,' and banged out of the room.[28]

On another occasion, when her mother has hurriedly left the room, Nicola's singing of 'Fidele's Dirge' having reminded her of Cousin Jon, whose plane has recently crashed, Ginty says 'in a special voice' that the dirge will 'always mean him' thereafter. She says this not because she really feels this way, but because 'it was the sort of thing Unity would have applauded and while it was in her head it had sounded so well and so sensitive, she'd even thought her family would be impressed'.[29] The falseness of this persona and the dangers inherent in a failure to be true to oneself, are not immediately clear to her, but later, when the psychological bonds she has forged for herself handicap her and 'force' her to act in a way which earns her the contempt of her family and temporary ostracism, she realises that she has gone as far down the path of Unity 'as it was safe to go'. To act the part of another being for too long is to risk the dissolution of one's true self, and this is a danger for the child in an 'exposed' world.

Ginty then ceases for the time being to play at being interesting. In *End of Term*, there is a suggestive, brief comment on Ginty:

> ... but since that shattering rehearsal (shattering, that is to say, for the unfortunate B. Evans) when Ginty had become Gabriel, she'd seemed in an odd way – not different – but more herself: as a transfer shows its bright colours when the concealing paper peels away.[30]

Ginty still suffers from a plasticity of character, a malleability, but this comment seems to hint that part of the difficulty in the child's quest for being is the lack of moral definition in the environment, for the moral atmosphere has a part to play in the shaping and defining of the identity. Ginty, allowed to fall under the influence of Unity, goes to the bad. Ginty, given the definition of the archangel Gabriel, is released to become more herself; it is as though with the aid of

positive and benevolent authority, the weaker beings may be helped
to be 'enough', or at least halted in the slide to becoming lesser enti-
ties. Rules and regulations, as Miss Cromwell, a teacher at Kingscote,
remarks, 'exist to protect the weak from the bullies and the foolish
from their folly'; they are there to enclose the unformed or undefined
being in a protective layer of authority.

Yet aid in the quest for definition in an environment perhaps far too
'exposed' can only have limited potency, and because Ginty still has
no self-knowledge – none of that 'scrupulous honesty' with herself
that we see in her younger sister Nicola, who one suspects is the effective protagonist of the series – she is still without a firm or concrete
identity. In *Peter's Room*, where the younger members of the family
and their neighbour Patrick get together to 'Gondal' as the Brontës
were wont to do, acting out fantasy adventures, getting under the
skins of other people, Ginty becomes not just one main character,
Crispian, but another called Rosina as well, which is perhaps telling in
its own way. Her sister, Ann, 'a kind girl', as Rowan says, thinks of
Ginty as being 'a little bit like Orsino in *Twelfth Night* – the one who
wore changeable taffeta because his mind was a very opal'; but Nicola,
who unlike Humpty Dumpty will not allow her words to slide around
meanings because reliability and responsiblity are part of her personal
code, says no: 'Chameleons are what she's like –'.[31] Ginty is not
merely temperamentally changeable, but something more dangerous:
what Forest implies here is that her being takes on the colour and
pattern of those she is with; she is not *enough* to withstand the being
of others whether good or bad, and is thus at the mercy of those
whose influence is for evil.

In the last but one novel so far, *The Attic Term*, Ginty's moral insuf-
ficiency is made clear; through her thoughtlessness and disregard for
rules, her boyfriend Patrick Merrick is expelled from school. It is not
so much the disobedience to rules as Ginty's moral slipperiness and
failure to realise that there is an ethical and moral code which loses
her the regard of the Merricks; in her inability to realise that there is
such a code, to distinguish between right and wrong, she displays a
lack of integrity, an integration of self and knowledge. Mr Merrick, in
a conversation with his son says:

'I don't *dis*like her – I think it's evens whether she goes to the good
or to the bad. But I doubt if it'll be very spectacular either way.'
'How *devastating*,' said Patrick, after a moment.
'It wasn't meant to be.'

'It sounds like the souls who can't be ferried over the Styx because
they've never been *enough –*'
'Perhaps she's always been able to hide too easily behind her mask.
Sometimes, when I look at her, I think of the Lady of Shalott.'
'The onion looking-glass lady? Why her?'
'... he said "*She has a lovely face*
God in his mercy lend her grace..."'
Patrick said nothing.[32]

The comparison of Ginty with the Lady of Shalott is interesting not
merely for the implied superficiality of the 'lovely face', and thus the
implications of being something which is mostly surface, but also
because the lady, who has lived her sheltered life representing
shadows, cannot cope with exposure to real life in the end. She is
overwhelmed by the three-dimensional reality of the world because
she herself is only two-dimensional, less real than they are, possessing
less sense of self. Furthermore, the lady, two-dimensional as she is, can
survive as long as she is enclosed in her tower, and hedged around by
dicta, *musts* and *must nots*. Yet, in breaking away from the spell and its
binding, she destroys the rules which permit her continuance, and,
protection withdrawn, she perishes. Ginty too, without adequate
identity, flounders in a world without clearly defined rules.

One is reminded by Mr Merrick's observation that Ginty's progress
in either direction is unlikely to be spectacular, of Alice's encounter
with the Cheshire Cat. Here, in response to her request for direction,
the cat answers that it all depends on where she want to go. 'I don't
much care where –' begins Alice, only to be interrupted by the cat,
who retorts smugly, and with Carroll's usual irony, that if she doesn't
care where she goes, then it doesn't matter where she goes, and if her
only care is getting *some*where, then all she has to do is keep on
walking. Translated into metaphysical terms, this suggests that
attaining the desired shape of being depends on having a clear notion
of one's moral direction. Without the comprehension of *why* precisely
it is that clarity of purpose is important, the individual is prone to
merely drifting because direction is of no significance, with the result
that the undirected individual – in this case, Ginty – will fail to
achieve anything very concrete in terms of identity.

This is also true for Lawrie, Ginty's younger sister, whose sense of
self is also seen to be frail, part of the reason for this being the refusal
to acknowledge the responsibility of choice, and throwing that
responsibility onto others. This may be seen in *End of Term*, where

Lawrie, who wants to play the Shepherd Boy in the school's Christmas Play and is not given the part, lets her twin, Nicola, who *has* been given it, pretend to be her in order to play in a school netball match. Her motives are partly altruistic, but at one layer of her mind, she hopes that Nicola will be caught, and have her part taken away as punishment:

> Lawrie tried hard to pretend she wasn't thinking that one ... There were some kinds of person you *couldn't* admit to being. (And if only Kempe, foul beast, had let her be the Shepherd Boy, she wouldn't have *had* to be that kind of person.)[33]

Where external forms of authority no longer have as much purchase or power to shape the self as before, that authority is transferred to the self, autonomy bringing with it responsibility. But here, Lawrie is seen to display a lack of responsibility for the self, allowing herself to think that circumstances are what make her into one kind or other of person, thus abjuring choice in the matter, even though she may not realise that this is what is happening.

While, on the one hand, Forest depicts the stage (mostly in school productions) as an area of immense fascination and interest, and also an arena which can enable self to be vicariously explored, it is also possible to see how acting might become an activity in which self can forget and so lose its own shape. We may recall that Fanny Price, in *Mansfield Park*, when asked to take part in the play *Lovers Vows* put up by the Crawfurds and Bertrams, refuses, saying in fright that she could not act any thing if she were to be given the world for it. Apart from the issue of ability, what Fanny really means is that she *will* not act. Not only is the play a morally dubious piece of literature, but for Fanny, acting is not an exploration of 'otherness', but a rendering up of her inner self and a taking on of another's being, something she feels to be fraught with moral danger. Of course, acting for Lawrie is not so heavily freighted with moral significance, but it is worth noting that next to Ginty, Lawrie, who has outstanding dramatic ability, is also the Marlow with least self-control and indeed, sense of self. And as noted earlier, in a world where self-knowledge and self-control are the only forms of authority left, this lack is a dangerous thing. While her facility in depicting other characters is wonderful, the degree of fluidity of self is perhaps too great, and Lawrie spends too little time in her own skin, in coming to terms with her real identity to be 'enough', any more than Ginty is. In *The Attic Term*, Ginty and Nicola have been given Conduct Marks, and Lawrie asks:

'Who are you going to be when Keith gives you out?' asked Lawrie, momentarily diverted ...

'Who'm I going to *be*?' said Nicola.

'*Be*. Like I'd be someone in the French Resistance being put up against a wall and shot if it was me.' ...

'There won't be enough time,' said practical Nicola.

'Yes, there will. Don't you remember when Marion Peters got one our second term? Keith went on for ages about how it reflected on the school as a whole when someone did something so serious that it merited a Conduct Mark –

'I'd forgotten all that.' Nicola considered. 'All the same, I shall still be me.'

'Oh honestly, it's *wasted* on you. I *wish* it was going to be me. Look, let me stand where you do in the line –'

'No,' said Nicola.

'Why not?'

'Because *no*. Finish.'

'But *why* not?'

'Because you're a disgusting little exhibitionist, *that's* why not,' said Ginty. 'If you want a Conduct Mark, get one of your own.'[34]

Nicola says she will still be herself, this pointing to a strong sense of reality as well as selfhood, while Lawrie's desire to act, to be someone else, also points to an escapism of sorts. Even 'reality' is something that is unable to confine or enclose her, but escape from this particular 'confinement' is also an escape from self, and this flight may result in a weakened self-image. In *The Thuggery Affair*, which is about drug smuggling, Lawrie, supposedly on her way to the police station to report the affair, is waylaid by a Ted, who takes her to a cinema. Earlier, she has ignored her mother's instructions to dress properly and neatly, and is using make-up; in the company of the Ted, she assumes the identity of a Sixties 'chick', and sits with him in the cinema 'profoundly interested to find herself behaving in a way no Marlow would dream of doing'. When she finally attempts to get away from him and go to the police station, climbing out of a window in the ladies' washroom, she is apprehended by the police, who, however, refuse to believe she is who she says she is, because of her behaviour and the outlandish way she is dressed. Ironically, though at this point she is no longer acting or exploring other forms of being, having placed herself temporarily outside the limits of the safe and the legal, her true identity is denied her for a time.

In a quasi-nightmare scene, Lawrie, while in a panic, gives a wrong name, 'Sophia Lawrence' (her real name is Lawrence Sybil, which she hates), which she then alters to Lawrence Sophia Marlow, further eroding her stock of credibility with the police inspector, who asks her if she can prove it. Lawrie is alarmed, never having had her identity doubted before. In checking the identity of the borrower of the library books Lawrie has with her, it is found that these have been borrowed in the name of Doris Gates, who helps the Marlows in their house, with the result that for a while, she is called Doris, given another identity altogether. The tenuousness of formal identity as seen here acts as sign to the frailty of self in the modern world.

Throughout the series it is implied that there are valid and invalid means by which one may depart from the 'enclosure' of self, and investigate 'otherness'. Understanding and affirming the being of others is important because, when validly undertaken, the understanding adds to one's own store of being, and, moreover, helps to give shape to the self. Imaginative investigation of being, as with Lawrie in her acting, is not wrong, but is perilous if not properly comprehended. It is possible to go too far and lose oneself completely, and this almost happens to Patrick, who, in the 'Gondaling' (the word is based on Emily Brontë's imaginary created world) which goes on in *Peter's Room*, desires to explore under the cover of this fictional personality the darkness of the traitor's soul, the feelings of cowardice and betrayal. This twist in the story line, which is made up as they go along, compels the narrative on to the path of suicide; as Patrick lifts the old pistol which is one of their 'props' to his head, Nicola, suddenly panicking, hits his hand, with the result that the pistol drops and a bullet which no one knew was there is fired through the window. Patrick has come near to losing himself in more ways than one.

Literature is a medium through which one may with validity explore the realm of otherness (and explore territory outside the legitimately defined spaces of childhood) without putting the self at risk in the same way, through immersing one's identity in another's. In literature, the boundaries between self and world-as-other are more palpable than they are in acting, where one is effectively 'other' when inhabiting a role. Literature provides a definition of sorts, stimulating growth and aiding in the contouring of identity, in this sense constituting an alternative and replacement authority where other kinds of authority have gone by the board, and this is where the choice of books is important.

Because literature helps to form one's moral vision by influencing one's view of the world – as Montaigne remarked, 'You are what you eat, and you are what you read.' – reading is shown to be of high significance in Antonia Forest's novels. Nicola is caught reading Mary Renault's *The Mask of Apollo*; while this is not completely banned as a morally dubious work, it comes under the school category of 'Limited', where age and maturity are factors that will supposedly aid in the reader's maintenance of an internal balance when assimilating a perhaps disturbing 'otherness'. Miss Cromwell asks Nicola if she realises why the book is 'limited'; Nicola 'hazard[s] politely, 'Because Nico liked men better than women, you mean?' upon which Miss Cromwell does not answer, but gives Nicola a course of 'bread-and-butter reading'. This diet of Dickens, Thackeray and Scott, Miss Cromwell hopes, will help repair any damage to faith in a sane and balanced world which Nicola might have suffered.

The problem of definition is also one which bothers Jane Gardam's Marigold Green, born into the same kind of world as that inhabited by the Marlows, where personal definitions have to be wrenched from the fabric of life and personal standards set up, there being no longer established and accepted canons of moral and ethical values by which to live. Marigold is known to the boys of the school where her father teaches as 'Bilgewater', their corruption of 'Bill's daughter'. Names are a part of definition, providing the individual with a way of thinking of the self, and she is thus given a dismal edition of herself to contemplate:

> 'In the end' says somebody, 'almost everything is appropriate,' and indeed the boys over the years have had a peculiar flair for hitting on the right word for a nick-name.
> Nick-name. Old Nick's name. Bilgewater.[35]

Definitions matter, Bilgewater feels, for they bend perception and, through perception, bend reality into new shapes. Names and the knowledge of the origins of words have power over being, the knowledge of a name giving one power over the named, thus bestowing both the power to banish and the power to transform being. She acknowledges what the names have made of her; it is implied that in the end, there is an appropriateness, a congruence between the nick-name and the nature of being; there is a sense that her nature has, in some vaguely apprehended but non-analysable way, been given a negative cast by the name given. Bilgewater is a nickname. The term 'nick name' is derived from 'Old Nick's name', meaning the devil's name; hence she feels doubly tainted, both by the appellation and the derivations of the very form of naming used.

Bilgewater is about the protagonist's search for power with which to break the control over her identity exerted by the psychological spell of misnaming which has been cast over her. The search for strength, for *enoughness*, to resist the image making of others which she finds so distressing, the search for a self-determined identity has to begin and end in herself, for here, again, authority has grown weak and impotent and is no longer able to enclose and mould the child.

When the book begins Bilgewater writes, 'I knew absolutely nothing about myself and others of my age.'[36] She has no proper home, no mother, her father is passive, if kind; and apart from Paula, the matron at the school, she has no one with whom she can talk things over. Undirected and unaware, she drifts, without attention to external things, until one day Paula pulls her up, asking how old she thinks she is (age and being do not appear to match) and saying that she is 'sick of [her] Marigold Green scumfishing about this world, scatty as Him'.[37] Whether 'Him' is supposed to refer to Bilgewater's father or to God, there lies in Paula's assessment of authority a criticism of laxity, irresponsibility, a failure on *someone*'s part, to take Bilgewater in hand and make something of her. So Paula takes it upon herself, though she is not Bilgewater's mother, to stop Bilgewater 'scumfishing', drifting, and to introduce some form of order into Bilgewater's too-emancipated life, beginning with a clearing up of the clothes left all over the place.

Bilgewater muses over the nature of experience as a shaping factor, whether through experience it is possible to gain power over the self:

> I began to reflect on the nature of experience and particularly of experience not advancing maturity. Experience. Experio. Experire. So many levels encompassing one definition ... Can some people experience and remain unchanged?
>
> No.
>
> ... But some people can experience and retain innocence. Some people can experience on a queer, shallow level in order to recount. For some, experience is only a vehicle, a pipe, a jug. Experience to such people is given only to be handed on. The creative artist I supposed was such a person, seeing, stretching for pen or brush or MS paper or a stage shouting, 'Here is my experience, COMPREHEND', and having shouted forgetting and surviving.[38]

One cannot experience and remain unchanged, but one can experience and yet remain without self-knowledge, without any new power over the self having been attained. The self may remain unshaped. Lawrie, discussed earlier, for example, is such a vehicle; one of those whose experience goes into her interpretations of dramatic parts, but which once having passed, leaves her unconscious and innocent of change. Lawrie feels, for instance, that it is more important, in the Christmas play, to make the audience feel religious than be so, oneself; she transmits experience, but is unaffected and untouched by it herself.

Bilgewater in Gardam's novel, however, comes to herself through experience that reveals to her the root of the problem: that in a way, she has been attempting to define her self using terms not fully comprehended, terms of existence to which she has not fully committed herself. She is not yet, in Marlow idiom, 'enough', because her strength such as it is, is not generated from personal conviction; she has yet to establish for herself a system of personal integrity, to decide what it means to be 'Marigold Green'. Somehow ending up in bed with Terrapin, one of the boys at her father's school, she says:

> 'I was quite enchanted with myself. I had always thought I had very strong views on sexual morality. I found I had nothing of the kind. Perhaps I should have been more carefully Prepared for Confirmation and not just relied on being father's daughter.'[39]

Yet, immediately following on this realisation, which removes the prop she has just become conscious of having used (i.e. her self-definition in terms of her father and his beliefs), there is a new awareness of precariousness, and an inner being stirs and claims attention. Terrapin tells her to take off her dress, but 'I found that I said no'. He turns to put off the light, but she knows, instinctively, that 'the light must not go out', and that she is in danger, through her lack of self-awareness, of losing herself before she has even had a chance to know the present self. It is too soon to become something different; like Alice with her pieces of mushroom, she feels that control over changes to the self is necessary to survival. When she emerges unscathed from this ordeal, it is to a more balanced existence where she can be at peace with herself, and her world is symbolically made whole as well when Paula, who had gone away, returns to marry her father, filling a gap in Marigold's existence. She becomes a defined being in a rather more defined and circumscribed world.

Fictional children, in all the modern novels for children looked at so far, have had to cope with exposure to a decline in moral certitude, and have thus had to exert themselves more than nineteenth-century children in order to develop the quality of concreteness, something recognizably and uniquely themselves. But, as is made clear in other twentieth-century novels for children – as, for example, Alan Garner's *Red Shift* and *The Owl Service*, and Robert Cormier's *The Chocolate War* and its sequel *Beyond the Chocolate War* – trying to find and hold the self together in twentieth-century society can be more harrowing and desperate a task than it is for the Marlows, Bilgewater, or the Grey family in *The Greengage Summer*, all of whom have at least some sort of sanity and recourse to kindness.

In the two Garner novels mentioned above, the case is different. The young protagonists inhabit narratives in which the rules governing children's literature have changed – to use Fred Inglis's phrase, there is no longer any 'promise of happiness'. The individual's hope of survival and peace lies in his ability to become a whole person, but this hope is a tenuous one and often frustrated, because the forms of authority that still exist have been rejected, and that very rejection has rendered yet more impotent and pathetic the erstwhile authorities of society, home and family. It is not a mere happening of chance that the hippie movement of the Sixties, so loudly and shrilly anti-estab-lishment in their mores and minds, should coincide with the movement within children's literature that threw down the barricades of class and should also decide to take as its subject matter the prob-lems of a traumatised young generation which owed its ills to the corruption and hypocrisy of the uncaring, bellicose, older generation.

There developed a tendency for the older generation, once depicted in fiction as sage, wise beings and the natural guardians of youth, to be shown as neurotic and unhelpful people,[40] people with problems of their own which incapacitated them and threatened to turn the young generation into sad replicas of themselves. The energetic anger of youth was directed at parents and representatives of authority, concentrating on the need for escape, the need for a brave new world.[41] The unfortunate aspect of this anti-establishmentarianism is that in discrediting authority and moral standards, the individual then finds himself with one less resource to turn to when in pain; because he has denied the power of God, parents and society to change things, to be of help, he is, for all practical purposes, alone. The rejected adult is powerless to help, for he cannot even get near the child.

Garner's *Red Shift* (1973), through the juxtaposition of three narratives, each set in a different historical period, shows the utter necessity for the citizen of the present to achieve ontological substantiality, and the near-utter helplessness of the individual in this matter because of the crumbling society he lives in. The first of the three narratives is set in the time of the Roman legions in Britain, the second at the time of the English Civil War, the third in the present. They are linked by the male protagonist in each case, Macey, Thomas and Tom, all of whom the reader understands to be analogues of each other (they are each of them subject to some kind of fits); but though the earlier two appear to have some psychic awareness of the future, Tom seems not to know of the others' existence at all. Macey is a berserker, and during the frenzy and Thomas's fits, they are aware of 'bluesilvers' ('I saw.' 'Saw what?' 'Blue. Silver. And red.'), which, the reader realises at the end of the novel, are the trains that represent connection and communication between the isolated.

During the novel, the trains are running, communicating, bringing Tom and his girlfriend Jan together, and they represent the hope that the expanding universe is still bridgeable, still ultimately knowable, that places and people are still reachable, and that the individual is not completely 'enisled' and forever alone. The moving trains are the rushing 'bluesilvers'; it is only when at the end, after Jan and Tom have found it impossible to bridge the gap between them, and the train stops for Jan to enter and leave forever, that one sees them clearly: 'The red doors closed. The blue and silver train. She stood at the window.' Communication is at an end. Tom and Macey can glimpse their analogues in other frames, can see the 'bluesilvers', and this ability to see each other is intended, I think, to indicate their sense of continuity and community. They are spiritual kin of each other, and belong in times when kinship and community still carry significance. In the church at Mow Cop Tom reads: 'Let there be no strife: for we be brethren,' a line also shouted by Macey in one of his berserker trances; and this line carries that sense of community which is missing in the present. For two men in the past, the word 'individuality' still retains its older meaning, opposite to that it bears in the present time. As mentioned in the introduction, this older meaning is that of 'inseparability', 'indivisibility', that one could not be divided from the larger body; today, it means the opposite: one who stands out from the masses.

Tom, however, is the child of his time, when individuality, whatever its benefits, also conveys a sense of isolation, apartness and alienation from society. (The Beatles' songs of the 1960s are full of this theme, in particular 'Eleanor Rigby', with its refrain about the lonely people and their lack of belonging.) The title *Red Shift* is a term taken from astronomy. The phenomenon of 'red shift', which the *OED* defines as the 'displacement of spectral lines to longer wavelengths in radiation from distant galaxies etc.', implies a growing distance between galaxies; and in the context of the novel, this comes to signify the dying of contact and communication between individuals. Tom belongs to a later period of history, one which is fragmenting and rendering everything less knowable, and his isolation renders him incommunicado from his analogues in other, less fragmented times.

Images of fragmentation and disintegration are found in the book, perhaps most memorably on the occasion where Tom presses his palms against the window till the glass breaks: 'He held the fragments like crushed ice. Shallow, pale lines crazed his skin. He felt nothing.'[42] Even the narrative structure of the text – with sections of each story interrupting each other, making it impossible to sustain a continuous line of story – suggests fragmentation, the failure of continuity. It is a text of the present, even as Tom is a citizen of the present; one of the ways in which the novel attempts to hint at the cracking context, the failure of traditional, enclosed narrative forms along with all traditional structures, is to show itself torn and broken as well. The narrative cannot speak of this openly: like Tom himself, it has been rendered inarticulate by the weight of all it has to say, by the accumulation of knowledge and sorrow, and it can only embody, formally, its own unspeakable meanings.

Barbara Hardy in *Forms of Feeling in Victorian Fiction* refers to a term coined by Ernst Robert Curtius: 'the topos of inexpressibility'. This, she says, 'is the device which in one stroke expresses powerful feeling and the impossibility of expressing it:' I cannot tell you how much, 'I cannot say what', 'Words fail me'.[43] This applies to Tom; his feelings exceed his ability to speak of them, and this disability is the result of too much knowledge, too much analysis, too much paralysis.[44] The text, too, is made dumb, unable to speak, for it is about the inability to speak and communicate, which is self-mutilating. The text can only gesture towards the truth of the matter, and because systems of understanding have broken down, the reader, too, is often bewildered, unable to comprehend what the novel and Tom cannot say.

The novel depicts a time in which the principles of enclosure or authority have broken down and become incapable of imparting comfort to the lost and alienated. The mood is almost existentialist:

nothing is fixed or significant and personal choice is so wide as to be terrifying. For the earlier analogues of Tom there is moral support to be derived from their respective communities in their search for identity and wholeness, even in the midst of chaos and confusion. Macey is upheld even in his distress over his fits by the thought that even this aberrant side to his being is of use to his 'brilliant mates', that his loss of self whenever he berserks, is at least not without meaning, for it enables him to protect his friends' lives. The loyalty to each other of the members of the community in which Thomas lives is also made manifest by the way in which, when the soldiers have overrun his village and demand that John Fowler be surrendered, the men keep silent and are killed for it even though they have no great love for him – it is simply that he is a part of them. In other words, their social identity is a form of stability.

Tom, however, has no such support, and neither has his girlfriend, Jan; and their importance to each other is accentuated because of this lack. Jan's parents are counsellors to other people, but ironically, are never there for her. Tom's parents are prurient emotional vampires who feed off him. Neil Philip, author of *A Fine Anger*, a sharp critical study of Garner's entire literary output, has noted Garner's use of modern electronic equipment to indicate distance between people of the twentieth century.[45] Though Jan's parents are counsellors, their counselling is impersonal, conducted through the medium of telephone and tape recorder.

'How can they stay sane, doing that work?'
'They never let themselves be involved. It's the training.'
'But they're always on call, especially with that thing.'
'What, the Tam? There are patients who'd rather talk to a phone than to Mum or Dad.'
'Get away.'
'They would ... A tape recorder doesn't want things from them.'
'A cassette confessor ... An automatic answering divine. God in the machine.'
'Don't be daft,' said Jan. 'It's only something that helps two people help a lot of others. It means they're never out of touch.'[46]

Though telephones are supposed to be a medium of communication, they enable Jan's parents to keep an emotional distance from those whom they counsel. God and the comfort of religion have been de-authorised, and instead of a golden calf, modern man has set up the electronic device to replace God. As Tom jeers, instead of a human priest they now have 'a cassette confessor … an automatic answering divine'. For Tom as well, his headphones are a means of distancing others, shutting them out, and the television turned up enables him not to hear his family.

At the root of Tom's fragmented personality is his loneliness, which is inspired by his family, his distance from people, and what appears to him to be a world far too open, one he is incapable of ever knowing fully because knowledge is always accumulating and the limits of the knowable receding. 'The boundary's undefined,' he says. The exposed individual sits shivering in the midst of chaos. Tom is supremely conscious of himself in direct relation to the expanding (and thus growing ever less knowable and familiar) universe, and fearful of the arbitrariness that brought Jan to him, because such arbitrariness fuels his suspicion that there is no truly secure, fixed thing around which he can crystallise a self:

> 'I love you.'
> 'Yes.' He stopped walking. 'That's all we can be sure of. We are, at this moment, somewhere between the M6 going to Birmingham and the M33 going nowhere. Don't leave me.'
> 'Hush.' said Jan. 'It's all right.'
> 'It's not. How did we meet? How could we? Between the M6 and the M33. Think of the odds. In all space and time. I'm scared.'[47]

As is shown in this conversation, Jan's love is the stable kernel of his existence, all the surety he has that there is any certainty in the world. Their truth to each other in the land of dreams without light or love or certitude or help for pain, is all there is to hold on to.

> 'For the moment, I have believed that there is a single person in all time and space who is honest, and that I have found her. I have believed that she accepted me, and that I could trust her. I have believed in perfection.'[48]

His belief in the unchanging nature of that love is all that stops him from falling apart, the sole hope for his future integrity and wholeness. 'I'm panicking,' he says, 'Love me. … Love is not love which alters when it alteration finds.' This quote is the only hint that Tom can give, the only way he can express his problem of a non-concrete or fixed self. Neil Philip has noted the underlying 'Tam Lin' story in

Red Shift, where the heroine has to take Tam Lin from the fairies and restore him to being by keeping hold of him no matter what shapes he is forced to take. Tom can only hint as much to Jan: that her love must not change no matter how he changes. Should she be able to do this, she will return him to himself. In the story of Macey in Roman Britain, the unnamed girl who is Jan's analogue is able to hold him through everything, which redeems him for himself. For Tom, however, this is not to be.

Jan too has need of security, for though she has a home and family, the family are never around. 'I've always wanted to hold something that matters,' she says when on one of their outings they find the votive axe that has been Thomas's 'thunderstone' and also Macey's possession. This 'thing that matters,' Jan calls the Bunty, and it becomes the symbol of security and continuance for both of them. Jan's family move away from the locality, a fact which undermines what little security Tom has left. Her home, formerly an emblem of safety and permanence (his family live in a caravan) is suddenly 'only a waiting room'.

One Saturday, as Tom waits at the station for Jan, he sees her with another man who, it turns out, she met in Germany before meeting Tom, and with whom she has had an affair. The knowledge of this destroys Tom, and he sells the Bunty to a museum, thus threatening Jan's spiritual wholeness as well. 'You sold what I'd lacked,' she says accusingly, but he takes away the last vestige of symbolic meaning invested in the Bunty: 'The axe was only a chunk of diorite.' Jan understands intuitively then that his sale of the Bunty was half-deliberate, a piece of revenge. She knows that in return for what he feels she has done to him, robbing him of his faith in her that was also his nucleus of self, he wants likewise to mutilate her, stop her from attaining wholeness of being and identity. Her response is designed to tell him that she recognises this: 'It would like to go now, please. It feels sick. It's had enough. It has a train to catch.' She is Jan no longer, only 'it', an object. Identity has been obliterated.

The fact of Tom's lack of wholeness and integrated coherent being emerges out of his incoherent conversation, especially as the narrative progresses and his failure to trust Jan riddles his confidence and sanity. He finds it almost, impossible, to communicate with anyone: 'He ran out of words,' Jan says early on in the book. When he writes letters to Jan they come in code, removing understanding by one degree, making communication more difficult. There is no *real* Tom; all his words are quotes. He quotes often from *King Lear*, words of madness that express him without their being his own. In their final conversation, nearly every sentence is a quote, a sign that 'Tom' no longer exists. He is without words, without being, an empty vehicle for the words of others.

Garner is not the only writer for children today whose works show forth the bleakness of the modern environment and the damage this can do to the self. Robert Cormier's novels are perhaps the most depressing and despairing there are for children today. The world no longer holds any havens of safety for the child anywhere, and the threat of disintegration of being is no longer insidious, but overwhelmingly present. In the over-exposed and open world of Cormier's novels, it seems that to triumph and maintain integrity and self is impossible. *I am the Cheese*, which was first published in 1977, is about the eradication of personality which is brought about by impersonal and uncaring authorities to whom the idea of being and humanity means absolutely nothing. Adam Farmer's father used to be a jounalist, who helped uncover a case of corruption in the government and testified against certain people; he therefore had to go into hiding with his family lest they be killed by others who fear exposure at the hands of Mr Farmer.

The structure of the text, as with *Red Shift*, is broken up and discontinuous, reflecting different levels of consciousness on the part of Adam Farmer, and also his disordered and broken personality. Sections of the narrative consist of the memories of the child, and other sections represent interviews with the state psychologist, who claims to be trying to help Adam reintegrate himself, to disinter the past from his present confusion and reconstruct his identity. However, as the reader discovers, the state psychologist is only there to ascertain whether Adam can recall anything else that may be useful to the state about the case which drove his family into hiding in the first place, and when he discovers that Adam knows nothing and can be of no further use, he submits a memo on the case recommending that Adam be 'eliminated' as the logical conclusion to the obliteration of self that the state has been cold-bloodedly undertaking.

The title of the novel, *I am the Cheese*, is doubly revealing. The title is taken from the nursery rhyme, 'The farmer in the Dell', with the obvious reference to their surname, 'Farmer'. In the rhyme, the cheese ends up first 'standing alone', and then being eaten; this is what happens to Adam, who is increasingly isolated as his family is first separated from their relatives and friends when they go into anonymity and a new life, and then as his parents are killed off in a supposed road accident, which is actually manufactured by the state. His personality and being is digested by the acid of what happens to him, and by the brainwashing he undergoes at the hands of the psychologist. But the title, with its equation of being: I am = the cheese, is also speaking about the erasure of self in a different way, about the substitution of identity that takes place, convincing the child he is something which in fact he is not, which substitution inculcates in him paranoia and fear.

Adam finds himself unable to distinguish clearly even in his memories, between his real identity, the assumed identity and the brainwashed identity, and this mental confusion infects the reader as well, inspiring a kind of terror in the reading of the text. Adam one day discovers that the name he goes under is in fact not his real name at all; his real name is Paul Delmonte. It also transpires that the powers-that-be had attempted to disguise the Delmontes, not only by getting rid of their surname (which shows their Italian origins), but also their religion: they are down on paper as Protestants when they are in fact Catholics. He also discovers that he has two birth certificates, one of which changes his birthday altogether, so that he is left with a sensation of unreality, feeling as if he has no real existence at all. In a similar fashion, his parents have been changed too. His mother especially, has altered from a calm and content woman to one who is forever peering out of windows from behind drawn curtains, apparently safely enclosed in anonymity but psychologically exposed and laid bare, feeling watched all the time.

The failure of the child, even one who *is* enough, to survive exposure to a corrupt society is also the subject of Cormier's two novels, *The Chocolate War*, and its sequel, *Beyond the Chocolate War*. These are deeply defeatist writings. The first is set in a Catholic school which is infested by a Mafia-like society called the Vigils. Brother Leon, the teacher in charge, holds a supposed charity sale of chocolates every year, which he and the Vigils, of course, benefit from. The story again looks at the subject of 'being enough'. Jerry Renault, the 'hero', makes a stand and refuses to sell the chocolates; the book is about the pressure which is increasingly brought to bear on him to do so. Behind the bare fiction of chocolate selling, the story is really, of course, about the attempt to corrupt the being of the child. Here, vigilance is not exerted by the adult guardians on behalf of Jerry: he is on his own.

The war is not about chocolate but about whether the child will be sufficient in himself to resist the attempt to drag him down. Jerry is 'enough', in that he does not give in, and never goes under, morally speaking, to Archie Costello and his thugs. None the less, being 'enough' in moral terms is still somehow unproductive of victory. In a fight with Archie at the close of the narrative, in which every reader confidently expects to find Jerry 'vindicated' and Archie crawling out of the arena the loser, Jerry is the one carried off half-dead. The evil flourishes like the green bay tree, and Jerry has to leave the school. The moral warfare continues in the sequel. Patterns of expectation set up by traditional, 'protected' children's novels, where the reader looks for moral triumph, are again exploded. Jerry, still courageous at the start of the novel, determined with his friend to bring down the Vigils, is defeated yet again, and this time dies in spirit though he remains uncorrupted.

The novels which I have been looking at so far examine the issue of 'being enough' in a world no longer bound about by authority and certitude, and attempt to trace the quest for being in such clouded contexts (the degree of clouding differs, of course, from novel to novel). They also indicate, occasionally, the elements of guidance to the child in search of identity that have replaced the older, plainer, system of ethics which was used by the eighteenth- and nineteenth-century child. These novels in their own way bemoan the passing of the security that came with the old order, even if that order was more stringent, less generous in the territorial space it allowed the child.

Conclusion (Contradiction)

An Introduction is to introduce people, but Christopher Robin and his friends, who have already been introduced to you, are now going to say Good-bye. So this is the opposite. When we asked Pooh what the opposite of an Introduction was, he said 'The what of a what?' which didn't help us as much as we had hoped, but luckily Owl kept his head and told us that the Opposite of an Introduction, my dear Pooh, was a Contradiction; and, as he is very good at long words, I am sure that that's what it is.

A.A. Milne, *The House at Pooh Corner*

In very many ways, children's literature today may be considered an emancipated one which enjoys most of the privileges that positive exposure can bring. The concept of *being* within children's literature has expanded. It does not any longer merely indicate the individual's conformity with standards of morality, spirituality or usefulness which a particular society in a particular time might decree, nor yet the obedient playing of a role designed by society. It is still a measure of worth, but the definition of worth has expanded to accommodate artistic creativity, the imaginative life, and in a way, the sheer *existence* of nature and people. People, in this new encompassing definition, *are*, and are worthy no matter which social class, race or IQ group they fall into. The socially deprived merit as much attention and are of as much value as those who are well-off, the Asian and African as much as the Caucasian, the mentally handicapped or the slow as much as the genius. Moreover, being no longer represents a static quality, but acts as an index of growth towards definition and shape. This expansion of the parameters of being is itself a testimony of emancipation.

Yet a few questions still need to be asked. The first, strangely enough, is whether this trend is altogether a good thing. In an age where people are extremely aggressive about what they deem to be their 'rights', the word 'freedom' possesses powerful resonances, and not everybody will readily concede that there should be any limits to what the child is free to experience and to know. Even if one allows that children should be permitted access to a world of violence and corruption, suffering and sex in literature, the failure to impose standards on writers who insist on taking these things as their subject matter must be considered a form of negligence. If writers contend that the child must have freedom to see and hear, then they have the responsibility of ensuring that the child emerge from the literary experience undiminished and unpolluted by doubt or fear of life and what it contains. They should not take cold from their exposure to the 'reality' of children's writers, should not be more distrustful of the world nor have their souls smudged by their reading.

Considered in this light, writers like Judy Blume and Robert Cormier are a menace to childhood. The popularity of that dreadful book, *Forever*, stems from its sexual explicitness; the writer obviously thinks that teenagers want to know about sex and feels justified in giving it to them in literary form by the present day contention that freedom is the right of the child. Yet, as Michele Landsberg has observed, the experience that is at the heart of the book is heartless, emotionally flat, a manual of teenage ineptness; it is about physical curiosity rather than poetry of the body and spirit, and surely damages the child in that it devalues and lessens the experience. This is exposure that is harmful and which (all in the name of freedom) the parent and publisher have not seen fit to guard the child from. *The Chocolate War* and its sequel are, similarly, exercises in emancipation which demonstrate that liberty can go too far. They are not thought-provoking; they go beyond disturbing the sheltered child, for they threaten his peace of mind and the balance of justice and morality he should have. The books show corruption and terrorism without the countering forces of justice and kindliness; the villains flourish and the good are defeated, and this harsh exposure to the adult world has left the child no spar to cling to.

Another question is whether children's literature as it stands today can truly be considered emancipated. Fictional children have been released from their iconography. They no longer have sweetness and light thrust on them, but can be mischievous without fearing instant hell-fire: Richmal Crompton's character William attests to this. With the horizons of possibility set further away, the imagination can roam in other dimensions, both scientific and moral. Furthermore, as children's literature has been set free from overt purpose, humour has entered into its creation, and laughter is an immensely liberating experience. Girls and boys are no longer forced into gender-based roles, but may find fulfilment in creative activity that has nothing to do with traditional conceptions of how girls and boys should behave and become. Both sexes are also enabled to partake of each other's identity. Tyke Tiler, for instance, in Gene Kemp's *The Turbulent Term of Tyke Tiler*, turns out at the story's end to have been a girl all along. Noel Streatfeild's Petrova, in *Ballet Shoes*, aspires to become a mechanic or pilot; Angus, in *The Bell Family*, wants to become a ballet dancer. Willmouse, in Godden's *The Greengage Summer*, is allowed by his understanding mother to wear a muff and dress dolls; his mother defends him to his disgusted uncle, saying that he is not a sissy.

All this stands on the credit side of the sheet. However, the burden of political and ideological correctness is a bind on children's literature which it could well do without. I am not saying that children should not be taught tolerance, consideration, egalitarianism and a consciousness of the needs of the environment, but that when these factors work to the exclusion of others, literature is in danger of returning to a state of unhealthy enclosure. Literature that embodies these principles is to be praised, but that which exists only to preach about racial equality and saving the whales is not literature but propaganda, and the two should be differentiated. Nicholas Stuart Gray's work in general is marvellously innovative and exciting, but his *Wardens of the Weir*, despite its apparently magical plot, is aimed at making children environment-conscious, and is deadly dull. Literature that is written solely in order to inculcate feminist principles is as limited as that written solely to inculcate religious ones. Books like *Little Black Sambo* have come under heavy criticism for their purportedly racist text, and are consequently not available in children's bookshops any longer. Though I have not been able to ascertain this from any printed source, I have been told of publishing policies in the Sixties and Seventies which punished the writer of stories about children with a privileged lifestyle. While the need was certainly there for a literature about children who did not own their own ponies and travel about in chauffeur-driven cars, but went to comprehensives and had to work part-time in order to earn some money, such policies (if this is true) have a tinge of reverse snobbery about them. One wonders, however, whether such vigilance in the cause of racial and social correctness is a trifle misplaced; if it is, then the wrong kind of censorship is being exercised, and enclosure of a negative cast is at work.

On the whole, however, the positive outweighs the negative. By far the greatest benefit to children's literature from its present aesthetic of freedom has been the wealth of fantasy literature that has grown up since fantasy attained admittance as an approved genre of writing for children. Today, classics in this genre abound: Lloyd Alexander's 'Prydain Chronicles', Susan Cooper's *The Dark is Rising* pentology, Pat O'Shea's *The Hounds of the Morrigan*, the short stories of Joan Aiken and Nicholas Stuart Gray, the marvellously imaginative and amusing novels of Diana Wynne Jones, Michael Ende's *The Neverending Story* (translated from the German) and so on. What precisely the child gets out of reading these highly magical books may be difficult to ascertain in quantifiable terms. But, apart from the quality of self-forgetfulness which Wordsworth noted right at the start of the nineteenth-century,

> Oh! give us once again the wishing cap
> Of Fortunatus, and the invisible coat
> Of Jack the Giant-Killer, Robin Hood,
> And Sabra in the forest with St. George!
> The child whose love is here, at least, doth reap
> One precious gain, that he forgets himself[1]

literature which has a flavour of the fantastic about it also accomplishes other things in the heart and mind of the child who is enabled to hear the horns of Elfland faintly blowing. Spiritual truths can be offered and accepted in a form which is non-didactic; the heart of the child experiences courage and pity and all the other greatnesses, which the world today finds more difficult to discuss in plain language than it once did, and emerges enriched in soul and being.

Notes

Introduction

1. Gaston Bachelard, *The Poetics of Space*, tr. Maria Jolas (Boston, 1969), pp. 211–12.
2. Frances Hodgson Burnett, *The Secret Garden* (Harmondsworth, Middlesex, 1951), p. 157.
3. Job, 1: 9–10 reads: 'Then Satan answered the Lord, "Does Job fear God for nought? Hast Thou not put a hedge about him and his house and all that he has, on every side?"' (This, and all future Biblical quotation, is from the Revised Standard Version of the Bible).
4. In Job 3: 23, Job cries out, 'What light is given to a man whose way is hid, whom God has hedged in?'
5. Antonia Forest, *The Cricket Term* (London, 1974), p. 80. All future references will be to this edition.
6. Edward Salmon, 'Should Children have a Special Literature?' reprinted from *The Parent's Review*, 5 [1890], in *A Peculiar Gift* (ed. Lance Salway) (Harmondsworth, Middlesex, 1976), p. 334.
7. Anon. 'Children's Literature', reprinted from *The Quarterly Review*, 13 (26 January 1860), ibid., p. 309.
8. Ibid., p. 314.
9. Oscar Wilde, 'The Happy Prince' [1888], reprinted in *Complete Shorter Fiction* (ed. Isobel Murray), (Oxford, 1979), p. 97.
10. D. H. Lawrence, 'Chaos in Poetry', reprinted in *Selected Literary Criticism* (ed. Beal) (London, 1955), p. 90.
11. Friedrich Nietzsche, *The Birth of Tragedy* (rev. 1886 edition), tr. Shaun Whiteside (Harmondsworth, Middlesex, 1993), p. 4.
12. Emily Brontë, *Wuthering Heights* [1847]: I am quoting from the Oxford World Classics edition (ed. Ian Jack), which follows the Clarendon Press edition of 1976. All future references will be to this edition (Oxford, 1995), p. 46.
13. The following summary of ideas may be found on pp. 267–8 of 'Jung, Literature and Literary Criticism', by Terence Dawson, in *The Cambridge Companion to Jung*, eds Polly Young-Eisendrath and Terence Dawson (Cambridge, 1997). I have applied the model over a time-frame much shrunken from that originally given. The section following immediately on this either quotes directly from the article or paraphrases sections of its argument.
14. I have summarised the five stages of the model here, though the finer points of the whole argument have been lost. The article is well worth reading in its entirety. It begins with a state where individuals have 'little or no concept of themselves as beings distinct from what society expects of them'. It then moves through stages where the individual begins (perhaps painfully) to separate himself from the 'other', construct his own

ethical/moral code, testing this against that held by society, arriving at 'the realization that the aura and authority with which one has invested all the collective norms and expectations within which one lives are of [one's] own making . . .'. This may result in alienation, for, as Dawson goes on to say, 'divested of all its mana, the world can seem utterly devoid of either certainty or meaning'. The fifth stage given 'begins with the initiation of a fresh dialectic with oneself, a conscious questioning of our innate tendencies, especially those of which we are least aware and which are revealed to us only through a searching analysis of our dreams and waking fantasies. The end of this long process is to know oneself not as a rebel or outsider, but as the specific human being that one is within one's own society. In this way, the process comes full circle, for the goal is a new integration with society, utterly different from the first stage by virtue of one's full consciousness of one's individual nature, function, and limitations'. Ibid., p. 267.

15. Henry Handel Richardson, *The Getting of Wisdom* [1910], (London, 1960), p. 86. Citation is from the Heinemann edition. All future references will be to this edition.
16. William Wordsworth, *The Excursion*, Book iv, ll. 1208–66.
17. William Wordsworth, *The Prelude*, Book i, ll. 17, 29–30.
18. Matthew Arnold, 'Heinrich Heine', in *Essays in Criticism* (1st Series, London, 1902), p. 161.
19. Northrop Frye, *The Secular Scripture* (Massachusetts and London, 1976), p. 166.
20. Mark Twain, *The Adventures of Huckleberry Finn* [1884]. Page references are to the University of California Press edition by Walter Blair. (London, 1985), p. 362.
21. Reprinted from *The Quarterly Review*, 13/26 (January, 1860) in *A Peculiar Gift* (ed. Lance Salway, Harmondsworth, 1976), p. 310.
22. See J. S. Bratton, *The Impact of Victorian Children's Fiction* (London, 1981), pp. 31–4.
23. Basil Willey, *Nineteenth Century Studies* (London, 1949), p. 52.
24. C. E. Montague, *Disenchantment* [1922] (Plymouth, 1968), p. 134.
25. Antonia Forest, *The Thuggery Affair* (London, 1965), p. 182.
26. Ibid., p. 182.
27. Humphrey Carpenter's *The Oxford Companion to Children's Literature* (Oxford, 1984), says of *Gumble's Yard*, that it was 'one of the first British children's books to try to deal with the subject of 20-cent. urban poverty' p. 233.
28. Ruth ap Roberts, in her fine study of Anthony Trollope's ethical stance, entitled *Anthony Trollope: Artist and Moralist*, has charted the rise of relativist morality and the rise of the concept of situational ethics in the nineteenth century. She notes for instance, the philosophical changes in the concept of casuistry from its initial pejorative overtones to its later implication of acceptance of new standards of right and wrong dependent upon specific predicament and individual perception and so forth.

Chapter 1

1. Felicity Hughes, 'Children's Literature: Theory and Practice' reprinted in *Children's Literature*, ed. Peter Hunt (London, 1990), p. 71.
2. E. E. Kellett spoke of 'the (largely imaginary) prudery and reticence of the Victorians [as being] chiefly due to this habit of family reading. It would take a tough father to read some modern novels aloud to his children.' *Early Victorian England* (London, 1934), p. ii, 48 n.
3. Sarah Trimmer, 'Observations on the Changes Which Have Taken Place in Books for Children and Young Persons', *The Guardian of Education* [1802]. Reprinted in *A Peculiar Gift*, ed. Lance Salway (Harmondsworth, Middlesex, 1976), p. 20.
4. George Moore complained in *Literature at Nurse or Circulating Morals* (London, 1885), p. 18, that 'never in any age or country have writers been asked to write under such restricted conditions.'
5. Charles Dickens, *Our Mutual Friend* [1864–5] (Oxford, 1989), p. 129.
6. According to Eugenia A. Ellison: 'Poets like Wordsworth grasped at the child as a figure of the ideal human condition, and it is due in large part to such writers that we have today a sizable body of child-centred literature and the twentieth century is continually more preoccupied with the analysis of the child.' *The Innocent Child in Dickens and Other Writers* (Texas, 1982), p. 11. While it is true that the emergence of a child-centred literature may in part be attributed to Wordsworth and the other poets of the Romantic school, the view of childhood as representing an ideal human condition and the portrayal of the child as an innocent was not directly responsible for the major changes which took place in children's literature in the nineteenth century.
7. The figure of the child did not of course disappear altogether from the English novel, but after the 1860s, it was not to figure quite as prominently. In a way, the American novel may be said to have taken up the figure of the child where the English novel had left off; Tom Sawyer was 'born' in 1876, and Huckleberry Finn and Maisie were soon to follow.
8. Cf. David Grylls, *Guardians and Angels* (London, 1978), pp. 24–8.
9. Cf. Harvey Darton, *Children's Books in England* (third edition, revised by Brian Alderson, Cambridge, 1982), pp. 51–67 on Puritan children's literature.
10. Quoted by David Grylls, *Guardians and Angels* (London, 1978), p. 26.
11. Gillian Avery, 'The Puritans and their Heirs' in *Children and Their Books*, eds Gillian Avery and Julia Briggs (Oxford, 1991), p. 106.
12. Juliet Dusinberre writes: 'Schiller, who had suggested connections between the child and the artist, shared Rousseau's idealism about children; both men influenced Wordsworth, whose "Intimations of Immortality" must be almost the most quoted text in the nineteenth century, appearing with wearisome regularity every time children are mentioned.' Ibid., p. 14. Eugenia Ellison also says that 'Wordsworth's Ode became a center of reference for writers of the nineteenth century as well as for many of the twentieth century.' *op. cit.*, p. 22.
13. Cf. James Holt McGavran, Jr.'s chapter 'Catechist and Visionary: Watts and Wordsworth in "We Are Seven" and the "Anecdote for Fathers"', in

Romanticism and Children's Literature in Nineteenth-Century England, ed. James Holt McGavran (Athens and London).

14. Susan Wolfson, *The Questioning Presence: Wordsworth, Keats and the Interrogative Mode in Romantic Poetry* (Ithaca, 1986), p. 43.

15. Juliet Dusinberre, *Alice to the Lighthouse* (London, 1987), p. 222.

16. Peter Coveney, *op. cit.*, p. 68.

17. Victor Watson, 'The Possibilities of Children's Fiction' in *After Alice*, eds Morag Styles, Eve Bearne and Victor Watson (London, 1992), p. 15.

18. Cf. Jerome Buckley, *Season of Youth* (Cambridge, Massachusetts, 1974), p. 19: '... to Wordsworth, the child was an entity in himself responsive to experiences that might alter the entire direction of his growing mind and eventually influence for better or for worse his whole maturity.'

19. *The Oxford English Dictionary* defines *glory* as 'resplendent majesty ... effulgence of heavenly light, imagined unearthly beauty' and so forth, all of which cannot be said to constitute precise descriptions of a state.

20. John Beer, in *Wordsworth in Time*, has referred to the 'aionic freedom' of the child 'dancing on a mountain top'. (London, 1979), p. 114.

21. J. A. Froude, *The Nemesis of Faith* [1849] (London and New York, 1904), p. 116.

22. George Eliot, *The Mill on the Floss* [1860]. Page references are to the Clarendon edition, ed. Gordon S. Haight (Oxford, 1979), p. 168.

23. F. H. Burnett, *Little Lord Fauntleroy* [1886] (New York and London, 1976), p. 95. Page references are to the Garland edition.

24. Ibid., p. 109.

25. Eleanor Porter, *Pollyanna* [1913] (Harmondsworth, Middlesex, 1969), p.152. All future references will be to this edition.

26. Kathleen Tillotson, *Novels of the Eighteen-Forties* (Oxford, 1954), p. 50.

27. Charles Dickens, Author's Preface to Third Edition, *Oliver Twist* [1837], ed. Kathleen Tillotson (Oxford, 1966), pp. lxi – lxii. All future references will be to this edition.

28. Ibid., p. lxii.

29. Ibid., p. lxiii.

30. Ibid., p. 7.

31. Janet Todd, *Sensibility: An Introduction* (London and New York, 1986), p. 3.

32. *Op. cit.*, p. 9.

33. Ibid., p. 29.

34. J. Hillis Miller in *Charles Dickens: the World of his Novels*, says, 'No novel could be more completely dominated by an imaginative complex of claustrophobia.' (Cambridge, Massachussetts, 1958), p. 43.

35. Charles Dickens, *The Old Curiosity Shop* [1841] (London, 1951), p. 3. Page references are to the Oxford University Press edition.

36. Ibid., p .3.

37. Ibid., p. 10.

38. F. H. Burnett, *The Secret Garden* (London, 1911), p. 179.

39. Peter Coveney, *The Image of Childhood*, p. 107.

40. Ibid., p. 82.

41. George Levine writes: 'We can see how incompatible with the realist effort to be tough-minded, disenchanted and faithful to the textures of experience was her [Charlotte Brontë's] commitment to the life of feeling.' *The*

Realistic Imagination (London, 1981), p. 182. I don't think this is incompatible; feeling and reason are intended to balance each other in *Jane Eyre*. Moderation and reason are supposed to order her feelings and to help direct them, the marriage of moderation and passion engendering the character.

42. *Op. cit.*, p. 37.
43. Ibid., p. 3.
44. Charles Dickens, *Master Humphrey's Clock* [1840] (Oxford, 1958), p. 8.
45. *Op. cit.*, p. 27.
46. Ibid., pp. 13–14.
47. Ibid., pp. 3–4.
48. Ibid., p. 39.
49. Ibid., p. 40.
50. In this context, it is interesting to recall Jerome Beatty's comment that '*Jane Eyre* conflates the themes and conventions of the "high" Romantic/ Byronic with those of the "lower", domestic/ Wordsworthian; by doing so it effects an "horizon change", a readjustment of expectations among novel readers that makes it an important literary landmark.' 'Jane Eyre at Gateshead: Mixed Signals in the Text and Context' in *Victorian Literature and Society*, eds J. R. Kincaid and A. J. Kuhn (Ohio, 1984). p. 168. Not only are tropes and conventions of two different traditions conflated, but also two different images of childhood.
51. *Op. cit.*, p. 37.
52. Ibid., p. 131.
53. 'She once told her sisters that they were wrong – even morally wrong – in making their heroines beautiful as a matter of course. They replied that it was impossible to make a heroine interesting on any other terms. Her answer was, "I will prove to you that you are wrong; I will show you a heroine as plain and small as myself, who shall be as interesting as any of yours." Hence Jane Eyre, said she in telling the anecdote . . .' Quoted by Elizabeth Gaskell in her *The Life of Charlotte Brontë*, ed. Alan Shelston (Harmondsworth, 1975), p. 308.
54. *Op. cit.*, p. 9.
55. Ibid., p. 12.
56. Ibid., p. 13.
57. Ibid., p. 20.
58. Ibid., p. 38.
59. Ibid., pp. 39–40.
60. E. Nesbit, *The Enchanted Castle* [1907] (London, 1964), p. 3.

Chapter 2

1. Dr. Masao Miyoshi, in his book *The Divided Self; A Perspective on the Literature of the Victorians* (New York, 1969), is concerned with showing the Victorian individual to be at war with himself, and discussing the Victorian's sense of alienation which is frequently expressed in the tropes of the split personality, perhaps best exemplified in the Jekyll and Hyde syndrome. I have borrowed his phrase 'the divided self' to indicate, in

addition to these ideas, a concept of being and selfhood that is compart-
mentalized in categories marked 'social', 'moral', and so forth. The fact of
such compartmentalization distinguishes between aspects of the self and
emphasises disintegration rather than wholeness; this is a form of analysis:
breakdown, which militates against the making of an integrated self,
where all aspects of being are conjoined.

2. See in this context T. E. Hulme, who writes of 'the search after an austerity,
monumental stability and permanence, a perfection and rigidity' which
leads to 'the use of forms which can almost be called geometrical'.
Speculations (London, 1987), p. 9.

3. Cf. Walter E. Houghton, *The Victorian Frame of Mind* (New Haven, 1957),
pp. 343–5.

4. Ira Bruce Nadel, 'The Mansion of Bliss' in *Children's Literature*, 10 (New
Haven and London, 1982), pp. 33–4.

5. Ibid., p. 35.

6. Claudia Nelson, *Boys will be Girls* (New Brunswick and London, 1991),
p. 143.

7. T. E. Hulme, *Speculations*, pp. 50–1.

8. André Gide, *Oscar Wilde: A Study* (trans. Stuart Mason) (Oxford, 1905),
pp. 27–8.

9. Cf. Houghton, *Victorian Frame of Mind*, p. 155.

10. P. L. Travers, *Mary Poppins* [1934] (London, 1971), p. 179. Page references
are to the Armada edition.

11. Quoted in Shirley Foster and Judy Simmons' *What Katy Read* (Houndmills,
Basingstoke, 1995), p. 86.

12. U. C. Knoepflmacher, 'The Balancing of Child and Adult: An Approach to
Victorian Fantasies for Children', in *Nineteenth Century Fiction*, 37 (March,
1983), p. 497.

13. Dennis Welland, in *Mark Twain in England*, says that Twain 'does this in
such a way to remind them [adults] even more sharply of what they now
are – no longer children, but adults who can watch the growing pains of
childhood with affectionate indulgence.' (London, 1978), p. 74. Welland
argues that the value of nostalgia is to remind parents of their responsibility of providing a secure framework for the child, but this is not
completely warranted by the author's avowed intention as quoted above.

14. J. A. Froude, *The Nemesis of Faith* [1849] (London and New York, 1904), p.
116.

15. Ibid., p. 30.

16. Nelson, *Boys will be Girls*, p. 150.

17. Marilyn Butler, *Romantics, Rebels and Reactionaries* (Oxford, 1981), p. 11.

18. Houghton, *Victorian Frame of Mind*, p. 10.

19. Tony Tanner, *Jane Austen* (London, 1986), p. 17.

20. Butler, *Romantics*, p. 96.

21. F. V. Bogel, *Literature and Insubstantiality in Later Eighteenth-Century
England* (New Jersey, 1984), p. 78.

22. Though Anne and Fanny feel themselves to be in danger of being
unplaced, they are, as Nina Auerbach notes in her essay, 'Jane Austen and
Romantic Imprisonment', in *Jane Austen: A Social Context*, ed. D.
Monaghan (London, 1981), p. 16, 'fixed points of knowledge' in their

environments, helping to restore order to their faltering societies.

23. Jane Austen, *Mansfield Park* [1814] (London, 1934), p. 35. Page references are to the Oxford University Press edition by R. W. Chapman.
24. Ibid., p. 395.
25. Ibid., p. 432.
26. Jane Austen, *Persuasion* [1818] (London, 1933), p. 5. Page references are to the Oxford University Press edition.
27. Ibid., p. 33.
28. Ruth Danon, *Work in the English Novel* (Kent, 1985), p. 1.
29. Maria Edgeworth, 'Lazy Lawrence' in *The Parent's Assistant* [1796] (London, 1907), p. 31.
30. And it is a calmly practical, not a charitable, world that Edgeworth shows. Benevolence by the rich is demonstrated by their willingness to give work, or the means to work, to the poor, and not money. As the lady who buys Jem's fossils says, it would encourage them to be lazy. Laura, the elder sister of Rosamund (of purple jar fame) constructs her charitable actions along such principles, giving the little lace maker money only for the express purpose of buying a new bobbin after hers has been spoiled, and ladies of *The Orphans* bestow flax on Mary to be spun.
31. Maria Edgeworth, 'Lazy Lawrence', *op. cit.*, p. 31.
32. Jane Austen, *Pride and Prejudice*, [1813] (London, 1932), p. 381. Page references are the Oxford University Press edition.
33. Quoted by Christopher Hill in *Reformation to Industrial Revolution* (Harmondsworth, Middlesex, 1969), p. 190.
34. Though Mrs. Charlesworth's *Ministering Children* has [rightly, I think] been disliked for its little do-good children who make their rounds of the cottages with baskets of food, there is a certain similarity in ethos to that found in Maria Edgeworth's novels where the children also perform in accordance with their conception of the 'duties' of acting particular to their class.
35. Thomas Carlyle, 'Signs of the Times' [1829], reprinted in *Selected Writings*, ed. Alan Shelston (Harmondsworth, Middlesex, 1971), p. 64.
36. See Butler, *Romantics*, pp. 102–3.
37. Houghton, *Victorian Frame of Mind*, p. 350.
38. Alan Sandison, *The Wheel of Empire* (New York, 1967), p. 104.
39. Cf. Houghton. *Victorian Frame of Mind*, pp. 341–7.
40. Hannah More, *Strictures on Female Education*, Ch. 1. Quoted by Vineta Colby in *Yesterday's Woman* (New Jersey, 1974), p. 121.
41. Isabella Beeton, *The Book of Household Management* [1860] (London, 1880), p. 17.
42. See J. S. Bratton's chapter entitled 'Books for Girls'; she writes, 'Here, too, the developments in fiction aimed at the moulding of aspirations and expectations to fit readers for a social role which was being newly defined.' *The Impact of Victorian Children's Fiction* (London, 1981), p. 148.
43. For further discussion of this see Judith Rowbotham's *Good Girls make Good Wives* (Oxford, 1989).
44. One finds the idea of self-sacrifice specifically linked to the need for a cohesive society in writings of the time. F. D. Maurice, elected to the post of Knightsbridge Professor of Casuistry, Moral Philosophy and Moral

Theology in 1866, wrote that '... no man ... no society, can stand upon selfishness. It must stand upon the opposite of selfishness ... So far as any family or any nation has ever been held together, it has been held by the might not of selfishness but of sacrifice.' *Epistles of St. John* [1857], p. 264; *Lectures on Social Morality* [1869], p. 385 ff.

45. *Little Women* was originally published in 2 volumes which appeared in October 1868 and April 1869, both called *Little Women*; the second part, was merely subtitled 'Part Second', though the English publication was called *Good Wives*. In 1880, the two volumes were combined into a single entity called *Little Women*, a format maintained in the Penguin edition [1989] edited by Professor Elaine Showalter from which page references will be taken hereafter. The second and third books in the series are *Little Men* (1871) and *Jo's Boys* (1886).

46. David Grylls, in *Guardians and Angels*, mentions the 'feeling of many Victorian authors that if maturity must lead to corruption it might be a kindness to kill children off – at least in the context of fiction' (London, 1978), p. 36. This suggests that the phenomenon of infant mortality so prominent in early children's fiction stems from a desire to keep children from growing up and losing the stable values of childhood, and has the effect of keeping them forever locked into childhood.

47. Charlotte Yonge, *The Daisy Chain* [1856] (London, 1902), p. 162. This, and all future page references, will be to the Macmillan edition.

48. Ibid., p. 162.

49. Girton, the first of the Cambridge colleges for women, was founded in 1869, Lady Margaret Hall in Oxford in 1878, and the University of London, though it first debated the idea of women students in 1862 (the vote resulted in a tie), and accepted 9 pioneering students in 1869, only received them on equal terms in 1879.

50. Charlotte Yonge, *The Daisy Chain*, p. 164.

51. Ibid., p. 164.

52. Ibid., p. 488.

53. Judith Rowbotham, *Good Girls make Good Wives* (Oxford, 1989), p. 34.

54. See also Shirley Foster and Judy Simmons' *What Katy Read* (Houndmills, Basingstoke, 1995) who make some similar points to those in the following section of *Little Women*, albeit within a feminist reading of the work. Their view that the text performs a delicate balancing act between the two value systems deserves serious consideration, though I myself feel that the balance gives way in favour of conformity in Jo's generation.

55. Letter to Sam May; quoted in Madeleine B. Stern's *Louisa May Alcott* (Norman, 1950), pp. 189–90.

56. L. M. Alcott, Preface to *Little Women* [1868] (London, 1907), p. vii.

57. Ibid., p. 72.

58. Ibid.

59. Ibid., p. 73.

60. Juliet Barker, *The Brontës: A Life in Letters* (Harmondsworth, Middlesex, 1997), p. 47.

61. L. M. Alcott, *Little Women*, p. 191.

62. L. M. Alcott, *Jo's Boys* [1886] (New York, 1962), p. 255. Page references are to the Collier edition.

63. L. M. Alcott, *Little Women*, p. 200.
64. Ibid., p. 32.
65. Ibid., p. 446.
66. See Beverly Lyon Clark's 'A Portrait of the Artist as a Little Woman': 'Jo's submersion in domesticity can be gauged in part, by the submersion of her fiction, including her domestic fiction.' *Children's Literature*, 17 (New Haven and London, 1989), p. 88.
67. L. M. Alcott, *Little Women*, p. 317.
68. Ibid., p. 401.
69. Ibid., p. 245.
70. Ibid., p. 319.
71 W. E. Houghton, *Victorian Frame of Mind*, p. 72.
72 E. Gaskell, from 'A letter to a young novelist' [1859], reprinted in *A Victorian Reader*, ed. Peter Faulkner (London, 1989).
73. L. M. Alcott, *Little Women*, p. 1.
74. Ibid., p. 447.
75. Henry James, Review of *Eight Cousins; or the Aunt-Hill* in *The Nation*, 14 October 1875. Reprinted in *Literary Reviews and Essays on American, English and French Literature by Henry James*, ed. Albert Mordell (New York, 1957), p. 245.
76. L. M. Alcott, *Eight Cousins* [1875] (London, 1906), p. 27.
77. Ibid., pp. 49–50.
78. L. M. Alcott, *Rose in Bloom* [1876] (London, 1938), pp. 340–1.
79. Houghton quotes a critic in the *Athenaeum* for 1835 as saying that 'a thorough-paced Utilitarian ... cannot exactly see the use of Painting and Music; flowers look pretty, but then flowers are of no use.' *Victorian Frame of Mind*, p. 115.
80. Juliet Dusinberre, *Alice in the Lighthouse*, p. 140.
81. Henry Handel Richardson, *The Getting of Wisdom* [1910] (London, 1931), pp. 270–1.
82. Ibid., pp. 271–2.
83. Ibid., p. 1.
84. Ibid., p. 153.
85. Ibid., p. 150.
86. Ibid., p. 221.
87. Ibid., p. 224.
88. Nina Auerbach, *Communities of Women* (Cambridge, Massachusetts and London, 1978), p. 3.
89. Arthurian myth, like Greek myth, tales of Robin Hood and tales from Chaucer, became increasingly popular in the nineteenth century as material for children, not only because of the heroic ideals represented in the first three, but because of the national heritage which they represented. In boys' magazines of the period one is constantly finding articles on English history or historical tales which were intended to appeal to, intensify and deepen the boys' sense of belonging and national pride, attempting to establish a new coherence in society by grounding its youth firmly in the ethos of a more stable period and welding it together through national sentiment.
90. J. R. Townsend, *Written for Children* (Harmondsworth, Middlesex, 1974), p. 111.

91. Thomas Hughes, *Tom Brown's Schooldays* [1857] (Ewell and London, 1947), p. 93.
92. Antonia Forest, *End of Term* (London, 1959), p. 85.
93. Thomas Hughes, *Tom Brown's Schooldays*, pp. 11–12.
94. Ibid., p. 91.
95. Ibid., p. 92.
96. Richard Jenkyns, *The Victorians and Ancient Greece* (Oxford, 1980), p. 213.
97. Charles Kingsley, *The Heroes* (London, 1859, second edition), pp. viii-xi.
98. Quoted by Richard Jenkyns, *The Victorians*, p. 336.
99. Also themes to be found in the modern historical fiction of Rosemary Sutcliff, whose individual heroes have to undergo some rite of passage that will gain them admittance to the ranks of their comrades; in her works, the Roman legionaries in Britain, like the various invader figures in *Puck of Pook's Hill*, find their roots there and marry and become part of the land.
100. Dusinberre, *Alice to the Lighthouse*, p. 173.
101. Leo Tolstoy, *War and Peace* (trans. L. and A. Maude) (London, 1942), p. 666.
102. Rudyard Kipling, *Puck of Pook's Hill* [1906] (London, 1924). Page references are to the Macmillan Pocket Kipling edition of 1924, p. 13.
103. Ibid., p. 11.
104. Ibid., p. 57.
105. One also finds in the novels of John Buchan, written for 'men and boys', themes of order and themes of excising the destabilizing elements of society and re-enclosing it in a circle of ideological correctness. This is true not only of the popular *The Thirty Nine Steps*, but also of *Mr. Standfast*, where the forces of disintegration are at work not only on the front itself, but attempting to stir up disaffection within the small towns and to create ideological difference where there was formerly homogeneity.
106. Rudyard Kipling, *Stalky and Co.* (London, 1899), p. 13. Page references are to the Macmillan edition.
107. Ibid., p. 17.
108. Ibid., p. 70.
109. Ibid., pp. 211–12.
110. Rudyard Kipling, *Kim* [1901] (London, 1944), pp. 264–5. Page references are to the Macmillan edition.
111. Sandison, *Wheel of Empire*, p. 97.
112. Kipling, *Kim*, pp. 403–4.
113. Charlotte Yonge's *Book of Golden Deeds*, highly popular in its time, retells this, and other heroic tales as exemplar to be emulated.
114. Fred Inglis, *The Promise of Happiness* (Cambridge 1981), p. 154.

Chapter 3

1. Gertrude Stein, 'Composition as Explanation' reprinted in *A Stein Reader*, ed. Ulla E. Dydo (Evanston, Illinois, 1993), p. 496.
2. Rosemary Jackson, *Fantasy: the Literature of Subversion* (London and New

York, 1981), p. 15. Jackson goes on to remark that through its 'misrule', fantasy permits ultimate questions about social order, and is unable to give 'affirmation to a closed, unified or omniscient vision.'

3. Quoted without source by Lance Salway, *A Peculiar Gift*, ed. Lance Salway (Harmondsworth, Middlesex, 1976), p. 109.

4. Sarah Trimmer, *The Guardian of Education. Volume II, January-August* [1803] review of *Mother Bunch's Fairy Tales*.

5. Jack Zipes, *Breaking the Magic Spell* (London, 1979), p. 14.

6. Newcastle Report on Popular Education [1861] reprinted in *English Historical Documents*, Vol. XII (1), ed. G. M. Young (London, 1956), p. 891.

7. Taunton Report on Endowed Schools [1867–1868] Ibid., p. 915.

8. Gillian Avery, with Angela Bull, *Nineteenth Century Children* (London, 1965), p. 41.

9. Edmund Burke, *A Philosophical Enquiry Into the Origin of Our Ideas of the Sublime and the Beautiful* [1757], ed. Adam Phillips (Oxford, 1990), p. 53.

10. Sarah Trimmer, *The Guardian of Education, Vol. II, Jan-August 1803*, review of *Histories and Tales of Past Times told by Mother Goose* quoted by Virginia Haviland in *Children and Literature, Views and Reviews*, ed. Virginia Haviland (London, 1973), p. 3.

11. Anon., *The History of Little Goody Two-Shoes*, published by John Newberry [1765], reprinted in *Masterworks of Children's Literature*, 3, p. 87.

12. Harvey Darton, *Children's Books in England* (third edition, revised by Brian Alderson, Cambridge, 1982), p. 99.

13. William Caldwell Roscoe, 'Fictions for Children', reprinted in *A Peculiar Gift*, ed. Lance Salway (Harmondsworth, Middlesex, 1976), from *Poems and Essays by the Late William Caldwell Roscoe* [1860], p. 23.

14. Isaac Watts, *The Improvement of the Mind*, part 2 (London, 1782), pp. 111–12.

15. John Ruskin, 'Fairy Stories' reprinted in *A Peculiar Gift*, ed. Lance Salway (Harmondsworth, Middlesex, 1976), p. 131.

16. S. Goldney, 'Fables and Fairy Tales' *Aunt Judy's Annual Volume*, ed. Juliana Horatia Ewing (London, 1885), p. 20.

17. An interesting comparison might be made with Ernst Cassirer's *Language and Myth* [1923] (tr. Susanne Langer) which looks at myth through etymology and language.

18. Andrew Lang, 'Modern Fairy Tales', *The Illustrated London News* (3 December 1892), 714.

19. Francis Paget, *The Hope of the Katzekopfs* (London, 1864), pp. 35–6.

20. Ibid., p. 82.

21. Ibid., p. 125.

22. Elizabeth Rigby, 'Children's Books' *The Quarterly Review*, (London, 1844). Reprinted in *Children and Literature, Views and Reviews*, ed. Virginia Haviland (London, 1973), p. 9.

23. Charlotte Brontë, *Jane Eyre* [1847] (Oxford, 1969), pp. 4–5.

24. Lewis Carroll, *Alice's Adventures in Wonderland* [1865] (London, 1920). All future page references in brackets are to the Macmillan edition of 1920.

25. The article is reprinted in *Aspects of Alice*, ed. R. Phillips (New York, 1971).

26. Humphrey Carpenter, *Secret Gardens* (London, 1985), p. 65.

27. With the rise of the nineteenth-century periodical for children, e.g. *Little*

Folks, The Boys Own Paper, et al., the child was further encouraged to participate actively in the 'making' of his literature; he was, for instance, encouraged to contribute letters and puzzles to the periodicals.

28. Dr. Dusinberre mentions, for instance, the *Pall Mall Gazette*'s inquiry [1898] which named *Alice in Wonderland* the winner. *Alice to the Lighthouse* (London, 1987), pp. 179–80.

29. R. L. Stevenson, Letter to W. E. Henley, included in *Letters of Robert Louis Stevenson*, ed. Sidney Colvin (London, 1911), Vol. 1, p. 49.

30. The name of the play written by J. M. Barrie was *Peter Pan* [1904]; the story, based on the play was named *Peter and Wendy* [1911] and a shortened version of this, *Peter Pan and Wendy* was published in 1915. The first and last chapters of the book were not in the original play.

31. J. M. Barrie, *Peter and Wendy* (London, 1911) p. 9.

32. Ibid., pp. 9–10.

33. F. H. Burnett, *A Little Princess* [1905] (Harmondsworth, Middlesex, 1961), p. 12. Page references are to the Puffin edition, which contains the full and unabridged text.

34. Ibid., p. 109.

35. E. Nesbit, *Harding's Luck* [1909] (London, 1930), p. 9. Page references are to the Ernest Benn edition.

36. Ibid., p. 280.

37. John Rowe Townsend, *Written for Children* (Harmondsworth, Middlesex, 1974, revised edition), p. 213.

38. W. E. H. Lecky, *The Map of Life: Conduct and Character* (London, 1899), pp. 240–2.

39. S. T. Coleridge, *Lectures on Shakespeare*, XI, quoted by William Walsh in *The Use of Imagination*, p. 24.

40. Cf. James Suchan's essay, 'Alice's Journey from Alien to Artist', in *Children's Literature, Vol. 7*. He writes: 'The fall into Wonderland proves to be a fall from identity or self, and the result is fragmentation or disorientation of the self. He also speaks of the apparent 'schizophrenia' in Alice: how she was 'very fond of pretending to be two people', and how she frequently speaks to herself to chastise herself.

41. Lewis Carroll, *Alice's Adventures in Wonderland*, pp. 19–20.

42. Cf. Juliet Dusinberre, *Alice to the Lighthouse*, (London, 1987), p. 8.

43. Lewis Carroll, *Alice's Adventures in Wonderland*, p. 143.

44. Stepping outside the boundaries of the safe and the known can be hazardous; as John Batchelor says in his essay, 'Dodgson, Carroll and the emancipation of Alice': 'it has been said [by Nina Auerbach] that although her size changes seem arbitrary and terrifying, she in fact directs them. But in the early episodes she doesn't "direct" them. She learns empirically that eating, drinking, and using the White Rabbit's fan cause them. But this weapon is, precisely, *un*directed (like a rogue missile)' ... *Children and Their Books* (eds Avery and Briggs) (Oxford, 1989), p. 185.

45. Frances Hodgson Burnett, *The Secret Garden*, p. 15.

46. Ibid., pp. 166–7.

47. Ibid., p. 12.

48. Ibid., p. 200.

49. Roderick McGillis, 'Secrets and Sequence in Children's Stories', *Studies in*

the Literary Imagination, 18 (1985), p. 38.
50. Robert Elbaz, *The Changing Nature Of The Self; A Critical Study of the Autobiographical Discourse* (Iowa, 1987), p. 8.
51. F. H. Burnett, *The Secret Garden*, p. 124.
52. Ibid., p. 28.
53. Ibid., p. 152.
54. The analogy of child and plant was not an unusual one. Froebel, in establishing the *kindergarten*, was thinking along those lines. Dr. Juliet Dusinberre, in *Alice to the Lighthouse*, speaks of Froebel's belief that 'education is a process of growth and development, a leading out of nature under the skill of an intelligent gardener.' p. 7.
55. Dr Dusinberre says of *The Secret Garden* that it 'shows two children escaping from the claustrophobic interior of a Victorian mansion full of outdated notions of child-rearing, and thriving in a garden with as much vigour as the plants which they tend'. Ibid., p. 7.
56. We may see a continuation of this notion in C. S. Lewis's 'Narnia' books, where to be grown up is to be prohibited from returning to the land of magic and enchantment. When Susan is banned from Narnia, it is because she has become too grown-up, interested in perfume and nylons and that sort of thing.
57. E. Nesbit, *New Treasure Seekers* [1904] (London, 1931), p. 311. Page references are to the Ernest Benn edition of 1931.
58. Humphrey Carpenter, *Secret Gardens: the Golden Age of Children's Literature* (London, 1987), p. 1.
59. E. Nesbit, *The Phoenix and the Carpet* [1903] (London, 1931), p. 295. Page references are to the Ernest Benn edition of 1931.
60. Arthur Ransome, *Secret Water* [1939] (Harmondsworth, Middlesex, 1969), p. 324. All references from Ransome's books will be taken from the Puffin editions.
61. The article may be found in *Signal 66*, September 1991 (Gloucester, 1991). It details the blending of the real and the poetical into a special kind of experience.
62. Arthur Ransome, *Winter Holiday* (Harmondsworth, Middlesex, 1968), pp. 244–5.
63. Arthur Ransome, *Peter Duck* [1932] (Harmondsworth, Middlesex, 1968), p. 101. Noted by Victor Watson in 'Poetry and Pirates', p. 156.
64. Neil Philip, *A Fine Anger* (London, 1981), p. 66.
65. In her case, social being; those who belong to the upper echelons of society, *are*; those who like Gwyn are servants, are untouchables: nonbeings.
66. Quoted by Virginia Haviland in *Children and Literature: Views and Reviews*, ed. Virginia Haviland (London, 1973), p. 96.
67. Rumer Godden, *The Greengage Summer* (London, 1958), pp. 17–18.
68. Ibid., p. 15.
69. Ibid.
70. Rosemary Sutcliff, 'History is People', in *Children and Literature, Views and Reviews* (ed. Virginia Haviland, London, 1973), p. 306.
71. Ibid., p. 41.
72. Ibid., p. 43.

73. Ibid., p. 57.
74. Ibid., p. 25.
75. Ibid., p. 22.
76. Ibid., p. 125.
77. Ibid., p. 49.
78. Ibid., p. 130.
79. Ibid., p. 131.
80. Ibid., p. 204.
81. Joan Aiken, 'Purely for Love', in *Children and Literature, Views and Reviews* (ed. Virginia Haviland, London, 1973), p. 151. In a similar vein, Jill Paton Walsh remarked, 'One does not rush to give *Anna Karenina* to friends who are committing adultery. Such impertinence is limited to dealing with children.' This was quoted by Michele Landsberg in *The World of Children's Books* (London, 1988), p. 182.
82. Ibid., p. 183.

Chapter 4

1. Rumer Godden, *The Greengage Summer* (London, 1958), p. 52.
2. Sheila Egoff, 'Precepts, Pleasures and Portents' in *Only Connect* (eds Egoff, Stubbs and Ashley) (Toronto, 1980), p. 430.
3. Anon. 'Children's Literature', in *A Peculiar Gift* (ed. Lance Salway), p. 314.
4. Louisa Alcott, *Jack and Jill* [1880] (Harmondsworth, Middlesex, 1991), p. 267. Page references are to the Puffin edition of 1991. This is a full and unabridged text.
5. C. S. Lewis, 'On Three Ways of Writing for Children', reprinted in *Only Connect*, p. 207.
6. Russell Hoban, 'Thoughts on Being and Writing' in *The Thorny Paradise*, ed. Edward Blishen (Harmondsworth, Middlesex, 1975), p. 75.
7. Russell Hoban, *The Mouse and his Child* [1967] (Harmondsworth, Middlesex, 1976), p. 18. All references will be to this edition.
8. Ibid., p. 19.
9. This has in part been fuelled by the revolution in children's literature, where writers who feel that the happy protected environment and aesthetics of, for example, *Swallows and Amazons*, are unreal and distasteful in that it ignores the alternative world of the socially and emotionally underprivileged. Such writers, turning to the world of the non-establishment, invest in realist aesthetics; for them, 'realism' is synonymous with the working class, the deprived and the marginalised, people with problems: classes of people who the authors feel have a real and continuing relationship with danger, hardship and suffering. Thus, many of the 'tell-it-like-it-is' children's authors of today expose the fictional child and the child reader to that same danger or suffering that they perceive to be the texture of the 'alternative' (i.e. non-establishment, non-stultifyingly comfortable) reality they are concerned with. The quality of uneasiness and even unhappiness experienced by the exposed child or youth can be thought-provoking and insightful, as in Garner's *Red Shift*, or can be chillingly defeatist, as with Cormier's *Chocolate War* books.

10. Sheila Egoff, 'Precepts, Pleasures and Portents' in *Only Connect*, p. 419.
11. Jason Epstein, 'Good Bunnies Always Obey' [1963]. Ibid., p. 81.
12. B. J. Craige, *Literary Relativity* (New Jersey, 1982), p. 20.
13. Matthew Arnold, 'The Literary Influence of Academics', in *Essays in Criticism*, 1st Series (London, 1875), p. 66.
14. Anon. 'Children's Literature' in *A Peculiar Gift* (ed. Lance Salway) (Harmondsworth, Middlesex, 1976), p. 306.
15. Matthew Arnold, *Culture and Anarchy* (ed. John Dover Wilson) (Cambridge, 1932), p.1.
16. Houghton, *Victorian Frame of Mind*, p. 138.
17. Sheila Egoff, 'The Problem Novel' in *Only Connect*, p. 367.
18. Fred Inglis, *The Promise of Happiness* (Cambridge, 1981), p. 82.
19. Humphrey Carpenter, *The Oxford Companion to Children's Literature* (Oxford, 1984), p. 188.
20. Sheila Egoff, 'Precepts, Pleasures, and Portents', p. 420.
21. In *The Ready-Made Family*, the 'problems' of divorce and the children caught in the middle are looked at, though the treatment of these is infinitely more subtle than Judy Blume's trite and awful *It's Not The End of the World*, or even Anne Fine's rather better *Goggle-Eyes* and *Madame Doubtfire*. Antonia Forest provides no simple solution to the family members' problem of adjusting to each other, but the reader emerges enriched and stimulated. *The Marlows and the Traitor* is about rescuing naval plans from one of its officers who has gone over to the Germans. *The Thuggery Affair* is about smashing a drug ring, and *Run Away Home* about helping a young boy to make his way back to his father; both of these could loosely be termed adventure stories, but what always makes the strongest impression on the reader is the sense of *truth* – of character, personality and speech – over which the stories are constructed, and from which they derive much of their plausibility. (If one thinks of the plots *in vacuo*, they appear rather unbelievable, but no one reading them thinks of this. Because the characters are real people, the situations in which they find themselves take on a part of their reality.)
22. Antonia Forest, *The Ready-Made Family* (London, 1967), p. 40.
23. Antonia Forest, *End of Term* (London, 1959), pp. 108–9.
24. Antonia Forest, *Falconer's Lure*, (London, 1957), p. 40.
25. Ibid., p. 40.
26. Antonia Forest, *Peter's Room* (London, 1961), p. 99.
27. Ibid., p. 95.
28. Antonia Forest, *Falconer's Lure*, p. 39.
29. Ibid., p. 135.
30. Antonia Forest, *End of Term*, p. 157.
31. Antonia Forest, *The Cricket Term* (London, 1974), p. 38.
32. Antonia Forest, *The Attic Term* (London, 1976), p. 218.
33. Ibid., p. 185.
34. Ibid., pp. 194–5.
35. Jane Gardam, *Bilgewater* [1976] (London, 1985), p. 12.
36. Ibid., p. 28.
37. Ibid., p. 68.
38. Ibid., p. 72.

39. Ibid., p. 154.
40. In his section on the teenage novel in *The Oxford Companion to Children's Literature*, Humphrey Carpenter mentions the post-Salinger generation of authors: Barbara Wersba, John Donovan, Paul Zindel, and so forth, whose novels are cluttered with parents who are drunks and social animals. What Michele Landsberg calls the 'Blumziger' school of teenage writing (Judy Blume and Paula Danziger), is full of divorced and mixed-up parents.
41. Sheila Egoff, in her essay 'The Problem Novel' (p. 367), writes, 'Alienation, hostility, egocentricity, the search for identity, the flouting of conventions – these things have evoked instant interest and sympathy from the young since the sixties. That was a period of general reaction against authority ... They brought into question power structures of all kinds – in government, in education, in the family itself. The stability of family life was taken for granted in children's literature until changes in life styles and the liberated attitude of the sixties made this convention seem mythical.' Cf. Fred Inglis, *The Promise of Happiness*, p. 32.
42. Alan Garner, *Red Shift* [1973] (London, 1975), p. 20.
43. Barbara Hardy, *Forms of Feeling in Victorian Fiction* (London, 1985), p. 12.
44. The Victorians set their faces against introspection and too great a degree of internal analysis because they felt this led to doubt which in turn paralysed action. In a similar way, Tom's introspection does just this.
45. Neil Philip writes: 'Garner expresses ... isolation though a number of ironic symbols ... most of which are communication devices ... television, tape recorder and telephones ... A number of these communication devices are ones which disturb or counter the natural progression of time: Jan's parents prefer to speak to an answering machine and then have their problems played back ...' *A Fine Anger* (Edinburgh, 1981), p. 92.
46. Alan Garner, *Red Shift* (London, 1975), p. 11.
47. Ibid., p. 8.
48. Ibid., p. 111.

Conclusion (Contradiction)

1. William Wordsworth, *The Prelude* [1850 revision], ed. E. de Selincourt (Oxford, 1926), p. 155.

Bibliography

Dates in square brackets are dates of first edition, where that is not the edition cited. Certain of the texts below which are not cited by name in the book itself have been included when they have been instrumental in forming the conclusions found therein. Where paperback editions of children's books have been cited, the author has been satisfied that these editions are neither abridged nor significantly altered from the original published text.

Abel, Elizabeth, Marianne Hirsch and Elizabeth Langland. (eds) *The Voyage In: Fictions of Female Development* (Hanover and London, 1983).

Aiken, Joan. 'Purely for Love' in *Children and Literature, Views and Reviews*, ed. Virginia Haviland (London, 1973).

Alcott, L. M. *Little Women* [1868] (London, 1907).

—— *Little Men* [1871] (London, 1911).

—— *Jo's Boys* [1886] (London, 1907).

—— *Eight Cousins* [1875] (London, 1906).

—— *Rose in Bloom* [1876] (London, 1938).

—— *An Old-Fashioned Girl* [1870] (London, 1907).

—— *Jack and Jill* [1880] (London, 1907).

Alderson, Brian. 'Tracts, Rewards and Fairies': the Victorian Contribution to Children's Literature' in *Essays in the History of Publishing, Longman 1724–1974*, ed. Asa Briggs (London, 1974).

Anstey, F. *Vice Versa* [1882] (Harmondsworth, Middlesex, 1981).

—— *The Brass Bottle* [1900] (Harmondsworth, Middlesex, 1946).

apRoberts, Ruth. *Anthony Trollope: Artist and Moralist* (London, 1971).

Ariès, Philippe. *Centuries of Childhood*, trans. R. Baldick (London, 1969).

Arnold, Matthew. 'Heinrich Heine' in *Essays in Criticism* (1st Series) [1865] (London, 1902).

—— *Culture and Anarchy* [1869] (Cambridge, 1932).

Auerbach, Nina. *Communities of Women* (Harvard, 1978).

—— 'Jane Austen and Romantic Imprisonment' in *Jane Austen: A Social Context*, ed. Donald Monaghan (London, 1981).

—— 'Alice and Wonderland: a Curious Child' in *Victorian Studies*, 17 (Sept 1973).

Austen, Jane. *Mansfield Park* [1814] (London, 1934).

—— *Persuasion* [1818] (London, 1933).

—— *Pride and Prejudice* [1813] (London, 1932).

Avery, Gillian. *Nineteenth Century Children: Heroes and Heroines in English Children's Stories, 1780–1900* (London, 1965).

—— 'The Puritans and their Heirs' in *Children and their Books*, eds Gillian Avery and Julia Briggs (Oxford, 1991).

—— *The Greatest Gresham* (London, 1962).

Avery, Gillian and Julia Briggs. (eds) *Children and their Books* (Oxford, 1991).

Bachelard, Gaston. *The Poetics of Space*, trans. Maria Jolas [1958] (Boston,

Massachusetts, 1994).

Bantock, G. H. *Studies in the History of Educational Theory, Vol. II: The Minds and the Masses 1760–1980* (London, 1984).

Barker, Juliet. *The Brontës: A Life in Letters* (London, 1997).

Barrett, G. C. 'That Cursed Barbauld Crew; Charles Lamb and Children's Literature' in *The Charles Lamb Bulletin* (Jan. 1979).

Barrie, J. M. *Peter and Wendy* (London, 1911).

Batchelor, John. 'Dodgson, Carroll and Alice' in *Children and their Books*, eds Gillian Avery and Julia Briggs (Oxford, 1991).

Bator, Robert. (ed.) *Signposts to Criticism of Children's Literature* (Chicago,1983).

Battiscombe, Georgina. *Charlotte Mary Yonge* (London, 1943).

Beatty, Jerome. 'Jane Eyre at Gateshead: Mixed Signals in the Text and Context', in *Victorian Literature and Society*, eds. James Kincaid and A. Kuhn (Ohio, 1984).

Beer, John. *Wordsworth in Time* (London, 1979).

Beeton, Isabella. *The Book of Household Management* [1860] (London, 1880).

Berman, Ronald. 'The Innocent Observer' in *Children's Literature*, 9 (New Haven and London, 1981).

Bettelheim, Bruno. *The Uses of Enchantment: the Meaning and Importance of Fairy Tales* (Harmondsworth, Middlesex, 1978).

Bingham, J. M. (ed.) *Writers for Children* (New York, 1988).

Blishen, E. (ed.) *The Thorny Paradise* (Harmondsworth, Middlesex, 1975).

Blume, Judy. *Forever* (New York, 1975).

Bogel, F. V. *Literature and Insubstantiality in Later Eighteenth-Century England* (New Jersey, 1984).

Bratton, J. S. *The Impact of Victorian Children's Fiction* (London, 1981).

Briggs, Julia. *A Woman of Passion: The Life of E. Nesbit 1858–1924* (Harmondsworth, Middlesex, 1989).

Briggs, K. M. *The Fairies in Tradition and Literature* (London,1967).

Bristow, Joseph. *Empire Boys* (London, 1991).

Brontë, Charlotte. *Jane Eyre* [1847] (Oxford, 1969).

Brontë, Emily. *Wuthering Heights* [1847] (Oxford, 1995).

Browning, Robert. *The Ring and the Book* [1868–1869] (Harmondsworth, Middlesex, 1981).

Buchan, John. *John MacNab* (London, 1925).

—— *Mr. Standfast* (London, 1919).

—— *The Thirty-Nine Steps* (London, 1915).

Buckley, Jerome. *Season of Youth* (Cambridge, Massachussetts, 1974).

Burnett, Frances H. *Little Lord Fauntleroy* [1886] (New York and London, 1976).

—— *A Little Princess* [1907] (Harmondsworth, Middlesex, 1961).

—— *Sara Crewe and Editha's Burglar* (London and New York, 1888).

—— *The Secret Garden* [1911] (Harmondsworth, Middlesex, 1951).

Butler, Francelia. (ed.) *Reflections on Literature for Children* (Connecticut, 1984).

Butler, Marilyn. *Romantics, Rebels, and Reactionaries*, (Oxford, 1981).

Cadogan, Mary and Patricia Craig. *You're a Brick, Angela!: A New Look at Girls' Fiction from 1839 to 1975* (London, 1975).

Carlyle, Thomas. 'Signs of the Times' [1829] reprinted in *Selected Writings*, ed. Alan Shelston (Harmondsworth, Middlesex, 1971).

Carpenter, Humphrey. *Secret Gardens: The Golden Age in Children's Literature*

(London, 1985).

Carpenter, Humphrey and Pritchard, Mari. (eds) *The Oxford Companion to Children's Literature* (Oxford, 1984).

Carroll, Lewis. *Alice's Adventures in Wonderland* [1865] (London, 1920).

—— *Through the Looking Glass* (London, 1872).

Cassirer, Ernst. *Language and Myth* [1923], trans. Susanne Langer (New York, 1953).

Charlesworth, Mrs. *Ministering Children* (London, 1854).

Clark, Beverly Lyon. 'A Portrait of the Artist as a Little Woman' in *Children's Literature 17*, (New Haven and London, 1989).

Colby, Vineta. *Yesterday's Woman* (New Jersey, 1974).

Collingwood, S. D. *The Life and Letters of Lewis Carroll* (London, 1898).

Collins, Philip. *Dickens and Education* (London, 1963).

Connell, W. F. *The Educational Thought and Influence of Matthew Arnold* (London, 1950).

Cook, Elizabeth. *The Ordinary and the Fabulous, an Introduction to Myths, Legends and Fairy Tales for Teachers and Story Tellers* (Cambridge,1969).

Coolidge, Susan. *What Katy Did* [1872] (London, 1907).

—— *What Katy Did at School* [1873] (London, 1907).

—— *What Katy did Next* [1886] (London, 1937).

Cormier, Robert. *The Chocolate War* [1975] (London, 1978).

—— *Beyond the Chocolate Wa*r [1985] (London, 1987).

—— *I am the Cheese* [1977] (London, 1979).

Coveney, Peter. *The Image of Childhood* (Harmondsworth, Middlesex, 1967).

Craige, B. J. *Literary Relativity* (New Jersey, 1982).

Crouch, Marcus. *Treasure Seekers and Borrowers* (London, 1962).

Croxson, Mary. 'The Emancipated Child in the Novels of E. Nesbit' in *Signal*, 14 (1974).

Danon, Ruth. *Work in the English Novel* (Kent, 1985).

Darton, Harvey. *Children's Books in England* (Cambridge, 1982).

Dawson, Terence. 'Jung, Literature and Literary Criticism' in *The Cambridge Companion to Jung*, eds Young-Eisendrath, Polly and Terence Dawson (Cambridge, 1997).

Dickens, Charles. *David Copperfield* (London, 1850).

—— *Great Expectations* (London, 1860).

—— *Hard Times* (London, 1854).

—— *The Life of Our Lord* [1849] (Southampton, 1987).

—— *Master Humphrey's Clock* [1840] (Oxford, 1958).

—— *The Old Curiosity Shop* [1841] (London, 1951).

—— *Oliver Twist* [1837] (Oxford, 1966).

—— *Our Mutual Friend* [1864–5] (Oxford, 1989).

—— 'Frauds on the Fairies' [1853] reprinted in *A Peculiar Gift*, ed. Lance Salway (Harmondsworth, Middlesex, 1976).

Dobrée, Bonamy. *Modern Prose Style* (Oxford, 1934).

Dusinberre, Juliet. *Alice to the Lighthouse: Children's Books and Radical Experiments in Art* (London, 1987).

Edgeworth, Maria, *The Parent's Assistant* [1796] (London, 1907).

—— *Rosamond* (London, 1856).

Egoff, Sheila. 'The Problem Novel' in *Only Connect*, eds Sheila Egoff, G. T.

Stubbs and L. F. Ashley (Toronto, 1980).
—— 'Precepts, Pleasures and Portents: Changing Emphases in Children's Literature', *Only Connect*, eds Shelia Egoff, G. T. Stubbs and L. F. Ashley (Toronto, 1980).
Elbaz, Robert. *The Changing Nature of the Self* (Iowa, 1987).
Eliot, George. *The Mill on The Floss* [1860] (Oxford, 1979).
Eliot, T. S. 'Huckleberry Finn: a critical essay' [1950], reprinted in *Only Connect*, eds Sheila Egoff, G. T. Stubbs and L. F. Ashley (Toronto, 1980).
—— *Collected Poems* (London, 1963).
Ellison, Eugenia A. *The Innocent Child in Dickens and Other Writers* (Texas, 1982).
Empson, W. *Some Versions of Pastoral* (London, 1935).
Epstein, Jason. 'Good Bunnies Always Obey' [1963], *Only Connect*, eds Sheila Egoff, G. T. Stubbs and L. F. Ashley (Toronto, 1980).
Farjeon, Eleanor. *Martin Pippin in the Daisy Field* (London, 1937).
—— *Martin Pippin in the Apple Orchard* (London, 1921).
Faulkner, Peter. (ed.) *A Victorian Reader* (London, 1989).
Forest, Antonia. *Autumn Term* (London, 1948).
—— *The Marlows and the Traitor* (London, 1954).
—— *Falconer's Lure* (London, 1957).
—— *End of Term* (London, 1959).
—— *Peter's Room* (London, 1961).
—— *The Thuggery Affair* (London, 1965).
—— *The Ready-Made Family* (London, 1967).
—— *The Cricket Term* (London, 1974).
—— *The Attic Term* (London, 1976).
—— *Run Away Home* (London, 1983).
Foster, Shirley and Judy Simmons. *What Katy Read* (London, 1995).
Fox, G. *et al.* (eds) *Writers, Critics and Children* (London, 1976).
Froude, J. A. *The Nemesis of Faith* [1849] (London and New York, 1904).
Frye, Northrop. *The Secular Scripture* (Massachusetts and London, 1976).
Gardam, Jane. *Bilgewater* [1976] (London, 1985).
—— *Crusoe's Daughter* (London, 1976).
Garner, Alan. *The Owl Service* [1967] (London, 1973).
—— *Red Shift* [1973] (London, 1975).
Gaskell, Elizabeth. 'Curious if True', in *Cousin Phyllis*, ed. Angus Easson (Oxford, 1981).
—— *The Life of Charlotte Brontë*, ed. Alan Shelston (Harmondsworth, Middlesex, 1975).
Gérin, Winifred. *Charlotte Brontë* (Oxford, 1967).
Gide, André. *Oscar Wilde: A Study*, trans. Stuart Mason (Oxford, 1905).
Gillespie, Joanna. 'Schooling through Fiction' in *Children's Literature*, 14 (New Haven and London, 1986).
Godden, Rumer. *The Greengage Summer* (London, 1958).
—— *The Peacock Spring* (London, 1978).
—— *The Battle of the Villa Fiorita* (London, 1963).
Goldney, S. 'Fables and Fairy Tales', in *Aunt Judy's Annual* (London, 1985).
Gosse, Edmund. *Father and Son* (London, 1907).
Gray, Nicholas Stuart. *Wardens of the Weir* (London, 1978).
Green, Martin. *Dreams of Adventure, Deeds of Empire* (London, 1980).

Green, Roger L. *Tellers of Tales* (London, 1946).

Grylls, David. *Guardians and Angels: Parents and Children in Nineteenth Century Literature* (London and Boston, 1978).

Haggard, H. Rider. *King Solomon's Mines* (London, 1878).

Hardy, Barbara. *Forms of Feeling in Victorian Fiction* (London, 1985).

Harrison, Bernard. 'Literature for Children: a Radical Genre', in *New Pelican Guide to English Literature*, 8 (Harmondsworth, Middlesex, 1983).

Hart-Davis, R. (ed.) *The Letters of Oscar Wilde* (London, 1962).

Hatch, Elvin. *Culture and Morality: the Relativity of Values in Anthropology* (New York, 1983).

Helson, Rosanna. 'The Psychological Origins of Fantasy for Children in Mid-Victorian England' in *Children's Literature*, 3 (New Haven and London, 1974).

Hepworth, Brian. *The Rise of Romanticism* (Manchester, 1978).

Hewins, Caroline M. 'The History of Children's Books' [1888], reprinted in *Children and Literature, Views and Reviews*, ed. Virginia Haviland (London, 1973).

Hill, Christopher. *Reformation to Industrial Revolution* (Harmondsworth, Middlesex, 1969).

Hilton, Mary, Morag Styles and Victor Watson. (eds) *Opening the Nursery Door* (London, 1997).

Hoban, Russell. *The Mouse and his Child* [1967] (Harmondsworth, Middlesex, 1976).

—— 'Thoughts on Being and Writing', in *The Thorny Paradise* (ed. Edward Blishen) (Harmondsworth, Middlesex, 1975).

Hollander, Anne. 'Reflections on Little Women', in *Children's Literature*, 9 (New Haven and London, 1981).

Hollindale, Peter. *Signs of Childness in Children's Books* (Woodchester, Stroud, 1997).

Houghton, Walter. *The Victorian Frame of Mind* (New Haven, 1957).

Housman, Laurence. *The Field of Clover* (New York, 1968).

Hughes, Felicity. 'Children's Literature: Theory and Practice', in *Children's Literature: The Development of Criticism*, ed. Peter Hunt (London and New York, 1990).

Hughes, M. V. *A London Child in the 1870s* (Oxford, 1977).

—— *A London Girl of the 1880s* (Oxford, 1946).

Hughes, Ted. 'Myth and Education' in *Children's Literature in Education* (St Albans, 1970).

Hughes, Thomas. *Tom Brown's Schooldays* [1857] (London, 1947).

Hulme, T. E. *Speculations* (London, 1987).

Hume, Kathryn. *Fantasy and Mimesis: Responses to Reality in Western Literature* (New York and London, 1984).

Hunt, Peter. (ed.) *Children's Literature: The Development of Criticism* (London and New York, 1990).

—— *Criticism, Theory and Children's Literature* (Oxford, 1991).

—— (ed.) *International Companion Encyclopaedia of Children's Literature* (London, 1997).

Inglis, Fred. *The Promise of Happiness: Value and Meaning in Children's Fiction* (Cambridge, 1981).

Iskandar, Sylvia Patterson. 'Readers, Realism and Robert Cormier', in *Children's*

Literature, 13 (New Haven and London, 1987).

Jackson, Rosemary. *Fantasy: The Literature of Subversion* (London, and New York, 1981).

James, Henry. *Literary Reviews and Essays on American, English and French Literature by Henry James*, ed. Albert Mordell (New York, 1957).

—— *What Maisie Knew* (New York, 1897).

Jan, Isabelle. *On Children's Literature* (London, 1973).

Janeway, Elizabeth. 'Meg, Jo, Beth, Amy and Louisa', in *Only Connect*, eds Sheila Egoff, G. T. Stubbs and L. F. Ashley (Toronto, 1980).

Jenkyns, Richard. *The Victorians and Ancient Greece* (Oxford, 1980).

Kellet, E. E. *Early Victorian England* (London, 1934).

Kelly, R. G. 'Terms for Order in some Late 19th Century Fiction for Children', in *Children's Literature*, 1 (New Haven and London, 1973).

Keyser, E. L. '"Quite Contrary": Frances Hodgson Burnett's *The Secret Garden*', in *Children's Literature*, 11 (New Haven and London, 1983).

Kingsley, Charles. *The Water Babies* (London, 1863).

—— *The Heroes* [1855] (London, 1859).

Kipling, Rudyard. *Puck of Pook's Hill* [1906] (London, 1924).

—— *Rewards and Fairies* (London, 1910).

—— *Kim* [1901] (London, 1944).

—— *Stalky & Co.* (London, 1899).

Knoepflmacher, U.C. and G. B. Tennyson. (eds) *Nature and the Victorian Imagination* (Berkeley, 1977).

—— 'The Balancing of Child and Adult: An Approach to Victorian Fantasy for Children', in *Nineteenth-Century Fiction*, 37 (Mar 1983).

Knowles, Murray and Kirsten Malmkjœr. *Language and Control in Children's Literature* (London and New York, 1996).

Koppes, P. B. 'Tradition and the Individual Talent of Frances Hodgson Burnett: a Generic Analysis of *Little Lord Fauntleroy*, *A Little Princess* and *The Secret Garden*', in *Children's Literature*, 7 (New Haven and London, 1979).

Kotzin, Michael, C. 'The Fairy Tale in England, 1800–1870', in *Journal of Popular Culture*, 4 (Summer, 1970).

Kuhn, Reinhard. *Corruption in Paradise: The Child in Western Literature* (Hanover and London, 1982).

Landsberg, Michele. *The World of Children's Books* (London, 1988).

Lang, Andrew. *Prince Prigio* (Bristol, 1889).

—— *Prince Ricardo* (Bristol, 1893).

Lawrence, D. H. *Selected Literary Criticism* (ed. Anthony Beal), (London, 1955).

Lecky, W. E. H. *The Map of Life. Conduct and Character* (London, 1899).

L' Engle, Madeleine, *A Wrinkle in Time* (New York, 1962).

Lemon, Mark. 'The Enchanted Doll', reprinted in *Masterworks of Children's Literature*, VI (London, 1985).

Levine, George. *The Realistic Imagination* (London, 1981).

Lewis, C. S. *Of This and Other Worlds* (London, 1982).

—— 'On Three Ways Of Writing For Children', reprinted in *Only Connect*, eds Sheila Egoff, G. T. Stubbs and L. F. Ashley (Toronto, 1980).

—— *A Grief Observed* (London, 1961).

—— *An Experiment in Criticism* (Cambridge, 1961).

—— *The Lion, the Witch and the Wardrobe* [1950] (Harmondsworth, Middlesex,

1959).

—— *Prince Caspian* [1951] (Harmondsworth, Middlesex, 1962).

—— *The Voyage of the Dawn Treader* [1952] (Harmondsworth, Middlesex, 1965).

—— *The Horse and his Boy* [1954] (Harmondsworth, Middlesex, 1965).

—— *The Magician's Nephew* [1955] (Harmondsworth, Middlesex, 1963).

—— *The Silver Chair* [1953] (Harmondsworth, Middlesex, 1965).

—— *The Last Battle* [1956] (Harmondsworth, Middlesex, 1964).

Little, Jean. *Mama's Going to Buy You a Mockingbird* [1984] (Harmondsworth, Middlesex, 1985).

Lloyd, Rosemary. *The Land of Lost Content* (Oxford, 1992).

Lochead, Marion. *The Renaissance of Wonder in Children's Literature* (Edinburgh, 1977).

Lodge, David. *Language of Fiction* (second edition) (London,1984).

Lurie, Alison. *Don't Tell the Grown Ups* (London, 1990).

Macdonald, George. *The Princess and the Goblin* [1872] (Harmondsworth, Middlesex, 1964).

—— *The Princess and Curdie* [1882] (Harmondsworth, Middlesex, 1966).

—— *At the Back of the North Wind* [1871] (Harmondsworth, Middlesex, 1984).

—— 'The Fantastic Imagination' [1908], reprinted in *A Peculiar Gift*, ed. Lance Salway (Harmondsworth, Middlesex, 1976).

MacDonald, Ruth. *Literature for Children in England and America from 1646–1774* (New York, 1982).

Manlove, C. N. *The Impulse of Fantasy Literature* (London, 1983).

Mayne, William. *Gideon Ahoy!* [1987] (Harmondsworth, Middlesex, 1989).

McGavran, James Holt Jr., 'Catechist and Visionary: Watts and Wordsworth in "We Are Seven" and the "Anecdote for Fathers"' in *Romanticism and Children's Literature in Nineteenth-Century England*, ed. J. H. McGavran Jr. (Athens, Georgia, 1991).

Meigs, C., A. T. Eaton, E. Nesbitt, R. H. Viguers (eds) *A Critical History of Children's Literature* (revised ed.) (London, 1969).

McGillis, Roderick. 'Secrets and Sequence in Children's Stories', in *Studies in the Literary Imagination*, 18 (1985).

McLeod, Karen. *Henry Handel Richardson: A Critical Study* (Cambridge, 1985).

Meyer, Susan E. *A Treasury of the Great Children's Book Illustrators* (New York, 1983).

Miller, J. Hillis. *Charles Dickens: the World of his Novels* (Cambridge, Massachussetts, 1958).

Milne, A. A. *Winnie the Pooh* [1926] (London, 1978).

—— *The House at Pooh Corner* [1928] (London, 1979).

Miyoshi, Masao. *The Divided Self* (New York, 1969).

Molesworth, Mary. *The Cuckoo Clock* (London, 1877).

—— *The Tapestry Room* (London,1879).

Monaghan, David. *Jane Austen: Structure and Social Vision* (London and Basingstoke, 1980).

—— (ed.) *Jane Austen: A Social Context* (London, 1981).

Montague, C. E. *Disenchantment* [1922] (Plymouth, 1968).

Montgomery, L. M. *Anne of Green Gables* [1908] (London, 1983).

—— *Anne of Avonlea* [1909] (London, 1983).

—— *Anne of the Island* [1915] (London, 1983).

—— *Anne of Ingleside* [1939] (London, 1983).
Moore, George. *Literature at Nurse or Circulating Morals* (London, 1885).
Moss, Anita. 'Varieties of Children's Metafiction', in *Studies in the Literary Imagination*, 18/2 (Atlanta, Georgia, 1985).
Mullan, John. *Sentiment and Sociability: The Language of Feeling in the Eighteenth Century* (Oxford, 1988).
Myers, Mitzi. 'Impeccable Governesses, Rational Dames and Moral Mothers: Mary Wollstonecraft and the Feminist Tradition in Georgian Children's Books', in *Children's Literature*, 14 (New Haven and London, 1986).
Nadel, I. B. '"The Mansion of Bliss" or the Place of Play; Victorian life and literature' *Children's Literature*, 10 (New Haven and London, 1982).
—— 'Renunciation; the "Perfect Freedom" of the Victorians' in *Interspace and the Inward Sphere*, eds Anderson and Weiss (Illinois, 1978).
Nelson, Claudia. *Boys Will be Girls* (New Brunswick and London, 1991).
Nesbit, Edith. *The Story of the Treasure Seekers* [1899] (London, 1958).
—— *The Wouldbegoods* (London, 1901).
—— *Five Children and It* (London, 1902).
—— *The Phoenix and the Carpet* [1903] (London, 1931).
—— *New Treasure Seekers* [1904] (London, 1931).
—— *The Story of the Amulet* (London, 1905).
—— *The Enchanted Castle* [1907] (London, 1964).
—— *The House of Arden* [1908] (London, 1929).
—— *Harding's Luck* [1909] (London, 1930).
—— *The Magic City* [1910] (London, 1930).
Newman, J. H. *The Idea of a University* [1873] (New York, 1959).
Newsome, David. *Godliness and Good Learning* (London, 1961).
Nietzsche, Friedrich. *The Birth of Tragedy* (1886; revised edition; trans. Shaun Whiteside, Harmondsworth, Middlesex, 1993).
Paget, Francis. *Hope of the Katzekopfs* (London, 1864).
Pearce, Phillippa. *Tom's Midnight Garden* (Oxford, 1958).
Philip, Neil. *A Fine Anger* (Edinburgh, 1981).
Phillips, R. (ed.) *Aspects of Alice* (New York, 1971).
Pollock, Linda. *Forgotten Children: Parent-Child Relations From 1500–1900* (Cambridge, 1983).
Porter, Eleanor. *Pollyanna* [1913] (Harmondsworth, Middlesex, 1969).
Prickett, Stephen. *Victorian Fantasy* (Sussex, 1979).
Quigly, Isabel. *The Heirs of Tom Brown: the English School Story* (London, 1982).
Ransome, Arthur. *Swallows and Amazons* [1930] (Harmondsworth, Middlesex, 1962).
—— *Peter Duck* [1932] (Harmondsworth, Middlesex, 1968).
—— *Winter Holiday* [1933] (Harmondsworth, Middlesex, 1968).
—— *Secret Water* [1939] (Harmondsworth, Middlesex, 1969).
Raverat, Gwen. *Period Piece* (London, 1952).
Rees-Williams, G. and B. *What I Cannot Tell My Mother Is Not Fit For Me To Know* (Oxford, 1981).
Reynolds, Kimberly. *Children's Literature in the 1890s and the 1990s* (Plymouth, 1994).
Richardson, Henry Handel. *The Getting of Wisdom* [1910] (London, 1931).
Riehl, Joseph, E. *Charles Lamb's Children's Literature* (Salzburg, 1980).

Rigby, Elizabeth. 'Children's Books' [1844] reprinted in *Children and Literature, Views and Reviews*, ed. Virginia Haviland (London, 1973).
Rilke, Rainer Maria. *Die Gedichte* (Frankfurt, 1986).
Ritvo, Harriet. 'Learning from Animals: Natural History for Children in the Eighteenth and Nineteenth Century', in *Children's Literature*, 13 (New Haven and London, 1985).
Roscoe, William Caldwell. 'Fictions for Children' [1855], reprinted in *A Peculiar Gift* (ed. Lance Salway) (Harmondsworth, Middlesex, 1976).
Rose, Jacqueline. *The Case of Peter Pan or the Impossibility of Children's Fiction* (London, 1984).
Rowbotham, Judith. *Good Girls make Good Wives* (Oxford, 1989).
Rousseau, Jean J. *Émile*, trans. P. D. Jimack (London, 1974).
Ruskin, John. 'Fairy Stories', reprinted in *Masterworks of Children's Literature*, VI (London, 1985).
Salinger, J. D. *Catcher in the Rye* (London, 1951).
Salmon, Edward. 'Should Children Have a Special Literature?' reprinted in *A Peculiar Gift*, ed. Lance Salway (Harmondsworth, Middlesex, 1976).
Salway, Lance. (ed.) *A Peculiar Gift: Nineteenth-Century Writings on Books for Children* (Harmondsworth, Middlesex, 1976).
Sandison, Alan. *The Wheel of Empire* (New York, 1967).
Scherf, Walter. 'Family Conflicts and Emancipation in Fairy Tales', in *Children's Literature*, 3 (New Haven and London, 1974).
Schneewind, J. B. 'Moral Problems in the Victorian Period', in *Victorian Studies*, 9, *Supplement* (Sept. 1965).
—— *Sidgewick's Ethics and Victorian Moral Philosophy* (Oxford, 1977).
Scudder, H. E. 'Books for Young People' [1867] reprinted in *Children and Literature, Views and Reviews*, ed. Virginia Haviland (London, 1973).
Shaw, W. D. *The Lucid Veil: Poetic Truth in the Victorian Age* (London, 1987).
Shepard, E. H. *Drawn From Memory; Drawn From Life* [1957, 1961] (London, 1986).
Sherwood, Martha. *The History of the Fairchild Family* (London, 1841).
—— *The Story of Little Henry and his Bearer*, reprinted in *Masterworks of Children's Literature*, 4 (London, 1984).
Shewan, Rodney. *Oscar Wilde: Art and Egotism* (London, 1977).
Sircar, Sanjay. 'The Victorian Auntly Narrative Voice and Mrs Molesworth's *Cuckoo Clock*', in *Children's Literature*, 17 (New Haven and London, 1989).
Stanley, A. P. *The Life and Correspondence of Thomas Arnold, D. D., Head Master of Rugby* (London, 1904).
Steele, M. Q. 'Realism, Truth and Honesty', in *Children and Literature, Views and Reviews*, ed. Virginia Haviland (London, 1973).
Stein, Gertrude. 'Composition as Explanation', reprinted in *A Stein Reader*, ed. Ulla E. Dydo (Evanston, Ill., 1993).
Steiner, George. *In Bluebeard's Castle* (London, 1971).
Stern, Madeleine B. *Louisa May Alcott* (Norman, 1950).
Stevenson, R. L. *Treasure Island* (London, 1882).
Stone, H. *Dickens and the Invisible World: Fairy Tales, Fantasy and Novel-Making* (Bloomington, 1979).
Strachey, Sir Edward. 'Nonsense as a Fine Art' [1888], reprinted in *A Peculiar Gift*, ed. Lance Salway (Harmondsworth, Middlesex, 1976).

Stretton, Hesba. 'Jessica's First Prayer', reprinted in *Masterworks of Children's Literature*, 5 (London, 1985).

Styles, Morag, Eve Bearne and Victor Watson (eds), *After Alice* (London, 1992).

—— *Talking Pictures: Pictorial Texts and Younger Readers*, (London, 1996).

Suchan, James. 'Alice's Journey from Alien to Artist', *Children's Literature*, 7 (New Haven and London, 1979).

Summerfield, G. *Fantasy and Reason: Children's Literature and the Eighteenth Century* (London, 1984).

Sutcliff, Rosemary. 'History is People', in *Children and Literature, Views and Reviews*, ed. Virginia Haviland (London, 1973).

—— *The Eagle of the Ninth* (London, 1954).

—— *The Silver Branch* (London, 1957).

—— *The Lantern Bearers* (London, 1959).

Tanner, Tony. *Jane Austen* (London, 1986).

Tennyson, Lord Alfred. 'The Princess', in *The Poems of Tennyson II*, ed. Christopher Ricks (London, 1987).

Thackeray, W. M. *The Rose and The Ring* (London, 1926 edn).

Thwaite, Ann. *Waiting for the Party: The Life of Frances Hodgson Burnett* (London, 1974).

Tillotson, Kathleen. *Novels of the Eighteen Forties* (Oxford, 1954).

Todd, Janet. *Sensibility: An Introduction* (London and New York, 1986).

Tolkien, J. R. R. *The Lord of the Rings* (London, 1955).

—— 'On Fairy Stories' in *Tree and Leaf* (Boston, 1965).

Tolstoy, Leo. *War and Peace* (trans. L. and A. Maude) (London, 1942).

Tompkins, J. M. S. *The Popular Novel in England, 1770–1800* (London, 1962).

Townsend, J. R. *Written for Children: An Outline of English Children's Literature* (London, 1965).

Travers, P. L. *Mary Poppins* [1934] (London, 1971).

Trease, Geoffrey. 'The Revolution in Children's Literature', in *The Thorny Paradise*, ed. Edward Blishen (Harmondsworth, Middlesex, 1975).

Trilling, Lionel. *The Liberal Imagination* (London, 1961).

Trimmer, Sarah. 'On the Care which is Requisite in the Choice of Books for Children' [1803], reprinted in *Children and Literature, Views and Reviews* (ed. Virginia Haviland) (London, 1973).

Trollope, Anthony. *The Prime Minister* [1876] (Oxford, 1973).

—— *The Last Chronicle of Barset*. [1867] (Oxford, 1989).

Twain, Mark. *The Adventures of Tom Sawyer* [1876] (Harmondsworth, Middlesex, 1986).

—— *The Adventures of Huckleberry Finn* [1884] (London, 1985).

Uttley, Alison. *A Traveller in Time* [1939] (London, 1963).

Vance, Norman. *The Sinews of the Spirit* (Cambridge, 1985).

Voigt, Cynthia. *Homecoming* (London, 1981).

Wall, Barbara. *The Narrator's Voice* (London, 1991).

Walsh, Jill Paton. *Goldengrove* [1972] (London, 1990).

—— *Unleaving* [1976] (London, 1990).

Walsh, William. *The Use of Imagination* (Harmondsworth, Middlesex, 1966).

Ward, Mrs. Humphrey. *Helbeck of Bannisdale* [1898] (Harmondsworth, Middlesex, 1983).

Watson, Victor. 'Poetry and Pirates – Swallows and Amazons at Sea', *Signal*, 66

(Sept. 1991, Gloucester).

—— 'The Possibilities of Children's Fiction', in *After Alice*, eds Morag Styles, Eve Bearne and Victor Watson (London, 1992).

Welland, Dennis. *Mark Twain in England* (London, 1978).

Wilde, Oscar. *The Happy Prince and Other Tales* [1888], reprinted in *Complete Shorter Fiction*, ed. Isobel Murray (Oxford, 1979).

Willey, Basil. *Eighteenth-Century Studies* [1940] (London, and New York, 1986).

—— *More Nineteenth-Century Studies: A Group Of Honest Doubters* [1956] (Cambridge, 1980).

Williams, Raymond. *Culture and Society* (Harmondsworth, Middlesex, 1961).

—— *The Country and the City* (London, 1973).

White, Dorothy N. *About Books for Children* (Oxford, 1949).

White, T. H. *The Sword in the Stone* (London, 1939).

Wordsworth, William. 'The Prelude' (1850 revised version), in *The Poetical Works of William Wordsworth*, ed. E. de Selincourt (Oxford, 1947).

—— 'The Excursion', in *The Poetical Works of Wordsworth* (Boston, 1982).

Yonge, Charlotte. 'Class Literature of the Last Thirty Years' [1867], reprinted in *Children and Literature, Views and Reviews*, ed. Virginia Haviland (London, 1973).

—— *The Daisy Chain* [1856] (London, 1902).

Young, G. M. *et al.* (eds) *English Historical Documents 1833–74*, 12 (1) and (2) (London, 1956).

Zipes, Jack. *Breaking the Magic Spell: Radical Theories of Folktale and Fairy Tale* (London, 1979).

—— *Fairy tales and the Art of Subversion: The Classical Genre for Children and the Process of Civilization* (London, 1983).

Index